The World of W.E.B. Du Bois

W.E.B. Du Bois
Archives, University Library, University of Massachusetts/Amherst.

The World of W.E.B. Du BOIS

A Quotation Sourcebook

Edited by MEYER WEINBERG

GREENWOOD PRESS
Westport, Connecticut • London

Library of Congress Cataloging-in-Publication Data

Du Bois, W. E. B. (William Edward Burghardt), 1868–1963.
   [Selections, 1992]
   The world of W.E.B. Du Bois : a quotation sourcebook / edited by
Meyer Weinberg.
     p. cm.
   Includes bibliographical references and index.
   ISBN 0–313–28619–1 (alk. paper)
   1. Du Bois, W. E. B. (William Edward Burghardt), 1868–1963—
Quotations. 2. Afro-Americans—Quotations, maxims, etc.
I. Weinberg, Meyer, 1920–   II. Title.
E185.97.D73A25 1992
305.896′07302—dc20   92–15481

British Library Cataloguing in Publication Data is available.

Library of Congress Catalog Card Number: 92–15481
ISBN: 0–313–28619–1

First published in 1992

Greenwood Press, 88 Post Road West, Westport, CT 06881
An imprint of Greenwood Publishing Group, Inc.

Printed in the United States of America

The paper used in this book complies with the
Permanent Paper Standard issued by the National
Information Standards Organization (Z39.48–1984).

10 9 8 7 6 5 4 3 2 1

TO THE MEMORY OF

ALBERT ANDERSON RABY

Contents

Acknowledgments   ix

Introduction   1

1. Through a Personal Prism   9

2. The Trouble I've Seen   31

3. Mother Africa   43

4. Education   53

5. Racism   79

6. Working Class   91

7. Forced Labor   101

8. Ruling and Other Classes   109

9. Women   125

10. Ideals and Realities   129

11. Literature   137

12. Reform, Radicalism, and Revolution   145

13. Christianity   161

14. Jews   173

15. White People   185

16. World Economy and Politics   189

17. War and Peace   199

18.   Some Other Countries   205

19.   Politics   215

20.   General   223

      References   261

      Index   265

Acknowledgments

I wish to thank David Graham Du Bois for his kind permission to reprint materials from the unpublished writings of W.E.B. Du Bois. For permission to quote from The Complete Published Works of W.E.B. Du Bois I am grateful to Kraus International Publications. John Bracey made a number of excellent suggestions while reviewing an early draft. Linda Deidman, the curator of the W.E.B. Du Bois Papers at the Library of the University of Massachusetts, Amherst, was unfailingly helpful, as were her staff. Betty Craker typed the complex manuscript, Anita Weigel used the computer to shape the work further, and Elise Young typed the subject index. All three have my deepest thanks. Copyeditor Linda Robinson insisted on clarity and definiteness in the interest of the reader. Production editor Lynn Sedlak Flint guided the work skillfully from manuscript to printer.

The World of W.E.B. Du Bois

Introduction

W.E.B. Du Bois stands preeminent among intellectuals of the United States in this century. None wrote more of enduring importance or continues to be as relevant for our own day. Equally significant, Du Bois was an activist intellectual—he organized, protested, laid out programs, petitioned, and raised questions of long-term strategy and short-term tactics. He mastered numerous forms of written expression: detailed scholarly investigations superior to many accepted models of research; vast investigative designs, stretching in one case over a century; editing of periodicals dealing more popularly with problems of the contemporary world; articles in learned and topical media; and sustained illumination in a new light of persistent issues ranging from the Reconstruction period of United States history to the relatively brief career of racism in world history. He was also a commanding speaker.

To study his life and writings is simultaneously to study African American history. His published works and his correspondence are *about* and *of* that history. But these are also part of the general history of the United States. Du Bois wrote a great deal with white Americans in mind. He did not strive only to free blacks from oppression; he also worked to warn all Americans that democracy for them was equally endangered by racism.

The major subjects of his writings range widely. Black people in the United States and the world were the foundation upon which the rest was built. He once wrote an essay contending that black colleges should start their curricula with special attention to black life and history. Then, the span of study should be broadened to include all of world civilization. This was, in fact, how Du Bois's own thought progressed. To study blacks alone was not to do justice to the broad humanity of all blacks and of others.

Black history from Africa forward appears throughout his writings. Although prominent leaders and individuals are mentioned, more fundamental is the great mass of poor blacks as historical actors. As slaves they hewed out a semblance of family and community life. When the historic moment materialized, they departed from the plantations and helped fill the ranks of the Union Army. After the Civil War, they constructed a new political order in the South and in the nation, despite their heritage of enslavement. Du Bois's readers and listeners came to know all this as a matter of pride.

Du Bois viewed lynching as institutionalized terror, perpetrated not by furtive foreigners but by homegrown murderers, abetted by Constitutional apologists. Committed in full view of local officers of the law, the outrages were declared beyond the purview of federal power. Occasional efforts by scattered legislators to subject them to federal jurisdiction invariably failed. Meanwhile, black Americans continued to be killed almost at random and, though frequently innocent of any crime, sacrificed on the altar of white supremacy. Du Bois never ceased to point up the hypocrisy of squaring lynching with democracy.

By democracy, Du Bois meant far more than the possession of certain civil rights and liberties. In the modern world, he insisted, democracy was either total or meaningless. No country, including the United States, could claim to be democratic while excluding entire populations from an effective voice in ruling themselves. Abolishing colonialism was part of the worldwide movement for democracy, as was the ending of racism in this country. Du Bois also meant by democracy the means whereby voters prepared to express informed and independent opinions. This required adequate education and steady employment consonant with a person's qualifications. The political power possessed by big business was illegitimate in a democracy, as he never tired of pointing out.

Du Bois taught one lesson among many throughout his long life. From time to time, he modified his statement of it or placed it in a novel context or put a heavier or lighter stress on it. That lesson was the two-ness of black life in America: the black as a member of a distinctive community anchored to race and the black as a member of the larger civic culture called America. The tension between the two originated in colonial times as white economic and political interest redefined a human whole into two antagonistic domains.

Du Bois saw black community life as an integral whole, culturally distinct and ethically equal to that of any other American community. He did not view it as a consolation prize for those darker people who failed to "make it" in white society. It was not second best but *another*.

To regard the black community as a complement to white society is to accord a certain permanence to it. Black community life could well endure for centuries longer, whatever democratic reforms America might enjoy. This belief was the nationalist kernel in Du Bois's thought. He never relinquished it. Repeatedly, Du Bois grasped a fundamental historical truth and made it a prism through which he examined and reexamined black life in America.

What does it mean to speak of "a black nation"? Until the Civil War, a black nation was possible in the United States. Indeed, during the 1850s and during the Civil War years, the term "Negro nation" appeared more than rarely in black writings. Black abolitionists, living in a two-ness of their own times, grew

increasingly impatient with their white colleagues. Frederick Douglass denounced those white abolitionists who might speak with him from a common
platform but then hurry to occupy a below-the-deck private room on a river
steamer on which Douglass was permitted only space on the deck, come rain
or shine. Delaney declared the superior right of blacks to edit antislavery newspapers, much to the chagrin of William Lloyd Garrison.

The war itself ended any possibility of a black nation. But this was not an
imposed resolution, forced upon black America. Rather, it was a self-determined
choice, based on a clear understanding that a new nation had emerged from the
Civil War. Its most novel feature was the challenge of incorporating a newly
created citizenry within the contours of a racist state. Jose Martí, the great Cuban
patriot, said that the emancipation from slavery and the endowing upon four
million persons the status of free persons was one of the grandest events of all
modern history. Only three years after this event, in 1868, Du Bois was born.

Du Bois thus matured in an America that shrank from its own grandeur while
seeking frantically to recreate old restrictions on its newest citizens. During the
1880s, Du Bois left the lovely heights of the Berkshires and began his lifelong
large-scale encounter with fellow blacks in the South and elsewhere. It was a
voyage of discovery whose disclosures never ceased to stir Du Bois.

There are those who measure Du Bois's consistency in this area. It is said,
for example, that he shuttled between segregation and integration. But the Du
Bois of the 1950s was as genuine as the Du Bois of the 1930s.

During the 1930s, Du Bois stressed the black side of two-ness as a matter of
collective self-defense. Seeing no effective government or industrial policy to
moderate the Great Depression which struck blacks with a special fury, he called
upon them to solidify their community and undergird it with a cooperative
economy. In school policy he preferred an end to segregation, but he was ready
to accept its continuation in the absence of any possibility of change. But he did
not advocate simple, passive acceptance. If blacks were not to have truly *common*
schools, then they must control the segregated ones. (Some thirty years later,
in 1966, black activists in Harlem were to make the same argument while raising
a call for community control.)

During the 1930s, also, Du Bois projected a vision of the ideal black higher
education. Likening black America to a separate nation, he rejected educating
its citizens in the substance of a foreign culture. It would be unthinkable for
French universities to use a foreign language and base their curricula on the
history, sociology, and economics of other countries. The black college in America, Du Bois contended, must start where it was and with the black condition
in America. The basic curriculum must concern itself with the problems and
prospects of black America. Only after that was attended to should the black
college go on to study world culture and society.

The 1930s were also the time that saw Du Bois produce his interpretive
masterpiece, *Black Reconstruction*. He had dealt with the subject before World
War I, but in the form of short, formal articles. Now, cascades of ideas flowed

as Du Bois traced a people first helping emancipate itself with its own armed power and then trying to create a new civil culture in the South. *Black Reconstruction* was the first extended historical work that portrayed blacks as initiators and leaders in the struggle for democratic life in America. Among other things, Du Bois showed that blacks were the originators of state-financed school systems in the South. He emphasized the crucial stake that poor blacks had in the existence of viable public schools.

The Du Bois of the 1930s was deeply aware of the black community, of the primacy of its problems, the need to strengthen black educational institutions, and the potential for leadership and political creativity among blacks. He treated the two-ness of black America during the Civil War, and during the short Reconstruction years as well, as a constructive element leading to cooperation between black and white, however fleeting. But he rejected any concept of black intellectual or cultural inferiority, and he combatted conceptions of black powerlessness.

The Du Bois of the 1950s hailed the *Brown* decision and urged blacks to accept it. But he warned of its destructive potential with regard to the teaching of the black culture and history in the formerly black schools. Underestimating the capacity of blacks to enforce the continuation of such instruction in desegregated public schools, he counselled black parents to take up the challenge and teach black history at home or in some private arrangement.

With the growth of self-organization during and after World War II, blacks proved able, for the second time in our history, to accommodate at least some of the public schools to the task of educating all black youths. By the 1960s, the demand for black studies demonstrated a growing confidence by blacks that public schools had the capacity to serve broader functions than to perpetuate a racist culture. Du Bois, of course, died in 1963, but in his shorter newspaper pieces and speeches and in his unpublished letters he had hailed the civil rights movement, especially as a black southern movement.

If Du Bois during the 1950s wrote less about the black community, it was not because of an underestimation of its importance. Quite the contrary. By 1960, black America was well on its way to a conscious self-hood that needed neither preaching nor pointing. Du Bois was supreme at both.

Two-ness, in his mind, was not overcome or abolished by the advent of the civil rights movement. Rather, it was raised to a new level. During the 1950s, for example, Du Bois began discussion—if only in book reviews and occasional articles—of the issue of class differences within the black community. He noted the relative recency of this differentiation and predicted that it would increase in the future, as indeed it has. Class differentiation, with its unequal apportionment of goods and services, was not welcomed by Du Bois. At the same time, however, he did not fear the accentuation of working-class consciousness among poorer blacks. It was the corrosive effect of economic privilege, not class consciousness, on the black community that concerned Du Bois.

No so-called white university ever honored itself by engaging Du Bois as a professor. Presumably, then, Du Bois possessed little knowledge that was truly intellectual. But such a presumption would be preposterous. The body of his work is immensely learned, but American academe has accepted knowledge of race only upon white authority. When white mainstream scholars pronounce on the subject, it is proper academic fodder. When, however, blacks write about it, the product is classified as "special-interest" and therefore not truly scholarship.

Ignorance feeds on itself. Thus, the very absence of race from American scholarly endeavor was seen as proving the irrelevance of race. Early in the twentieth century, while Du Bois wrote about the failure of American education for young black Americans, philosopher John Dewey remained silent on the issue of race. Even though he wrote volubly about education and democracy, he failed to write a single sentence about the undemocratic manner in which blacks were deprived of an education. This was the case even though Dewey was an invited attendee at the founding convention of the NAACP. Still, in his academic specialty, he found no occasion to deal with race. To Du Bois, on the other hand, racism was one of the central concerns of his life. No wonder that until 1942 no "white" American university, North or South, employed a tenured black classroom professor. Racial ignorance was safe in academe.

There is little reason to think that Du Bois was emotionally shattered by his exclusion from white academe. There was more originality in his *Black Reconstruction* than in the dozens of dreary doctoral dissertations and proper monographs written by faculty in the history departments of many universities. He managed to receive some grants, but otherwise he was deprived of a daily routine that could have deepened and broadened his productivity. Leaves for research were rare in black colleges, as Du Bois and his colleagues knew to their sorrow. Heavy teaching schedules and inadequate libraries, along with very modest salaries, determined that little research would be done by faculty. But Du Bois was not fatalistic about the matter. He fought it as another obstacle placed in blacks' way by a racist society.

Throughout his writings Du Bois left many observations that are relevant to continuing problems of black America. Thus, contemporary discussions of the "underclass" proceed frequently in isolation from historical factors. Du Bois, however, was writing of the special recalcitrance of black poverty at the opening of the twentieth century. He spoke often of the centuries of unpaid labor by black workers, furthering the case for reparations in our own day. Some sixty years ago Du Bois was writing about the particularities of South African race policy. His readers were—and are—distinctively well supplied with perspective on a supremely racist state system. No American, or other, writer conceptualized so well the entire system of racism. Even today, conventional sociological and psychological accounts of racism pale before the richness and specificity of Du Bois's explication.

Despite this extraordinary record, the average college student in the United States barely knows the name Du Bois. Or, if one does, it is as the author of a prescient sentence in a book written in 1903. No mention is made that he lived and wrote for another sixty years and that he developed one of the most impressive bodies of literature in American history.

At no time during Du Bois's life were many of his books in print. Except for *Souls of Black Folk* (1903), only the last-published work or two were in print at any given time. Publishers printed small numbers of his books because the market was so small for works concerned with black themes. Few black people could afford to buy books, and not many who could afford it were in the habit of doing so. It was, in fact, only in 1986 that the complete published works of Du Bois were in print for the first time. The set of thirty-seven volumes, published by Kraus International and edited by Herbert Aptheker, is a monument to a central figure in American culture. Only now can we hope to study his total published contribution. Because of the previous scarcity and outright unavailability of his works, numerous historians and other scholars were deprived of the opportunity to study them closely. The present situation has changed greatly for the better.

Yet, the bulk of Du Bois's unpublished works is even greater. Consisting primarily of letters, the largest part of them was released during 1980 in the form of 89 microfilm reels, each one containing the equivalent of a single printed volume. The originals of all the microfilm reels are located in the Archives of the University of Massachusetts at Amherst. These unpublished materials have been utilized extensively in the present work. The University of Massachusetts Press has published five volumes from the unpublished materials. Three of these consist of correspondence; one, of selected material on racism; and another on prayers for young students which Du Bois wrote early in his academic career.

Du Bois wrote thousands of letters, many of them replying to inquiries. Among others, historians such as Merle Curti and the young C. Vann Woodward expressed gratitude to Du Bois for his scholarly writing. His opinions and ideas about research problems and possible sources were solicited. Nehru of India, Albert Einstein, and other world figures either wrote him or received letters from Du Bois. But most were not well-known, a number barely literate, and many needed personal help of one kind or another. Invariably, they were respectful as he was in replying.

Requests for financial help were turned down but succinct advice often accompanied the declination. Seemingly without exception he supplied bibliographical references to anyone who asked. Young black artists, writers, or sculptors could expect encouragement but also searching questions. To inquiries about the desirability of going to college, Du Bois almost always counselled younger people as to its indispensability.

Du Bois held few grudges against others or against himself. His letters show him, without comment, helping the same man find a job who several years before had denounced Du Bois as a faker. He was both self-critical and self-forgiving.

Du Bois had no great difficulty changing his mind, even on important matters. Nor did he do so in a tortured way. Characteristically, when changing his mind, he tended to cite a reason rather than to criticize someone else for having misled him. This feature of his thinking is plainest in his correspondence.

The present book introduces scholars, students, and the general reader to the principal themes discussed by Du Bois during the nearly 35,000 days he lived. The goal is not to exhaust his writings but to direct attention to significant places in his writings that will keep readers busy for some time. The quoted extracts are as short as possible and as long as necessary.

To aid the reader in a journey through more than a thousand quotations, three things have been done. First, the quotations have been grouped into twenty chapters, nineteen of them dealing with fairly specific topics; the twentieth chapter deals with issues not covered in the preceding nineteen. Second, preceding each quotation is a several-word heading designed to summarize the main sense of the quotation. All the headings are the work of the editor but incorporate, wherever possible, words from the quotations. Third, an index to the quotations has been constructed. Index entries stress not so much the main sense of quotations as distinctive Du Boisian ways of stating matters. Especially striking phrases and characteristic expressions are highlighted. Yet, all these aids do not fully relieve the reader of the responsibility of remembering. As you turn these pages, be prepared to copy memorable sentences or quotations. There will be no lack of them.

Working with these Du Bois materials has been a great honor. He was a voice and mind of a great people and should be celebrated as a national treasure. I hope this book will help achieve this goal.

1

Through a Personal Prism

1. AGE OF ANXIETY

These are times when, in spite of ourselves, we are suspicious of everybody. I can remember in the 30 years when I drove a car that every time I halted to let a person cross the street, inevitably, I was regarded with great distrust. And so it is today about everything.

To Paul Partington, April 10, 1961; microfilm reel no. 75, frame no. 525; W.E.B. Du Bois Papers, University of Massachusetts, Amherst.

2. AGING

The most disquieting sign of my mounting years is a certain garrulity about myself, quite foreign to my young days. I find a growing tendency to fix innocent listeners with my stern eyes, despite their all too evident longing to escape, and to tell what life has meant to me.

"The Shadow of Years," *Crisis* 15 (February 1918) 167–71; *Selections* From the Crisis, vol. 1 (1983) 150.

3. APPETITE

I have always grave suspicion of those who do not eat the first thing in the morning.

To Lurlani Smith, February 4, 1937; microfilm reel no. 48, frame no. 137; W.E.B. Du Bois Papers, University of Massachusetts, Amherst.

4. ART AND REALITY

I am so glad to hear that you have returned to the piano. After all, one has to get out of this world and get into something real at least now and then. My refuge is that eternal novel which I have been working on for some time.

To Grace Goens, April 17, 1953; microfilm reel no. 69, frame no. 828; W.E.B. Du Bois
   Papers, University of Massachusetts, Amherst. [His three-volume novel, *The Black
   Flame*, was published 1957–1961.]

5. AUTOBIOGRAPHY

Autobiographies do not form indisputable authorities. They are always in-
complete, and often unreliable. Eager as I am to put down the truth, there are
difficulties; memory fails especially in small details, so that it becomes finally
but a theory of my life, with much forgotten and misconceived, with valuable
testimony but often less than absolutely true, despite my intention to be frank
and fair. Mostly my life today is a mass of memories with vast omissions, matters
which are forgotten accidentally or by deep design.

Autobiography (1968) 12.

6. BITTER WORLD

Do not waste time being bitter. This is a bitter world but we have got to live
in it, and things are not usually quite as bad as we fear.

To Marina Armattoe, March 29, 1955; microfilm reel no. 71, frame no. 205; W.E.B.
   Du Bois Papers, University of Massachusetts, Amherst.

7. BLACK AT HARVARD

Toward whites [at Harvard] I was not arrogant. I was simply not obsequious,
and to a white Harvard student of my day, a Negro student who did not seek
recognition was trying to be more than a Negro. The same Harvard man had
much the same attitude toward Jews and Irishmen.

Autobiography (1968) 136.

8. BLACK FOLK SONGS

[After graduating from high school] I heard . . . for the first time the Negro
folk songs. . . . I was thrilled and moved to tears and seemed to recognize something inherently and deeply my own.

Autobiography (1968) 106.

9. BLACK IS BEAUTIFUL

You will meet . . . curious little annoyances. People will wonder at your dear
brown and the sweet crinkley hair. . . . You must know that brown is as pretty
as white or prettier and crinkley hair as straight even though it is harder to comb.
The main thing is YOU beneath the clothes and skin—the ability to do, the will
to conquer, the determination to understand and know this great, wonderful,
curious world.

Letter to Yolande, his daughter, who was attending school in England, October 29, 1914; *Correspondence*, I, 208.

10. BOLSHEVIK

I stand in astonishment and wonder at the revelation of Russia that has come to me. I may be partially deceived and half-informed. But if what I have seen with my eyes and heard with my ears in Russia is Bolshevik, I am a Bolshevik.

"Russia, 1926," *Crisis*, 33 (November 1926) 8; *Selections from* The Crisis, vol. 2 (1983) 452.

11. BONE OF THE BONE

I . . . am bone of the bone and flesh of the flesh of them that live within the Veil.

The Souls of Black Folk (1903) viii.

12. BOOTED

After only two years' experiment [as a teacher] I left Wilberforce [University]. I was not kicked out, but that was only because I moved before the inevitable swing of the boot.

"The Future of Wilberforce University," *Journal of Negro Education*, 9 (October 1940) 553–70; *Writings by W.E.B. Du Bois in Periodicals Edited by Others*, vol. 3 (1982) 97.

13. BOURGEOIS LEADERS

Many of our younger Negro thinkers believe that the essential difficulty with American Negro leadership today is that [it] is "bourgeois"; that is, that it believes in the achievement of Negro emancipation by the accumulation of wealth and capital secured through the exploitation of the poor by the rich. This is a serious matter, and it has undoubtedly a partial basis of truth. I can trace my own dawning realization of this in the last twenty years until I began to face an impasse in my thinking some ten years ago. I did not mince or mouth the fact. I was not born like so many of my fellows, knowing all things for all time; nor did my change in orientation come suddenly . . . because I had read "a book of Marx."

Pittsburgh Courier, December 11, 1937; *Newspaper Columns by W.E.B. Du Bois* (1986) 255.

14. BOYHOOD

My boyhood seems, if my memory serves me rightly, to have been filled with incidents of surprisingly little importance such as brooks with stones across, grass, and gate-posts.

"Something about Me" (1890) *in* Aptheker (ed.), *Against Racism* (1985) 17.

15. BROADENING TRAVEL

[While living and studying in Europe, 1892–1894] . . . I met men and women as I had never met them before. Slowly they became, not white folks, but folks. The unity beneath all life clutched me. I was not less fanatically a Negro, but 'Negro' meant a greater, broader sense of humanity and world fellowship. I felt myself standing, not against the world, but simply against American narrowness and color prejudice, with the greater, finer world at my back.

Autobiography (1968) 157.

Of greatest importance was the opportunity which my *Wanderjahre* in Europe gave of looking at the world as a man and not simply from a narrow racial and provincial outlook. This was primarily the result not so much of my study, as of my human companionship, unveiled by the accident of color. . . . I had reached the habit of expecting color prejudice so universally, that I found it even when it was not there.

Autobiography (1968) 159.

16. CAPTAINS OF SOULS

[In 1896] I was ready to admit that the best of men might fail. I meant still to be captain of my soul, but I realized that even captains are not omnipotent in uncharted and angry seas.

Autobiography (1968) 193.

17. CLEAR SIGHT

I'm an optimist but I've got eyes.

"Next Steps," May 13, 1933; microfilm reel no. 80, frame no. 519; W.E.B. Du Bois Papers, University of Massachusetts, Amherst.

18. CLOTHES DESIGNING

I do not altogether like your plan of designing dresses, clothing, etc., chiefly because only the very rich people are able to wear beautifully designed clothes and work for such a class of capricious, changeable and to a very large extent vulgar people is not at all attractive.

To daughter Yolande Du Bois, June 19, 1915; microfilm reel no. 79, frame no. 714; W.E.B. Du Bois Papers, University of Massachusetts, Amherst.

19. COMING SOUTH

So I came to a region where the world was split into white and black halves, and where the darker half was held back by race prejudice and legal bonds, as well as by deep ignorance and dire poverty. But facing this was not a lost group, but at Fisk a microcosm of a world and a civilization in potentiality. Into this world I leapt with enthusiasm. A new loyalty and allegiance replaced my Americanism: henceforward I was a Negro.

Upon arrival at Fisk (1885); *Autobiography* (1968) 108.

20. COMMON SCHOOL STUDENTS

[In summer 1886 I taught in East Tennessee log cabin schools.] My first school was the second held in the district since Emancipation [in 1865]. I touched immediately the lives of the commonest of mankind—people who ranged from barefooted dwellers on dirt floors, with patched rags for clothes, to rough, hard-working farmers, with plain, clean plenty.

Autobiography (1968) 114.

21. COMPULSORY SELF-DEFENSE

In my younger years, I had no idea of becoming a "Negro" editor or a Negro Leader, or a Negro sociologist. But . . . I had no choice. My work as "assistant instructor" in the University of Pennsylvania was successful, but I had as much chance of a professorship there as a snowball in Hell. I lost no time being sorry for myself but accepted with enthusiasm my job of being a Negro.

Amsterdam News, June 12, 1943, *Newspaper Columns by W.E.B. Du Bois* (1986) 528.

22. CONSISTENCY

I am not worried about being inconsistent. What worries me is the Truth.

"Segregation in the North," *Crisis* 41 (April 1934) 115–17; *Selections from* The Crisis, vol. 2 (1983) 745.

23. CONTROVERSIAL

I am at present . . . what is called in America "a controversial person" because I insist that a man can be a Socialist or a Communist or anything else that he so desires and that punishment and discrimination because of belief is barbarism.

Letter to E. Sylvia Pankhurst, May 4, 1955; *Correspondence*, III, 380.

24. COST OF LIVING

Can you give me recommendations as to a good laundry? Mrs. Du Bois told me to ask you. The laundry which I am using at the Hotel Theresa charges me twenty-two cents per shirt. At that rate I fear bankruptcy.

To Mrs. J. Rosamond Johnson, October 13, 1944; microfilm reel no. 56, frame no. 276; W.E.B. Du Bois Papers, University of Massachusetts, Amherst.

25. COURTESY TO BLACKS

The sea was calm throughout the trip. . . . The passengers were rather more courteous than I expect Americans to be. . . . (1958).

Autobiography (1968) 11.

26. DOCTORS

I find in my own experience that it is almost impossible to get a physician to give me rational advice which shall keep me from getting ill. He insists on writing a prescription.

"On the Modern Physician," *Medical Review of Reviews* 73 (January 1917) 9; *Writings by W.E.B. Du Bois in Periodicals Edited by Others*, vol. 2 (1982) 105.

27. EARLY TO RISE

I arise here [in Atlanta] with the sun, getting my mile walk by half-past seven, and I am sitting in my office bright and perky by eight; somewhere between nine and eleven, I go to bed.

To Alice Dunbar Nelson, December 15, 1934; microfilm reel no. 42, frame no. 802; W.E.B. Du Bois Papers, University of Massachusetts, Amherst.

28. EQUALITY WITH WHITES

I have given a wrong impression . . . if I have led people to believe that I want the colored people to have simply equality with other people—what I have tried to ask for is justice, treatment according to desert and I have tried to put especial emphasis upon this. I want the colored people to have the right to develop according to their capacity and I certainly would be disappointed if they did not develop much higher things than the white race has developed to.

Letter to Miss M. B. Marston, March 11, 1907, *Correspondence*, I, 127.

29. EVENTUAL VICTORY HERE

Curiously enough, while I'm criticized as being very anti-American, as a matter of fact I never had the slightest doubt but that we were going to gain our equality here in America, and therefore I wasn't going to take refuge in France or Germany or anywhere else. I was coming right back here to do the fighting.

"Oral History Manuscript," May 24, 1960; microfilm reel no. 88, frame no. 1652; W.E.B. Du Bois Papers, University of Massachusetts, Amherst.

30. EXERCISE

I find that I get my exercise and keep fit principally through my walking. I walk down to the office (three miles) every morning and often back again at night.

To daughter Yolande Du Bois, November 3, 1915; microfilm reel no. 79, frame no.
  7167; W.E.B. Du Bois Papers, University of Massachusetts, Amherst.

31. EXILE

I just cannot take any more of this country's treatment. We leave for Ghana
October 5th and I set no date for return. If I were you I'd try to buy nothing
more but save and in time leave. . . . Chin up, and fight on, but realize that
American Negroes can't win.

To Grace Goens, September 13, 1961; microfilm reel no. 75, frame no. 242; W.E.B.
  Du Bois Papers, University of Massachusetts, Amherst.

32. EXILE?

This is my native land. I shall never live elsewhere. I could not if I would.
I would not if I could.

Russia and America: An Interpretation (1950, unpublished); microfilm reel no. 85, frame
  no. 477; W.E.B. Du Bois Papers, University of Massachusetts, Amherst.

We are leaving Oct. 5th for West Africa where I am going to plan an En-
cyclopedia Africana. We shall be gone several months and perhaps longer.

To Virginia Banks, September 21, 1961; microfilm reel no. 75, frame no. 9; W.E.B.
  Du Bois Papers, University of Massachusetts, Amherst.

33. EXPLOITATION

I have hitherto lived very careful[ly] to keep out of commercial enterprises
which had for their object the exploitation of colored people. On the other hand,
I am very much interested in commercial and industrial organization which will
be organized and run for the benefit of the mass of Negroes.

To A. S. Frissell, April 25, 1922; microfilm reel no. 10, frame no. 1099; W.E.B. Du
  Bois Papers, University of Massachusetts, Amherst.

34. EXPORTING RACISM

One annoyance I met . . . all over Europe: the landlord would hasten to inform
me beamingly that "Fellow Americans had just arrived." If there was one thing
less desirable than white "fellow Americans" to me, it was black "fellow
Americans" to them.

Autobiography (1968) 159.

35. FBI AND DU BOIS

Subject favors equality between the white and colored races.

W.E.B. Du Bois File, May 1, 1942.

He is considered to be respectable.

W.E.B. Du Bois File, November 12, 1942.

Very studious.

W.E.B. Du Bois File, February 13, 1943.

Considered to be one of the most outstanding and competent negroes in Atlanta.

W.E.B. Du Bois File, February 27, 1953.

Peculiarities: Wears pointed goatee.

W.E.B. Du Bois File, December 29, 1950.

Du Bois reportedly very critical of capitalistic system and stated socialism is coming to the U.S.

W.E.B. Du Bois File, May 29, 1958.

Peculiarities: Wears mustache and pointed goatee.

W.E.B. Du Bois File, June 18, 1960.

Distinguishing characteristics: Wears Van Dyke beard or goatee; precise and cultured.

W.E.B. Du Bois File, April 30, 1956, p. 57.

36. FUND RAISING

During my whole career, I have tried not to be put in a position where collecting money from philanthropists would be any considerable part of my work. For that reason I have always declined to be candidate for the presidency of any college or organization, where I had to raise funds. This kind of work interferes, to my mind, with study and investigation, and inevitably puts the scholar under obligation to the rich men and to business interests.

Letter to Merle Curti, June 4, 1958; *Correspondence*, III, 430.

37. GARBAGE

The stuff which you have put in the front hall is not classed garbage and the garbage collector will not handle it. You will have to arrange for its removal yourself as Henry has no facilities for taking care of it. It should not remain in the hall during the weekend and if you can't get rid of it I shall ask Henry to put it on your landing.

To Mr. Shaeffer, October 28, 1960; microfilm reel no. 74, frame no. 775; W.E.B. Du Bois Papers, University of Massachusetts, Amherst.

38. GRANDFATHERS

I am very much pleased to get your letter this morning. You must remember that grandfathers are human and have their disappointments and discouragements and do not like to be forgotten.

To his granddaughter Du Bois Williams, January 17, 1946; microfilm reel no. 59, frame
no. 716; W.E.B. Du Bois Papers, University of Massachusetts, Amherst.

39. GROWING UP BLACK

I found myself . . . in school, making it a sort of point of honor to excel white
students every time I could in anything. It came chiefly from just working harder.
I began to recognize that in some way, for some reason—I wasn't clear at all
about it—I sort of had to justify myself.

"Oral History Manuscript," May 5, 1960; microfilm reel no. 88, frame no. 1599; W.E.B.
Du Bois Papers, University of Massachusetts, Amherst.

40. HABIT

I average three cigarettes a day, and I have a jigger of whiskey usually every
night before I go to bed.

Interview with Al Morgan, June 4, 1957; microfilm reel no. 72, frame no. 933; W.E.B.
Du Bois Papers, University of Massachusetts, Amherst.

41. HARVARD UNIVERSITY

I have conducted classes and given lectures at Yale, Vassar and Princeton at
the invitation of the University authorities, but never has Harvard invited me on
any occasion except in the case of student organizations. My *Suppression of the
Slave Trade to America* became the initial volume of the Harvard Historical
series over sixty years [ago]. The University has never in any way mentioned
this rather unusual happening. Last year a Harvard man wrote the President on
his own initiative on some recognition of my work. No action followed. I have
heard from Negro graduates of Harvard some disparaging remarks made by
professors about the undesirability of encouraging any other Negro students of
my "bitter" type. I have gotten the impression that Harvard was not particularly
proud of me.

Letter to Corliss Lamont and Kyrle Elkin, February 4, 1958; *Correspondence*, III, 422.

[While attending Harvard] I did not seek contact with my white fellow students.
On the whole I rather avoided them. I took it for granted that we were training
ourselves for different careers in worlds largely different. There was not the
slightest idea of the permanent subordination and inequality of my world. Nor
again was there any idea of racial amalgamation. I resented the assumption that
we desired it.

Dusk of Dawn (1940) 101.

42. HATEFUL ATLANTA

It took but a few years of Atlanta to bring me to hot and indignant defense
[of my people]. I saw the race-hatred of the whites as I had never dreamed of

it before—naked and unashamed! . . . I held back with more difficulty each day my mounting indignation against injustice and misrepresentation.
Darkwater (1920) 21.

43. HONESTY

Honesty is one of my greatest failings.

To Maud Owens, February 19, 1929; microfilm reel no. 28, frame no. 1384; W.E.B. Du Bois Papers, University of Massachusetts, Amherst.

44. HOUSEHOLD FINANCE

You could probably do as well and more cheaply with electric apparatus than with a gas stove. You can get a good percolator coffee pot for about $5.00 and that will boil water for eggs. You can get a grill for $7.00 or $8.00. It will not pay to pay less for either of these articles; but an $8.00 grill will cook bacon and eggs and toast sandwiches.

To daughter Yolande, October 8, 1935; microfilm reel no. 45, frame 93; W.E.B. Du Bois Papers, University of Massachusetts, Amherst.

45. INHERITING ENEMIES

You are evidently also beginning to realize that there are disadvantages as well as advantages in having parents who are well known. You inherit not only my friends but my enemies and no one can live a life without unfortunately making a fairly large collection of the latter although we may do this unconsciously and unwillingly.

To daughter Yolande, November 25, 1921; microfilm reel no. 9, frame no. 670; W.E.B. Du Bois Papers, University of Massachusetts, Amherst.

46. INSUFFICIENT HUMILITY

In Nashville . . . I accidentally ran into a white woman. I jostled her . . . and I turned and raised by hat and begged her pardon. The woman was furious. Of course, I couldn't understand. But you see, I didn't beg her pardon in the right way. I spoke to her as though I was an equal, instead of showing that kind of humility that I should have.

"Oral History Manuscript," May 24, 1960; microfilm reel no. 88, frame no. 1641; W.E.B. Du Bois Papers, University of Massachusetts, Amherst.

47. INSULATION

I have . . . availed myself of but few of my opportunities to make friends of white folk because of an almost uncontrollable distaste for giving the slightest chance to anyone to resent me or my presence.

Pittsburgh Courier, August 29, 1936; *Newspaper Columns by W.E.B. Du Bois* (1986) 109.

48. INSULT

It is not that I care so much about riding in a smoking-car, as the fact that behind the public opinion that compels me to ride there, is a denial of my *manhood*.

"An Open Letter to the Southern People," (1887), series 3/C, Folder no. 5501, *Unpublished Articles*, p. 7; W.E.B. Du Bois Papers, University of Massachusetts, Amherst.

49. INTERRACIAL INTERACTION

Few colored people of prominence in America have less social intercourse with white people than I. Not that I am prejudiced against them but I have plenty of companionship with my own people.

To S. M. Kitchen, September 23, 1929; microfilm reel no. 28, frame no. 873; W.E.B. Du Bois Papers, University of Massachusetts, Amherst.

50. JOB SEEKING

I began a systematic mail campaign. I wrote to no white institution—I knew there were no openings there.

Autobiography (1968) 184.

51. LAST SPEAKER

If ever on an American program I came elsewhere than at the end, I should be quite unable to speak from sheer surprise, and this from no conscious design, but by half-unconscious reasoning.

"The Negro Ideals of Life," *Christian Register* 84 (October 25, 1905) 1197–99; *Writings by W.E.B. Du Bois in Periodicals Edited by Others*, vol. 1 (1982) 269.

52. LEADERSHIP

I think I may say without boasting that in the period from 1910 to 1930 I was a main factor in revolutionizing the attitude of the American Negro toward caste. My stinging hammer blows made Negroes aware of themselves, confident of their possibilities and determined in self-assertion. So much so that today common slogans among the Negro people are taken bodily from the words of my mouth.

Autobiography (1968) 295.

53. LECTURING

I make my living in part by lecturing. I prepare my lectures with great care, taking time and trouble writing, re-writing and arranging them. I spend on an average of one hundred dollars cash each year for books upon which my information is based. . . .

To Harry E. Davis, January 17, 1941; microfilm reel no. 52, frame no. 787; W.E.B. Du Bois Papers, University of Massachusetts, Amherst.

You will please . . . ask the people not to arrange banquets, or receptions on the night of the lecture. I appreciate their kindness, but after lecturing I am too tired to do anything else but go to bed.

To M. G. Allison, February 19, 1921; W.E.B. Du Bois Papers, University of Massachusetts, Amherst.

I put a good deal of time into my lectures, writing them as carefully as I would write a book and then committing them partially to memory.

To Theodora Peck, March 30, 1949; microfilm reel no. 64, frame no. 255; W.E.B. Du Bois Papers, University of Massachusetts, Amherst.

Since I read most of my lectures I should like to have in the lecture room a reading stand, breast high. A table will not do and interferes with my delivery.

To Leon Ritz, April 6, 1954; microfilm reel no. 70, frame no. 554; W.E.B. Du Bois Papers, University of Massachusetts, Amherst.

My custom in meetings like your[s] . . . is to write out my words and commit them partially to memory; then I read my manuscript slowly and clearly. This with entrance and exit occupies most of a half hour and leaves the audience willing to hear more, which is the time to stop.

To Mary Endicott, January 26, 1960; microfilm reel no. 74, frame no. 113; W.E.B. Du Bois Papers, University of Massachusetts, Amherst.

54. LIFELONG HABITS

I do not apologize for living long. High on the ramparts of this blistering hell of life, I sit and see the Truth. I look it full in the face, and I will not lie about it, neither to myself nor to the world.

National Guardian, February 17, 1958; *in* Aptheker (ed.), *Newspaper Columns by W.E.B. Du Bois* (1986) 1003.

55. LIVING A LONG TIME

In all my plans and dreaming, I do not remember ever thinking of a long life.

Autobiography (1968) 13.

56. LOVE OF COUNTRY

It would not be true for me to say that I "love my country," for it enslaved, impoverished, murdered and insulted my people. Despite this I know what America has done for the poor, oppressed and hopeless of many other peoples, and what indeed it has done to contradict and atone for its sins against Negroes. I still believe that some day this nation will become a democracy without a color-line.

In Battle for Peace (1952) 163.

57. MARRIAGE

Marriage is rather serious business because in the ordinary course of events you have to live a long time with the person you marry and outside of being in love with them you have got to be good friends and interesting companions. . . . I have a sort of feeling that pity and sympathy in your case very largely supplies lack of any very strong affection. . . .

To daughter Yolande, August 29, 1923; microfilm reel no. 11, frame no. 896; W.E.B. Du Bois Papers, University of Massachusetts, Amherst.

58. MIRAGE

When a person goes to work and for the first time earns money, he feels tremendously rich. So that he ought to take certain precautions in order not to overspend.

Letter to Henrietta Shivery, September 7, 1934; *Correspondence*, II, 8.

59. MUSIC AT HARVARD

But I did have a good singing voice and loved music, so I entered the competition for the Glee Club. I ought to have known that Harvard could not afford to have a Negro on its Glee Club travelling about the country. Quite naturally I was rejected.

"A Negro Student at Harvard at the End of the 19th Century," *Massachusetts Review* 1 (Spring 1960) 439–58; *Writings by W.E.B. Du Bois in Periodicals Edited by Others*, vol. 4 (1982) 321.

60. MY FUNERAL

Two or three Negro spirituals: chorus, one strophe and one repetition of the chorus, no more:

"Let us cheer the weary Traveller"
"Brethren, my way, my way's cloudy"
"My Lord, what a Mourning."

The Schiller's Ode to Joy, Beethoven's music
Finally, one of the great Funeral Marches:
    Saul, Siegfried, or some other. . . .

To Shirley Graham Du Bois, June 26, 1957; microfilm no. 79, frame no. 605; W.E.B.
    Du Bois Papers, University of Massachusetts, Amherst.

61. MY NAME

My name is pronounced in the clear English fashion: Du, with u as in Sue;
Bois, as oi in voice. The accent is on the second syllable.

To Chicago Sunday Evening Club, January 20, 1939; microfilm reel no. 49, frame no.
    1171; W.E.B. Du Bois Papers, University of Massachusetts, Amherst.

62. MY TEACHERS

I was extremely emotional on the race problem while I was a student at Harvard
and my emotion was curbed by the philosophy of William James and the historical
research under [Albert Bushnell] Hart. They did not quench; they directed it.

Letter to Ben F. Rogers, Jr., December 20, 1939; *Correspondence*, II, 204.

63. NOBLE

I remember how as a boy I resented being expected to sing lustily about the
"Land of the Noble, Free." I knew quite a few Americans who were not noble
and I certainly was not free.

"Social Medicine" (1950); *in* Aptheker (ed.), *Against Racism* (1985) 266.

64. OLD AGE

I am sixty years of age. Naturally, most of my work is done.

To Henry Allen Moe, August 11, 1928; microfilm reel no. 25, frame no. 606; W.E.B.
    Du Bois Papers, University of Massachusetts, Amherst.

As people get older time goes faster and they do not know how much rushed
by.

Letter to his daughter, Yolande, November 15, 1954; *Correspondence*, III, 372.

I think I have felt particularly in the last twenty-five years a certainty of
judgement and depth of knowledge concerning this world which is new, inspiring
and astonishing. I began to realize what an omniscient God who has lived a
million years must have accumulated in the shape of knowledge, and how near
that knowledge may make him omnipotent.

Amsterdam News, February 27, 1943; *Newspaper Columns by W.E.B. Du Bois*
    (1986) 505.

I had . . . for some years begun to canvass the possibility of a change in work. This, of course, is not easy when a person is over 60 years of age. If he has not had the grace to die before this, he ought, in accordance with prevalent public opinion, at least be willing to stop acting and thinking. I did not agree with that.

1934; *Autobiography* (1968) 299–300.

I would have been hailed with approval if I had died at 50. At 75 my death was practically requested.

Autobiography (1968) 414.

65. PAST AND PRESENT

I remember once offering to an editor an article which began with a reference to the experience of last century. "Oh," he said, "leave out the history and come to the present." I felt like going to him over a thousand miles and taking him by the lapels and saying, "Dear, dear jackass! Don't you understand that the past *is* the present; that without what *was*, nothing *is*? That of the infinite dead, the living are but unimportant bits?"

The World and Africa (1947, 1965) 80.

66. PERSONAL HISTORY

The eldest daughter . . . was quite white, and she went to Vassar and graduated there before they knew that she was colored. I remember years after going there, and some of the professors were arguing that she ought to have told them. I said, "Why?" "Why should you tell people who your great-grandfather was?"

"Oral History Manuscript," May 24, 1960; microfilm reel no. 88, frame no. 1640; W.E.B. Du Bois Papers, University of Massachusetts, Amherst.

67. PERSONA NON GRATA

Most persons who have wealth and are in the habit of giving us subscriptions are inimical to my attitude and particularly to my frank and unpopular writing and talking. I do not know rich people. I am not persona grata to the great Foundations, so that even in good times, I can not do much for those who need and deserve help, while in bad times like this, I am quite powerless.

To Elizabeth Prophet, May 18, 1931; microfilm reel no. 35, frame no. 686; W.E.B. Du Bois Papers, University of Massachusetts, Amherst.

68. PREDILECTIONS

My best virtue—grit; my worst fault—sensitiveness; my favorite song—Go Down Moses; my pet vanity—a beard; my favorite food—bread and milk; my favorite drink—ginger ale; my favorite sport (outdoor)—walking; my favorite sport (indoor)—reading; my favorite character in history—Toussaint L'Ouverture.

To Cyril Clemens, June 2, 1938; microfilm reel no. 49, frame no. 26; W.E.B. Du Bois
    Papers, University of Massachusetts, Amherst.

69. PULLMAN PORTER

I remember the fussy old woman who always had something to do or ask whenever the porter appeared:
"Oh Porter, Porter! Is that the Missouri River?"
The Porter was polite and imperturbable:
"It is a portion of it, Madame."

Amsterdam News, June 5, 1943; *Newspaper Columns by W.E.B. Du Bois* (1986) 526.

70. QUALIFIED

I speak with no authority: no assumption of age nor rank; I hold no position, I have no wealth. One thing alone I own and that is my own soul. Ownership of that I have even while in my own country for near a century I have been nothing but a "nigger." On this basis and this alone I dare speak, I dare advise.

"China and Africa," *Peking Review* 1 (March 3, 1959) 11–13; *Writings by W.E.B. Du
    Bois in Periodicals Edited by Others*, vol. 4 (1982) 294.

71. QUOTE, UNQUOTE

You had an editorial in which I am quoted as saying that "The Puritans and Pilgrims were prostitutes and jailbirds from the streets of London, etc. . . . ." I said nothing of the sort. What I said was "that among the people who settled America, there were not only the Puritans and Negroes but even prostitutes and jailbirds."

To the Editor of the *Detroit Free Press*, October 15, 1930; microfilm reel no. 31, frame
    no. 59; W.E.B. Du Bois Papers, University of Massachusetts, Amherst.

72. RACISM AND ANTI-SEMITISM

The race problem in which I was interested cut across lines of color and physique and belief and status and was a matter of cultural patterns, perverted teaching and human hate and prejudice, which reached all sorts of people and caused endless evil to all men. So that the ghetto of Warsaw helped me to emerge from a certain social provincialism into a broader conception of what the fight against race segregation, religious discrimination and the oppression by wealth had to become if civilization was going to triumph and broaden in the world.

"The Negro and the Warsaw Ghetto," *Jewish Life* 6 (April 1952) 14–15; *Writings by
    W.E.B. Du Bois in Periodicals Edited by Others*, vol. 4 (1982) 175.

73. RACISM AND WAR

I appealed to the last meeting of peace societies in St. Louis, saying, "Should you not discuss racial prejudice as a prime cause of war?" The secretary was sorry but was unwilling to introduce controversial matters!

"The African Roots of the War," *Atlantic Monthly* 115 (May 1915) 707–14; *Writings by W.E.B. Du Bois in Periodicals Edited by Others*, vol. 2 (1982) 101.

74. RACISM ELSEWHERE

I had experienced on French soil less prejudice of color and race than anywhere else in the world.

Autobiography (1968) 18.

75. RELAXATION

I have just returned from a month in Europe, a week in Czechoslovakia and three weeks in Paris, where I sat in the Luxembourg Gardens and wrote short stories as a diversion.

To Fernando Ortiz, September 18, 1950; microfilm reel no. 65, frame no. 409; W.E.B. Du Bois Papers, University of Massachusetts, Amherst.

76. RESERVED MANNER

In general thought and conduct I became quite thoroughly New England. It was not good form in Great Barrington to express one's thoughts volubly, or to give way to excessive emotion. . . . There was on the street only a curt "good morning" to those who you knew well and no greetings at all from others. . . . This was later reinforced and strengthened by inner withdrawals in the face of real and imagined discriminations.

Autobiography (1968) 93.

77. RIGHTS AND DUTIES

I am by birth and law a free black American citizen. As such I have both rights and duties. If I neglect my duties my rights are always in danger. If I do not maintain my rights I cannot perform my duties. . . . Whenever I meet personal discrimination on account of my race and color I shall protest. If the discrimination is old and deep seated, and sanctioned by law, I shall deem it my duty to make my grievance known, to bring it before the organs of public opinion and to the attention of men of influence, and to urge relief in courts and legislatures. I will not, because of inertia or even sensitiveness, allow new discriminations to become usual and habitual. To this end I will make it my duty without ostentation, but with firmness, to assert my right to vote, to frequent places of public entertainment and to appear as a man among men. I will religiously do this from time to time, even when personally I prefer the refuge of friends and family.

"A Philosophy for 1913," *Crisis* 5 (January 1913) 127; *Selections from* The Crisis, vol.
        1 (1983) 47.

78. SCHOOL DAYS

I had, as a child, almost no experience of segregation or color discrimination. My schoolmates were invariably white; I joined quite naturally all games, excursions, church festivals; recreations like coasting, swimming, hiking and games. I was in and out of the homes of nearly all my mates, and ate and played with them. I was as a boy long unconscious of color discrimination in any obvious and specific way.

Autobiography (1968) 74–75.

79. SELF-CENSORSHIP

A week ago, your publicity agent . . . sent me a copy of Langston Hughes' *Famous Negro Music Makers* and asked my comment. I wrote her today saying that I could not conceive of a reputable publishing house [such as Dodd, Mead and Co.] issuing this book and omitting Paul Robeson. No Negro in the world has done so much to make Negro music known over the globe as Robeson. I said that if in this omission you followed the advice of Hughes I am bitterly disappointed in him as an honest man and that I had known him for 35 years. I published some of his first work. I added that if this omission was forced on him by the policies of your firm, I regard your action as beneath contempt.

Letter to Edward H. Dodd, Jr., September 27, 1955; *Correspondence*, III, 387.

80. SENSE OF HUMOR

You are a very patient sort of person and your salvation like mine depends upon your very lovely sense of humor. Without that, I am sure we should both of us jump off the nearest and highest branch.

To Emma Groves, October 9, 1930; microfilm reel no. 31, frame no. 398; W.E.B. Du
        Bois Papers, University of Massachusetts, Amherst.

81. SILENT REPRESSION

For me it is practically impossible to get publicity for anything I do or say or write. Even the Negro press is closed [to me].

To George Padmore, January 27, 1955; microfilm reel no. 71, frame no. 643; W.E.B.
        Du Bois Papers, University of Massachusetts, Amherst.

82. SMART BUT YOUNG

My rapid advancement [in school] made me usually younger than my classmates, and this fact remained true in high school and at college and even when

I began my life work it influenced my attitudes in 'many ways. I was often too young to lead in enterprises even when I was fitted to do so, but I was always advising and correcting older folk.

Autobiography (1968) 76.

83. SNOBS

[In my boyhood home in Great Barrington] I cordially despised the poor Irish and South Germans, who slaved in the [woolen and paper] mills, and annexed the rich and well-to-do as my natural companions. Of such is the kingdom of snobs!

Darkwater (1920) 10.

84. SPEAKING FEES

Please for heaven sakes secure me a decent fee. One Hundred Dollars would be fine; $50 acceptable, and I would not throw $25 in the waste basket.

To Alice Dunbar Nelson, September 30, 1930; microfilm reel no. 31, frame no. 1064;
     W.E.B. Du Bois Papers, University of Massachusetts, Amherst.

85. SPEAKING GRATIS

If I begin the practice of appearing where I am invited at my own expense, even though the cause is good, I should not only be bankrupt but dead in a short time.

To B. Andrew Rose, September 16, 1931; microfilm no. 34, frame no. 498; W.E.B. Du
     Bois Papers, University of Massachusetts, Amherst.

86. STEREOTYPE

[As a student] I never saw a picture of anybody who was colored or black who had done anything in the world. Always well-dressed white men.

"Oral History Manuscript," May 5, 1960; microfilm reel no. 88, frame no. 1604; W.E.B.
     Du Bois Papers, University of Massachusetts, Amherst.

87. STUDY OF BLACK PROBLEMS

I laid down in public session in 1899, a broad program of scientific attack on this problem . . . and appealed to Harvard, Columbia and Pennsylvania, to take up the task. Needless to say, they paid not the slightest attention to this challenge and for 25 years thereafter not a single first-grade college in America undertook to give any considerable scientific attention to the American Negro.

Autobiography (1968) 199.

88. SUPPORTERS

It is possible that in some far off day much praise will come to my memory; although even that is not certain, for history plays curious tricks. Today, at any rate, I have a few fine and loyal friends; I have a small audience which, while it does not particularly like me personally, approves and applauds my work; but there is a company of Negroes entirely ignorant of my work and quite indifferent to it; there are very many of the envious and jealous; and there is an appalling number of those who actively dislike me and hate me.

To M. V. Boutté, December 27, 1927; microfilm reel no. 21, frame no. 911; W.E.B. Du Bois Papers, University of Massachusetts, Amherst.

89. THE TEACHER

[There was] a certain lack of sympathy and understanding which I had for my students. I was for instance a good teacher. I stimulated inquiry and accuracy. I met every question honestly and never dodged an earnest doubt. I read my examination papers carefully and marked them with sedulous care. But I did not know my students as human beings. They were to me apt to be intellects and not souls.

Autobiography (1968) 283.

90. TEACHING NEGROES

I see no reason to commit suicide because no white university has ever offered me a chair. That is their loss not mine. I have spent a quarter of a century teaching Negro students in Negro schools. I am proud of it.

Chicago Defender, November 29, 1947; *Newspaper Columns by W.E.B. Du Bois* (1986) 745.

91. THEORY AND PRACTICE

During the last few years I have been spending about twelve or fifteen dollars a year with you for cleaning and pressing of clothes. I find this year that apparently you no longer hire colored helpers on your delivery wagons. I think that it is only fair that in the future I confine my patronage to those who reciprocate by hiring colored people.

To Stoddard's, Atlanta, July 16, 1941; microfilm reel no. 53, frame no. 387; W.E.B. Du Bois Papers, University of Massachusetts, Amherst.

92. UNIVERSITY OF PENNSYLVANIA

. . . It would have been a fine thing if after this difficult, successful piece of work [*The Philadelphia Negro*], the University of Pennsylvania had at least offered me a temporary instructorship. . . . But then, as now, I know an insult when I see it.

Autobiography (1968) 199.

93. WALL PAPER

I should like a crimson wall paper in my room, dark red, or something of that sort. The woodwork can be white or if possible black.

To Yolande Du Bois Williams, January 9, 1940; microfilm reel no. 52, frame no. 302;
    W.E.B. Du Bois Papers, University of Massachusetts, Amherst.

94. WASHING DIRTY LINEN

[A subscriber to *Crisis* magazine wrote me as editor, complaining that NAACP had picketed in London against lynching in the U.S.A. and protested that such dirty linen should not be washed in public. I replied that] I was going to wash that linen anywhere that I got soap and water. . . .

"W.E.B. Du Bois—A Recorded Autobiography" (1961) 3 (Folkways Records).

95. WEALTH AND POVERTY

I grew up in the midst of definite ideas as to wealth and poverty, work and charity. Wealth was the result of work and saving and the rich rightly inherited the earth. The poor, on the whole, were themselves to be blamed. They were unfortunate and if so their fortunes could easily be mended with care. But chiefly, they were "shiftless," and "shiftlessness" was unforgivable.

Autobiography (1968) 80.

96. WEDDING COSTS

As to the size and cost of the wedding: We must be careful not to be so ostentatious and showy as to be vulgar. The expense ought to be well within our economic situation. I am especially alarmed about the number of bridesmaids. It seems to me that fifteen is beyond all possibility. . . . We have decided that two hundred ought to be the outside limit for persons invited to the reception. Even this is an awful mob, and the thought of feeding them makes me feel weak. . . .

To daughter Yolande, January 13, 1928; microfilm reel no. 25, frame no. 368; W.E.B.
    Du Bois Papers, University of Massachusetts, Amherst. (Five hundred people
    attended the reception, and there were sixteen bridesmaids. See letter to Mildred
    Bryant Jones, April 13, 1928; frame no. 845.)

97. WEDDING ETIQUETTE

At a Six O'clock wedding no one knows how to dress; whether for afternoon or evening. For a Seven O'clock wedding, the ushers would probably have as much difficulty in providing proper dress, as in the afternoon. The tuxedoes would not be acceptable. . . . For an afternoon wedding, all they need is a cut-away coat with a white vest or a vest of the same material and dark or striped trousers.

To Countee Cullen, his prospective son-in-law, January 31, 1928; microfilm reel no. 25, frame no. 146; W.E.B. Du Bois Papers, University of Massachusetts, Amherst.

98.   WHITE COMPANIONS

In the case of white companions . . . we could not talk together, we lived in different worlds. . . . Thus, I did not seek white acquaintances, I let them make the advances, and they therefore thought me arrogant. In a sense I was, but after all I was in fact rather desperately hanging on to my self-respect, I was not fighting to dominate others; I was fighting against my own degradation. I wanted to meet my fellows as an equal; they offered or seemed to offer only a status of inferiority and submission.

Autobiography (1968) 283.

99.   WHITE WORKERS

I was bitter at lynching, but not moved by the treatment of white miners in Colorado or Montana. I never sang the songs of Joe Hill, and the terrible strike at Lawrence, Massachusetts [in 1912], did not stir me, because I knew that factory strikers like these would not let a Negro work beside them or live in the same town. It was hard for me to outgrow this mental isolation, and to see that the plight of the white workers was fundamentally the same as that of the black, even if the white worker helped enslave the black.

Autobiography (1968) 305.

100.   WORLD SERIES

I want to thank you very much for your kindness in making it possible for me to get tickets for the fifth World Series ball game. I enjoyed the game very much, and it was the first World Series I have ever attended.

To William B. Graham, October 15, 1947; microfilm reel no. 60, frame no. 67; W.E.B. Du Bois Papers, University of Massachusetts, Amherst. [The Yankees beat the Dodgers, 2–1, and won the series, 4 games to 3.]

101.   WORLD WAR I

I was swept off my feet during the [first] world war by the emotional response of America to what seemed to be a great call to duty. The thing that I did not understand is how easy and inevitable it is for an appeal to blood and force to smash to utter negation any ideal for which it is used. . . . I am ashamed of my own lack of foresight. . . .

To Kirby Page, June 24, 1930; microfilm reel no. 32, frame no. 796; W.E.B. Du Bois Papers, University of Massachusetts, Amherst.

2

The Trouble I've Seen

102. BARRED

The National Bar Association was started because the American Bar Association would not and still refuses to allow Negroes to become members.

Phylon 2 (Fourth Quarter 1941); *Sections from* Phylon (1980) 152.

103. BLACK BARBERS

The business [of barbering] became unpopular with Negroes because it compels them to draw a color line. No first-class Negro barber would dare shave his own brother in his shop in Philadelphia on account of the color prejudice.

The Philadelphia Negro (1899) 116.

104. BLACK CODES

Passed directly after Lee's surrender . . . these labor codes . . . attempted to reestablish slavery without a slave trade.

"The Economic Revolution in the South," in Booker T. Washington and Du Bois, *The Negro in the South* (Philadelphia, Penn.: George W. Jacobs Co., 1907) 77–122; *Writings by W.E.B. Du Bois in Periodicals Edited by Others*, vol. 2 (1982) 62.

105. BLACKS IN MILITARY

[After World War I] I heard from the mouths of soldiers the kind of treatment that black men got in the American army; I was convinced and said that American white officers fought more valiantly against Negroes within our ranks than they did against the Germans. . . . I collected some astonishing documents of systematic slander and attacks upon Negroes and demands upon the French for insulting attitudes toward them.

Autobiography (1968) 274.

106. BUYING LAND

But it is precisely in this black belt that it is most difficult to buy land; here it is that the capitalistic culture of cotton with a system of labor peonage is so profitable that land is high; moreover in many of these regions it is considered bad policy to sell Negroes land because a fever of land owning "demoralizes" the labor system so that in the densest black belt of the south the percentage of land holding is often least among Negroes—a fact that has led to curious moralizing on the shiftlessness of black men.

"The Economic Future of the Negro," *Publications of the American Economic Association*, Series 3, 7 (1906) 219–41; *Writings by W.E.B. Du Bois in Periodicals Edited by Others*, vol. 1 (1982) 352.

107. CASTE SYSTEM

Alone and among modern countries the United States has set up in the twentieth century a legal system of caste among its citizens. This body of law interferes with marriage and the family, with education, health, work, and wealth.

Color and Democracy (1945) 90.

108. CHEATING

I have seen, in the Black Belt of Georgia, an ignorant, honest Negro buy and pay for a farm in installments three separate times, and then in the face of the law and decency the enterprising American who sold it to him pocketed money and deed and left the black man landless, to labor on his own land at thirty cents a day.

The Souls of Black Folk (1903) 170.

109. COLORED PICTURES

Colored people almost never see pictures of their racial compatriots done in color so that neither they nor white people interested would always realize that a white and black print portrayed a brown person. This is the reason that I deliberately spent $96 to make the public realize that the man . . . was brown in color. I think it was good advertisement for our racial aims although I admit it was a costly one.

To Elmer Adler, September 25, 1941; microfilm reel no. 52, frame no. 363; W.E.B. Du Bois Papers, University of Massachusetts, Amherst.

110. CONVICT LEASING

From 1876–1904 the State of Georgia has received from traffic in criminals a net income over expenses of nearly nine hundred thousand dollars from the sale of criminals to private contractors. . . . The sinister increase of this blood money is the greatest single cause of persistent crime in Georgia, since it makes the object of the whole prison system money and not reform of criminals or prevention of crime.

Some Notes on Negro Crime Particularly in Georgia (1904) 60–61.

In the South road-building, mining, brickmaking, lumbering and to some extent agriculture depend largely on convict labor. . . . The state is supplying a demand for degraded labor and especially for life and long term laborers and . . . almost irresistibly the police forces and sheriffs are . . . [pushed] to find black criminals in suitable quantities.

Morals and Manners among Negro Americans (1914) 42–43.

111. DEATH OF CHILDREN

In some cities of the United States half the colored children die before they reach the age of one year.

"Negro Mortality," *Hampton Negro Conference Annual Report* 2 (September 1906) 81–
84; *Writings by W.E.B. Du Bois in Periodicals Edited by Others*, vol. 1 (1982)
327.

112. DEPRESSION

[During the Depression of the 1930s] the rate of unemployment among Negroes was twice, three times, and four or more times as high as white unemployment. In Harlem . . . sixty-four of every hundred men were out of work, and four out of every five heads of families were jobless. Yet, in October 1932, 74 percent of all the unemployed in Harlem were not receiving any relief at all.

Mansart Builds a School (1959) 341.

113. THE DIFFERENCE

A Negro can today run a small corner grocery with considerable success. Tomorrow, however, he cannot be head of the grocery department of the department store which forces him out of business.

The Negro in Business (1899) 25.

114. DISCRIMINATION

[With reference to the American Association of University Professors:] I think that the persistent policy which you follow in spite of our protest of holding your meetings, national and local, in places where your Negro members are not allowed to attend is not only unfair but contemptible. I do not wish, therefore, any further connection with an organization that persists in such conduct.

To Ralph E. Himstead, March 13, 1945; microfilm reel no. 56, frame no. 1059; W.E.B.
Du Bois Papers, University of Massachusetts, Amherst.

115. ECONOMIC PROBLEMS

The problem of work, the problem of poverty, is today the central, baffling problem of the Northern Negro.

The Black North in 1901 (1901) 42.

116. FORCED LABOR

In considerable parts of all the Gulf States, and especially in Mississippi, Louisiana, and Arkansas, the Negroes on the plantations in the back-country districts are still held at forced labor practically without wages.

The Souls of Black Folk (1903) 151.

117. GREAT WHITE WAY

An actor with such wide world recognition as Ira Aldrich could not play in New York because white actors would not play beside him. Even as late as 1917 when Mrs. Norman Hapgood tried to stage Ridgley Torrence's plays in New York there was a great outcry against permitting white and black actors to appear on the same stage. . . . It has been only in the last decade that white and black actors could appear on the New York stage without protest.

To editor of *New York Times*, 1947; microfilm reel no. 60, frame no. 467; W.E.B. Du Bois Papers, University of Massachusetts, Amherst.

118. HARMING BLACKS

Murder, killing and maiming Negroes, raping Negro women—in the 80's and in the southern South, this was not even news; it got no publicity; it caused no arrests; and punishment for such transgression was so unusual that the fact was telegraphed North.

Autobiography (1968) 122.

119. HOTELS

In 1910, colored men could be entertained in the best hotels in Cleveland, Detroit and Chicago. Today, there is not a single Northern city, except New York, where a Negro can be a guest at a first-class hotel. Not even in Boston is he welcome; and in New York, the number of hotels where he can go is very small.

"Segregation in the North," *Crisis* 41 (April 1934) 115–17; *Selections from* The Crisis, vol. 2 (1983) 746.

120. HOUSING

So far as actual sleeping space goes, the crowding of human beings together in the Black Belt is greater than in the tenement district of large cities like New York.

"The Problems of Housing the Negro: III. The Home of the Country Freedman," *Southern Workman* 30 (October 1901) 535–42; *Writings by W.E.B. Du Bois in Periodicals Edited by Others*, vol. 1 (1982) 119.

The alleys of Charleston [S.C.] . . . are probably the vilest human habitations in a civilized land.

"The Problems of Housing the Negro: V. The Southern City Negro of the Lower Class," *Southern Workman* 30 (December 1901) 688–93; *Writings by W.E.B. Du Bois in Periodicals Edited by Others*, vol. 1 (1982) 134.

121. HUMAN BONFIRES

Human bonfires have been made [of Negroes] in three or four cases: one in Georgia, one in Mississippi, and one in Louisiana. In Louisiana the victim was a nice old man of the "uncle" type which the white South particularly loves. A theatrical company playing "Potash and Perlmutter" made an excursion to the entertainment and several society women were present.

"The Lynching Industry," *Crisis* 9 (February 1915) 196, 198; *Selections from* The Crisis, vol. 1 (1983) 90.

122. INNER CULTURE

[Blacks] . . . bent to the storm of beating, lynching and murder, and kept their souls in spite of public and private insult of every description; they built an inner culture which the world recognizes in spite of the fact that it is still half-strangled and inarticulate.

Black Reconstruction (1935) 667.

123. JAPANESE AMERICANS

Ten thousand Americans of Japanese descent, torn from their homes, despoiled of their savings and threatened with mob law have been settled in south central Arizona on 17,000 acres of land. . . . No American community welcomes these folk.

Amsterdam News, March 4, 1944; *Newspaper Columns by W.E.B. Du Bois* (1986) 582.

124. JOY AND BITTERNESS

Negro joy has today no natural spontaneity. Cynicism, bitterness among colored folk, is much more spontaneous than ebullient joy. But the motions of joy and carefree abandon must still be gone through with. They pay. They are almost the only things that do pay among Negroes, in music and vaudville, and even in books and writings. It is, nevertheless, more and more a pose - a method of earning a living. After and when the New Negro art enjoys a real freedom with a compensatory chance of livelihood, there will pour forth a flood of bitter recrimination and tragedy which will astonish the more complacent white world.

"What the New Negro Is Thinking," December 27, 1931; microfilm reel no. 80, frame
    nos. 466–467; W.E.B. Du Bois Papers, University of Massachusetts, Amherst.

125.   JUSTICE AND EDUCATION

The Negro is a problem, not only because he does not get justice, but because
his continuing lack of education hinders him from seeking and obtaining justice.

Amsterdam News, November 6, 1943; *Newspaper Columns by W.E.B. Du Bois* (1986)
    568.

126.   LIBRARY OF CONGRESS

I will venture to say there has not been a single week in the last ten years
when colored people who have tried to dine in the cafeteria of the Library of
Congress have not been either refused or segregated or insulted in some way.

Letter to Oswald Garrison Villard, January 12, 1929; *Correspondence*, I, 387–388.

127.   LURKING VIOLENCE

It is hard to realize in a law-abiding community how the fear of physical
violence broods in the air in the South. No Negro can feel himself safe from it.

"Violations of Property Rights," *Crisis* 2 (May 1911) 28–32; *Selections from* The Crisis,
    vol. 1 (1983) 7.

128.   LYNCHING

Condemn lynching men, and not merely lynching Negroes.

"Douglass as a Statesman" (1895); *Writings by W.E.B. Du Bois in Periodicals Edited
    by Others*, vol. 1 (1982) 29.

Remember that in the lynching like that at Athens, Georgia, of the six or
seven thousand people, nine-tenths are church members in good standing, Ma-
sons, Elks, Odd Fellows, business men, and even philanthropists. There is not,
there can not be today in Athens a single white man of prominence who cannot
put his hand upon a murderer, or who would refuse to shake hands and recognize
socially that same murderer. This is the real lynching problem.

"Diary of Journey" (1921), Series 3/C, Folder no. 5515, pp. 6–7, *Unpublished Articles*;
    W.E.B. Du Bois Papers, University of Massachusetts, Amherst.

[In May 1917] a Negro was publicly burned alive in Tennessee under circumstances unusually atrocious. The mobbing and burning were publicly advertised
in the press beforehand. Three thousand automobiles brought the audience,
including mothers carrying children. Ten gallons of gasoline were poured over
the wretch and he was burned alive, while hundreds fought for bits of his body,
clothing, and the rope.

Dusk of Dawn (1940) 251.

The South reached the extraordinary distinction of being the only modern civilized country where human beings were publicly burned alive.

Black Reconstruction (1935) 700.

Lynching continued in the United States but raised curiously enough little protest. Three hundred twenty-seven victims were publicly murdered by the mob during the years 1910 to 1914, and in 1915 the number leaped incredibly to one hundred in one year. The pulpit, the social reformers, the statesmen continued in silence before the greatest affront to civilization which the modern world has known.

Dusk of Dawn (1940) 223.

Before the wide eyes of the mob is ever the Shape of Fear. Back of the writhing, yelling, cruel-eyed demons who break, destroy, maim and lynch and burn at the stake is a knot, large or small, of normal human beings and these human beings at heart are desperately afraid of something. Of what? Of many things but usually of losing their jobs, of being declassed, degraded or actually disgraced; of losing their hopes, their savings, their plans for their children; of the actual pangs of hunger; of dirt, of crime. And of all this, most ubiquitous in modern industrial society is that fear of unemployment.

"The Shape of Fear," *North American Review* 223 (June 1926) 291–304; *Writings by W.E.B. Du Bois in Periodicals Edited by Others*, vol. II (1982) 284.

It is still a national shame and disgrace that at least every month in the United States a human being is murdered by mobs without judicial trial or any adequate attempt to ascertain his guilt.

To Jessie D. Ames, February 10, 1938; microfilm reel no. 48, frame no. 505; W.E.B. Du Bois Papers, University of Massachusetts, Amherst.

129. LYNCHING AS TERROR

The lynching of Negroes was mainly an attempt to terrorize them and grew directly out of the disfranchisement of 1876. There was practically no lynching in the south before the war and very few attempts to punish crime in this way between 1865 and 1885. . . . Lynching began to rise as a method of keeping the Negro in his place.

The Black Man and the Wounded World (unpublished), chapter 8, "The Challenge"; W.E.B. Du Bois Papers, Fisk University.

130. MACHINERY OF SUPPRESSION

Policies of suppression and repression, common in colonies and in slums, easily transport themselves to treatment of other minorities, whose oppression is not due directly to economic causes. We have all seen how racial antipathy evolves policies of religious intolerance; how economic exploitation is transmitted into color prejudice; how any refusal to submit to dominant cultural patterns, current at the particular time, tends to bring into use the whole machinery of suppression, which is born of economic exploitation.

"Human Rights for All Minorities," April 29, 1947; microfilm reel no. 80, frame no. 983; W.E.B. Du Bois Papers, University of Massachusetts, Amherst.

131. MASS MEDIA

There was a time when all allusions to Negroes in the public press were chiefly to ridicule, caricature, gross invective, or maudlin pity. This has not wholly passed away, especially in the South and in the dispatches of the Associated Press.

"Hopeful Signs for the Negro," *Advance* 44 (October 2, 1901) 327–28; *Writings by W.E.B. Du Bois in Periodicals Edited by Others*, vol. 1 (1982) 152.

132. MEETINGS

Meetings of Negroes in the Black Belt are always looked upon with suspicion, and they are stopped by a very simple expedient: somebody goes and shoots at the Negroes secretly and at the slightest sign of resistance, the whole organization of the Black Belt is called into being. This organization consists of all the law officers of the county, and all the white men near and in neighboring counties and states.

To the Editor of the N.Y. *World*, Nov. 20, 1919; microfilm reel no. 7, frame no. 1165; W.E.B. Du Bois Papers, University of Massachusetts, Amherst.

133. NATIONAL OPPRESSION

Whenever a nation oppresses a people it does not gather to itself simply the advantages of the privileged; it also gathers the distinct disadvantages of being always conscious of injustice and being continually compelled to act against its own conscience and against its own deeper wish.

"The Significance of Henry Hunt," October 10, 1940; microfilm reel no. 80, frame no. 777; W.E.B. Du Bois Papers, University of Massachusetts, Amherst.

134. NEW CIVIL WAR

It must be remembered and never forgotten that the civil war in the South which overthrew Reconstruction was a determined effort to reduce black labor as nearly as possible to a condition of unlimited exploitation and build a new class of capitalists on this foundation. The wage of the Negro worker, despite the war amendments, was to be reduced to the level of bare subsistence by taxation, peonage, caste, and every method of discrimination. This program had to be carried out in open defiance of the clear letter of the law.

Black Reconstruction (1935) 670.

135. NEW YORK CITY

No Negro in 1910 could sit in the orchestra of a theater, or get a meal at a first-class restaurant. . . . Negroes were not excluded from white churches, but they were not expected to attend.

"John Haynes Holmes, the Community Church and World Brotherhood," *Dedication Book in Celebration of the New Building of the Community Church of New York, October 17, 1948: 1825-1948* (New York: Community Church Publications, 1948) 36–37; *Writings by W.E.B. Du Bois in Non-Periodical Literature Edited by Others* (1982) 265.

136. PEOPLE AND THINGS

In the beautiful new business block built by the Prudential Insurance Company in Atlanta, Ga., is a great marble corridor. Within this are two passenger elevators and a freight elevator. On the latter is this sign: *"For Negroes and other large Packages."*

"The Savings of Black Georgia," *Outlook* 69 (September 14, 1901); *Writings by W.E.B. Du Bois in Periodicals Edited by Others*, vol. 1 (1982) 109.

137. PERSONALITY

Seldom if ever do we meet black folk. Black folk are not pictured in papers and they are not talked about except in bulk. The emergence of personality, therefore, of the Negro race is an unlikely thing attended with great difficulty and often almost an accident.

"The Social Significance of Booker T. Washington" (ca. 1920), Series 3/C, Folder no. 5513, p. 4, *Unpublished Articles*; W.E.B. Du Bois Papers, University of Massachusetts, Amherst.

138. POLICE

The Police system of the South was originally designed to keep track of all Negroes, not simply of criminals; and when the Negroes were freed and the whole South was convinced of the impossibility of free Negro labor, the first and almost universal device was to use the courts as a means of reenslaving the blacks.

The Souls of Black Folk (1903) 178–179.

139. POVERTY

Most human beings are so poor that they have never really lived. Most of the ability, genius and power of the human race is starved to death and is never able to give its vast treasure to humanity. And this because we pretend to think Poverty is necessary and inevitable.

Amsterdam News, September 19, 1942; *Newspaper Columns by W.E.B. Du Bois* (1986)
   467.

140. PUBLIC OPINION

[There is a] widespread feeling all over the land, in Philadelphia as well as
in Boston and New Orleans, that the Negro is something less than an American
and ought not to be much more than what he is.

The Philadelphia Negro (1899) 284.

In the South . . . less than one-fifth of the population would give Negro workers
an even chance at jobs; and throughout the nation only 42 percent. Three-fourths
of the Southerners would not work beside the Negro at the same job, and
throughout the nation only 43 percent would be willing that a Negro should get
a better job than a white man, even though he were better qualified.

Color and Democracy (1945) 92–93.

141. RAILROADING

We protect and defend sensational cases where Negroes are involved. But the
great mass of arrested or accused black folk have no defense. There is a desperate
need of nationwide organizations to oppose this national racket of railroading to
jails and chain-gangs the poor, friendless and black.

In Battle for Peace (1952) 153.

142. SIT-IN STRIKERS

[The southern student sit-in strikers] haven't put their finger on what is the
great problem, of course, mob violence and lynching and injustice in the courts
and disfranchisement—but they have put their finger on the one thing that most
people don't think about: the dozens and hundreds of petty insults that you get
every day, and that are unnecessary. They're carried on by people that are just
careless and mean.

"Oral History Manuscript," May 24, 1960; microfilm reel no. 88, frame no. 1654;
   W.E.B. Du Bois Papers, University of Massachusetts, Amherst.

143. SOUTHERN COURTS

The Southern courts have erred in two ways: One, in treating the crime of
whites so leniently that red-handed murderers walk scot-free and the public has
lost faith in methods of justice. The other, in treating the crimes and misde-
meanors of Negroes with such severity that the lesson of punishment is lost
through pity for the punished.

"The Negro and Crime" (1899); *Writings by W.E.B. Du Bois in Periodicals Edited by
   Others*, vol. 1 (1982) 58.

144. SOUTHERN SMALL TOWN

Thus the pattern of race segregation and control was laid down and kept rigid. None transgressed in wages paid, credit given or character of social contacts. Strangers were watched and warned. Crops and wealth were divided by long arranged rule. Mobs could suddenly be gathered and lynchings arranged by whites. Riots and murders were carried out by rule. One or two white policemen watched the Negroes. These towns by the thousands in the South kept the interracial pattern intact, held political control of the state, and were the center of stern religious dogma. It was no empty joke to assert in this land, "Man made the city, God made the country, but the Devil made the small town."

The Ordeal of Mansart (1957) 199.

145. STILL NOT FREE

Despite compromise, war, and struggle, the Negro is not free. In the backwoods of the Gulf States, for miles and miles, he may not leave the plantation of his birth; in well-nigh the whole rural South the black farmers are peons, bound by law and custom to an economic slavery, from which the only escape is death or the penitentiary.

The Souls of Black Folk (1903) 46.

146. SUPPRESSING DISSENT

I do not think that many of the persons in Europe interested in good causes know under what reign of terror we now live in the United States. No citizen can get a passport for travel abroad unless in the first place he promises to say nothing and not to take part in any activity which the present government of the United States does not want said or done.

To E. Sylvia Pankhurst, September 29, 1954; microfilm reel no. 70, frame no. 970; W.E.B. Du Bois Papers, University of Massachusetts, Amherst.

147. U.S. CONSTITUTION

By the second decade of the 20th century, a legal caste system based on race and color had been openly grafted on the democratic constitution of the United States.

Autobiography (1968) 231.

148. URBAN DEVELOPMENT

The Atlanta rich have wrung city taxes out of poor blacks and poor whites and then squandered wealth to lay mile on mile of beautiful boulevard through silent and empty forests with mile on mile of nine-inch water mains and sewers of latest design, while here and there rise grudgingly the spreading castles of

the Sudden Rich; but in the city's heart . . . the children sicken and die, because
there is no city water, and five thousand black children sit in the streets, for
there are no seats in the schools.

"The South," *Crisis* 13 (April 1917) 268–70; *Selections from* The Crisis, vol. 1 (1983)
    131.

149. VAGRANCY LAWS

Vagrancy laws aimed at the idle Negroes in city and town and [were] designed
to compel them to work on farms, going so far in several states as to reverse
the common law principle and force the person arrested for vagrancy to prove
his innocence.

"The Economic Revolution in the South," *in* Booker T. Washington and W.E.B. Du
    Bois, *The Negro in the South* (Philadelphia, Penn.: George W. Jacobs Co., 1907)
    77–162; *Writings by W.E.B. Du Bois in Periodicals Edited by Others*, vol. 2
    (1982) 66.

150. WATCHING YOU

Negroes traveling abroad are under special watch of the State Department and
would be liable to persecution and loss of jobs when they return, if they made
any criticism on race relations in the United States. Usually, the only colored
people who can get passports are those who promise to say the right things.

To Louis Harding Horr, February 27, 1956; microfilm reel no. 71, frame no. 1225;
    W.E.B. Du Bois Papers, University of Massachusetts, Amherst.

151. WORLD WAR I

Anti-Negro prejudice was rampant in the American army and the [Negro]
officers particularly were subjected to all sorts of discrimination [while in France].
. . . Colored officers were refused at officers' clubs. . . . Clashes of white and
colored soldiers ended in bloodshed in a number of cases.

"The Black Man in the Revolution of 1914–1918," *Crisis* 17 (March 1919) 218–23;
    Selections from The Crisis, vol. 1 (1983) 175, 176.

3

Mother Africa

152. AFRICA

No one can write [only] a few words about Africa because Africa is three or four times the size of the United States and no one word would be true of all parts of it.

To H. M. Jackson, December 9, 1925; microfilm reel no. 15, frame no. 782; W.E.B. Du Bois Papers, University of Massachusetts, Amherst.

153. AFRICAN DEATHS

Africa has no monopoly on cruelty, and more Negroes have died under European rule than ever died under Negro rule.

To Albert Schweitzer, July 31, 1946; microfilm reel no. 59, frame no. 489; W.E.B. Du Bois Papers, University of Massachusetts, Amherst.

154. AFRICAN HERITAGE

Among Negroes of my generation there was not only little direct acquaintance or consciously inherited knowledge of Africa, but much distaste and recoil because of what the white world taught them about the Dark Continent. There arose resentment that a group like ours, born and bred in the United States for centuries, should be regarded as Africans at all. They were, as most of them began gradually to assert, Americans.

Autobiography (1968) 343.

155. AFRICAN NEEDS

Africa is full of poor people who have not money to pay missionaries, and who need capital, education and medicine far more than religion.

To Jessie Sheperd, September 5, 1927; microfilm reel no. 23, frame 61; W.E.B. Du
Bois Papers, University of Massachusetts, Amherst.

156. AFRICAN NEWS CENSORSHIP

African news in 1915 was very carefully kept from knowledge of American
Negro newspapers by being omitted in cable dispatches. The best proof of this
is that in the *Crisis* which I edited from 1910 to 1934, there was no notice of
the Nyasaland uprising [led by John Chilembwe], although I was especially
interested in Africa. If the *Crisis* did not notice it, you can be pretty sure that
no other Negro papers did.

To George Shepperson, October 10, 1951; microfilm reel no. 67, frame no. 487; W.E.B.
Du Bois Papers, University of Massachusetts, Amherst.

157. AFRICAN AMERICAN STUDIES

[At Atlanta University between 1896 and 1914] there were . . . no special
undergraduate courses which touched the Negro except incidentally. In teaching
United States history we gave attention to the Negro but there was no course in
the history of the Negro in the United States. Also there were no courses on
Africa or African history.

To John Hope Franklin, April 11, 1940; microfilm reel no. 51, frame no. 555; W.E.B.
Du Bois Papers, University of Massachusetts, Amherst.

158. ANCIENT EGYPT

Egypt was by blood and cultural development a part of the history of Africa
and Negro Africa must be explained certainly in part by the history and development of Egypt.

Black Folk Then and Now (1939) 38.

159. ANTHROPOLOGY

Modern anthropology and social science have done excellent work, but it is
on the whole to the discredit of these sciences that they have so easily loaned
themselves to manipulation as servants of administration. Anthropology in recent
years has been called upon, not so much to state the truth and lay down reasonable
ideals of development, as to tell the administration what scientific paths it may
follow so as to keep peace with the natives and appease public opinion at home.
And especially has it joined the administration in discrediting the educated African and belittling his cooperation in science and social development.

Black Folk Then and Now (1939) 255.

160. BLACK ARMS

So far as Africa has been conquered by white Europe, this has been mainly by means of black soldiers, and Africa is held in subordination today by black troops.

Black Folk Then and Now (1939) 378.

161. BLACK AFRICA

Men of all races are welcome to Africa if they obey its laws, seek its interests and love their neighbors as themselves, doing unto others as they would that others should do unto them. . . . Our wealth and labor belong to us and not to thieves at home nor abroad. Black Africa welcomes the world as equals; as masters, never; we will fight this forever and curse the blaspheming Boers and the heathen liars from Hell.

"A Proposed Declaration of Independence of the Peoples of Africa," Nov. 1, 1951; microfilm reel no. 67, frame no. 312; W.E.B. Du Bois Papers, University of Massachusetts, Amherst.

162. BLACKS AND AFRICA

Whenever we [American Negroes] try, as of course we must try, to help our fellow Africans in other parts of the world, our work is looked upon as interference and with that attitude goes usually the assumption that we are busybodies who must be ignored. As a matter of fact, time will prove, if it has not already proven, that the fight which descendants of American slaves have made in the United States is one part of the most significant in the world and that its results are of importance not simply for themselves and for Americans but for all people of the world who are today in contact and commerce with the darker races. We American Negroes have not only the wish but the duty to do all we can in the interpretation of interracial problems for the benefit of the world and particularly for Great Britain, the leading world colonial power.

Letter to E. Sylvia Pankhurst, July 31, 1946; *Correspondence*, III, 133.

163. CAPITALISM IN AFRICA

What I am afraid of in the case of [Ghana's] Nkrumah and [Nigeria's] Azikiwe is that they will think that they can save West Africa by a species of reformed capitalism in which benevolent white industrialists will have a philanthropic share. In that direction I am convinced lies disaster.

To George Padmore, March 25, 1955; microfilm reel no. 71, frame no. 649; W.E.B. Du Bois Papers, University of Massachusetts, Amherst.

164. COLONIAL LAND

One of the first objectives of European investors in Africa was to gain ownership of the land. This effort had two purposes: to establish plantations on which cocoa, coffee, tobacco, grain and other profitable products could be raised; and to sequester enough land to make it impossible for the native to live without working for the outside capitalists.

"Black Africa Tomorrow," *Foreign Affairs* 17 (October 1938) 100–10; *Writings by W.E.B. Du Bois in Periodicals Edited by Others*, vol. 3 (1982) 57.

165. COLONIZATION

Some few efforts, as in Liberia and Sierra Leone, were made early in the nineteenth century to establish independent Negro countries, but this was before it was realized [by European powers] that political domination was necessary to full exploitation.

The World and Africa (1947, 1965) 33.

166. CONGO

The wealth of Belgium is primarily the wealth of black Congo, and that wealth is being used to curb the labor movement in Belgium and everywhere else it can. It is no answer for Belgium to point to its mission schools and hospitals, or even to its black priests and converts. Religion in the Congo, all unconscious of the function forced on it by capitalism, is making a humble, docile class of profitable black labor to underbid white labor everywhere.

Pittsburgh Courier, August 29, 1936; *Newspaper Columns by W.E.B. Du Bois* (1986) 110.

First Belgium confiscated all native rights to land ownership. Then they subsidized all chiefs and put labor under vast corporations in which Britain and America invested. They curbed education to elementary instruction under Catholics, with few exceptions. They gave the natives training in skills of a higher grade than in South Africa or the Rhodesias, but kept wages low and did not give enough education to permit training even for physicians; and for a long time they refused to let Negroes enter Belgium higher schools at home.

The World and Africa (1947, 1965) 281.

167. CULTURAL LEVELS

The level of culture among the masses of Negroes in West Africa in the fifteenth century was higher than that of northern Europe, by any standard of measurement—homes, clothes, artistic creation and appreciation, political organization, and religious consistency. . . . What stopped and degraded this development? The slave trade.

The World and Africa (1947, 1965) 163.

168. DUST UNTO DUST

I am happy to address you this morning as a citizen of the Republic of Ghana. All the logic of my life leads me to this place. My great-grandfather was carried away in chains from the Gulf of Guinea. I have returned that my dust shall mingle with the dust of my forefathers.

To Kwaku Boateng, February 17, 1963; microfilm reel no. 79, frame no. 1015; W.E.B. Du Bois Papers, University of Massachusetts, Amherst.

169. ECONOMIC POWER IN AFRICA

The power of British and especially American capital when it once gets a foothold is tremendous. But of course I realize that once political power is in your hands that you can curb capital, providing your own bourgeoisie permits it. I am watching the struggle with great interest.

To George Padmore, December 19, 1954; microfilm reel no. 70, frame no. 959; W.E.B. Du Bois Papers, University of Massachusetts, Amherst.

170. ETHIOPIA

Ethiopia . . . is a state socialism under an Emperor with almost absolute power. He is a conscientious man. But what will follow his rule? A capitalist private profit regime or an increasingly democratic socialism; or some form of communism? (1955).

The World and Africa (1947, 1965) 270.

171. EUROPE IN AFRICA

It demanded the right to exploit and develop an unexploited land, pointing out that already Africa is furnishing vast quantities of necessary materials. . . . When Italy and Germany call for a share of these raw materials what they really mean is the control of the labor back of the raw material, and it is this demand of the countries of modern Europe and America to have at their disposal the cheapest human toilers, that makes the real problem of Africa, just as it makes the problem of Asia and the South Seas.

Black Folk Then and Now (1939) 235.

172. EXPLOITATION AND REVOLT

The result of exploitation of Africa in the first half of the 20th century was revolt in the second half, from Tunis to the Cape of Good Hope.

The World and Africa (1947, 1965) 266.

173. FATAL HARM

What . . . was the greatest hurt of slavery which American inflicted on Negroes? It was not compulsory toil. . . . It was not too little food or ragged clothing. . . . It was not altogether personal assault and treatment as subhumans. All these hurt. But the fatal harm was the entire break of millions of Negroes with their past. Their language, their memories. . . . Their ideals and dreams: their habits of eating, bathing, playing and even thinking. Their concept of good and bad, right and wrong. In some matters this break was not complete.

"Negro Culture," undated; microfilm reel no. 81, frame no. 1447; W.E.B. Du Bois
Papers, University of Massachusetts, Amherst.

174. GARROTING AFRICA

The methods by which this continent has been stolen have been contemptible and dishonest beyond expression. Lying treaties, rivers of rum, murder, assassination, mutilation, rape and torture have marked the progress of Englishman, German, Frenchman, and Belgian on the dark continent. The only way in which the world has been able to endure the horrible tale is by deliberately stopping its ears and changing the subject of conversation while the deviltry went on.

Africa—Its Place in Modern History (1930) 42.

175. HERITAGE

My whole link with my African ancestors was built up from family tradition, while I was in high school and after. It was inextricably mingled with Dutch and French cultures, the English language and the Jewish Old Testament.

"Negro Culture," undated; microfilm reel no. 81, frame no. 1447; W.E.B. Du Bois
Papers, University of Massachusetts, Amherst.

176. HISTORICAL PERSPECTIVE

In the European middle ages when Africa became more or less separated from direct contact with Europe, nevertheless, African culture filtered into Europe, and legend and story and song came out of the dark continent. There was then no question of racial inferiority based upon color.

"The Negro's Fatherland," *Survey* 39 (November 10, 1917) 141; *Writings by W.E.B. Du Bois in Periodicals Edited by Others*, vol. 2 (1982) 111.

177. KENYA

In Kenya particularly, the theft and monopoly of the best land by whites, and the attempt to reduce the mass of labor to semi-slavery is one of the worst results of British penetration. It is a history characterized by oppression and deliberate hypocrisy.

People's Voice, January 3, 1948; *Newspaper Columns by W.E.B. Du Bois* (1986) 841.

178. LOSS IN AFRICA

We American Negroes often excuse our lack of interest in Africa by saying that we have lost nothing in Africa. We are mistaken, we have lost the chance to be treated as men because as long as caste and race discrimination is by common consent practiced in colonial regions in Africa and Asia, it will be current in America. The European aristocracies which are built and derive living and luxury from debasement of black men in Africa are not going to recognize Negroes as men in America and the Americans who ape European aristocrats are going to imitate race hate as their passport to superiority.

"A Program of Emancipation for Colonial People," in Merze Tate (ed.), *Trust and Non-Self-Governing Territories* (Washington, D.C.: Howard University Press, 1948) 96–104; *Writings by W.E.B. Du Bois in Non-Periodical Literature Edited by Others* (1982) 263.

179. LOW AND HIGH

All over Africa either the land has been taken or the market monopolized so that the people are forced to work for the planters and miners at the lowest wage which will keep them alive and reproducing. The raw material thus cheaply produced has been transported to Europe and America and the resulting profit, based on starvation wages in the colonies, has been immense, ample to allow the manufacturer and trader to pay their European and American labor comparatively high wages.

"Africa Today," *New Africa*, February 1949; *Writings by W.E.B. Du Bois in Periodicals Edited by Others*, vol. 4 (1982) 104.

180. PAN-AFRICANISM

It is . . . imperative that the colored peoples of the world, and first of all those of Negro descent, should begin to concentrate upon this problem of their economic survival, the best of their brains and education. Pan-Africa means intellectual understanding and cooperation among all groups of Negro descent in order to bring about at the earliest possible time the industrial and spiritual emancipation of the Negro peoples.

"Pan-Africa and New Racial Philosophy," *Crisis* 40 (November 1933) 247, 262; *Selections from* The Crisis, vol. 2 (1983) 722.

The idea of one Africa to unite the thought and ideals of all native peoples of the dark continent belongs to the twentieth century and stems naturally from the West Indies and the United States. Here various groups of Africans, quite separate in origin, became so united in experience and so exposed to the impact of new culture that they began to think of Africa as one idea and one land. Thus late in the eighteenth century when a separate Negro Church was formed in Philadelphia it called itself "African"; and there were various "African" societies in many parts of the United States.

The World and Africa (1947, 1965) 7.

Ghana must . . . be the representative of Africa. . . . All the former barriers of language, culture, religion and political control should bow before the essential

unity of race and descent, the common suffering of slavery and the slave trade
and the modern color bar. . . . Ghana should lead a movement of black men for
Pan-Africanism. . . . The consequent Pan-Africa . . . should avoid subjection to
and ownership by foreign capitalists who seek to get rich on African labor and
raw material, and should try to build a socialism founded on old African com-
munal life. . . . (1957).

The World and Africa (1947, 1965) 296, message to Kwame Nkrumah, prime minister
of Ghana.

181.   PAN-AFRICAN MOVEMENT

No one feels more unhappy than I over the failure of American Negroes to
stand fully back of the Pan-African Movement. I think their cooperation will
come in time; but I have not been able to accomplish it as yet.

To T. R. Makonnen, November 9, 1948; microfilm reel no. 62, frame no. 1068; W.E.B.
Du Bois Papers, University of Massachusetts, Amherst.

182.   PATERNALISTIC SCHOLARS

[With reference to the International African Institute, London:] I note . . . with
distress that your organization apparently has not planned for using the work of
African scholars; that they have no place on your board of directors and that
your whole attitude continues to be the attitude of superior people who are
working for inferiors because they know so much more than these inferiors can
ever be expected to learn. . . . This is a mistaken and utterly indefensible attitude.

To Edwin W. Smith, January 31, 1945; microfilm reel no. 57, frame no. 427; W.E.B.
Du Bois Papers, University of Massachusetts, Amherst.

183.   SOUTH AFRICA

In Southwest Africa [Namibia] the mandate commission of the League of
Nations severely blamed . . . South Africa for murdering with airplanes and
bombs, over a hundred men, women and children in 1920 for non-payment of
taxes.

To Major Roberts, November 14, 1946; microfilm reel no. 59, frame no. 462; W.E.B.
Du Bois Papers, University of Massachusetts, Amherst.

Without doubt, South Africa is today the most discouraging part of the world
and that is saying a good deal.

To Mary Louise Hooper, February 21, 1958; microfilm reel no. 72, frame no. 655;
W.E.B. Du Bois Papers, University of Massachusetts, Amherst.

184.   WHITES OUT

The withdrawal of whites from Africa like any sudden social change would
bring difficulties and even momentary disaster, but in the long run it would

restore the dignity and initiative of the black race and give them that independence and self-rule which made Belgium and France and all free countries.

To Albert Schweitzer, July 31, 1946; microfilm reel no. 59, frame no. 489; W.E.B. Du Bois Papers, University of Massachusetts, Amherst.

4

Education

185. ATHLETES

The three men of the football team who are enrolled in . . . [Sociology 471] have been present in class only twice and have never recited nor handed in reports although a fourth of the semester is already gone. I have, therefore, dropped their names from the class roll. I do not want sociology to interfere with football and I certainly do not intend that football should interfere with sociology. It is conceivable that a college course should be arranged so as to accommodate undergraduate sports but this is in no wise permissible in a graduate course by serious men and women.

To John P. Whittaker of Atlanta University, October 12, 1940; microfilm reel no. 51, frame no. 232; W.E.B. Du Bois Papers, University of Massachusetts, Amherst.

186. ATLANTA UNIVERSITY STUDIES

From 1900 to this day, no book of importance has been published on . . . American Negro problems which has not depended in some degree on our work at Atlanta from 1896 to 1914.

"Ho! Everyone That Thirsteth!" May 26, 1958; microfilm reel no. 81, frame no. 1188; W.E.B. Du Bois Papers, University of Massachusetts, Amherst.

187. BARGAINING

There is a more or less clearly expressed attitude in many Southern [black] colleges, that since the Negro professor must teach in the South that he should accept almost any wage offered him.

Amsterdam News, June 27, 1942; *Newspaper Columns by W.E.B. Du Bois* (1986) 443.

188. BLACK COLLEGE PRESIDENTS

The presidents of the colored state schools when they met each other, laughed themselves to tears at their experiences in making white morons do what they were determined not to do. But the game also had its risks and tragedies; sometimes a Negro president found himself replaced by a less scrupulous rival who bid lower for power. . . . In the background ever loomed black public opinion which flared unexpectedly in the path of many a black educational politician who proved too yielding in letting down the standards of the colored school.

Worlds of Color (1961) 11.

189. BLACK COLLEGES

There is not a single adequately endowed and reasonably equipped Negro college in the United States.

"Lecture in Baltimore" (1903); *in* Aptheker (ed.), *Against Racism* (1985) 75.

There are in the United States today about five institutions, which by reason of the number of students and grade of work done, deserve to rank as Negro colleges.

"Atlanta University," *in* Edwin D. Mead (ed.), *From Servitude to Service* (Boston, Mass.: American Unitarian Association, 1905) 155–97; *Writings by W.E.B. Du Bois in Periodicals Edited by Others*, vol. 2 (1982).

It is not only illogical but it is an indictment of the Negro college that the chief studies of the Negro's condition today are not being done by Negroes and Negro colleges. The center of gravity as well as the truth of investigation should be brought back to the control of an association of Negro colleges; and this not for the purpose of creating a Negro science or purely racial facts; but in order to make sure that the whole undistorted picture is there and that the complete interpretation is made by those most competent to do it, through their own lives and training. (1941)

Autobiography (1968) 3, 4.

190. BLACK COLLEGIANS

There are today less than 2,750 living Negro college graduates in the United States; and less than 1,000 Negroes in college. . . . The mass of so-called "normal" schools for the Negro are doing simply elementary, common school work, or at most, high school work with little instruction in methods.

The Negro Common School (1901) 117.

191. BLACK EDUCATION

The object of Negro education must be Negro culture; to let no part of our rich experience in this land be lost or die; to preserve our history and experience;

our poetry, song and rhythm; our biography and art; our ancient folkways. This is not in opposition to whites, rather in sympathy and fulfillment. . . . We face . . . the preservation and cultivation of Negro talent not simply among our rich and well-to-do, but even more among the vast numbers of our poor and outcast; among those locked by the thousands in our jails and penitentiaries.

"Ho! Everyone that Thirsteth!" May 26, 1958; microfilm reel no. 81, frame no. 1190; W.E.B. Du Bois Papers, University of Massachusetts, Amherst.

192. BLACK LITERACY

While officially we are 85% literate . . . this is doubtless an overstatement when census methods are taken into account and it is certain that attendance reports in Southern Negro public schools are purposely exaggerated.

To Edwin R. Embree, October 1, 1940; microfilm reel no. 51, frame no. 1163; W.E.B. Du Bois Papers, University of Massachusetts, Amherst.

193. BLACK PRINCIPAL

Remember that the principal of a [poor black] school is between two fires; he must satisfy the white folks first of all, or lose his job. He must satisfy the colored folks, and he must satisfy his own conscience, if he has one. Under the present circumstances, it's a pretty hard job: and he can use a great deal more sympathy than he gets. Try, therefore, to be charitable.

Letter to Henrietta Shivery, October 16, 1934; *Correspondence*, II, 9. The addressee taught in a school in Meridian, Mississippi.

194. BLACK SCHOOLING

The extension of the New England Ideal of universal education to black folk [after the Civil War] was an easy and momentous step. Nevertheless, only part of the church accepted it. The Catholics and the Episcopalians did practically nothing. The southern white Methodists and Baptists naturally took no part. The Presbyterians took but a small part.

"Will the Church Remove the Color Line?" *Christian Century* 48 (December 9, 1931) 1554–56; *Writings by W.E.B. Du Bois in Periodicals Edited by Others*, vol. 2 (1982) 313.

195. BLACK TEACHERS

There are, at present about 100 colored teachers in the schools of greater New York.

To E. Washington Rhodes, December 29, 1922; microfilm reel no. 11, frame no. 71; W.E.B. Du Bois Papers, University of Massachusetts, Amherst.

Negroes teach in the public schools of the North. There are perhaps 200 of them teaching in the public schools of New York City, and perhaps an equal number in Chicago, several in Cleveland, Boston and other cities. They are not segregated but teach white and colored pupils alike.

To Mrs. C. B. Shelvin, April 13, 1928; microfilm reel no. 26, frame no. 425; W.E.B. Du Bois Papers, University of Massachusetts, Amherst.

196. BLACK YOUTH

George Walker: You can't even teach your boys and girls the plain truth. That's the tragedy of colored youth today, I know. It's not just being poor; it's not just being kicked and insulted; it's coming to realize that this is a world where goodness and truth just don't exist. Or, if they do, you can never prove it.

Worlds of Color (1961) 309.

197. CCNY

I would advise you very strongly to seek a position in the College of the City of New York as teacher. There never has been a [black] teacher there which is additional reason for having one.

To C. L. Maxey, Jr., May 18, 1926; microfilm reel no. 19, frame no. 323; W.E.B. Du Bois Papers, University of Massachusetts, Amherst.

198. COLLEGE TRAINING

One never knows what one might have done without the training which he received. Certainly, I cannot imagine any of my writing being possible without the training which I received in College.

To Oscar E. Ferguson, January 22, 1929; microfilm reel no. 28, frame no. 418; W.E.B. Du Bois Papers, University of Massachusetts, Amherst.

199. COLONIAL EDUCATION

In some colonies education is emphasizing class differences by giving special training only to chief's sons and thus erecting a social aristocracy; in other areas, effort is being made to confine native education to vernacular tongues, which will keep the natives from knowledge of modern literature and modern cultural patterns.

Color and Democracy (1945) 42.

200. COMMON EDUCATION

I should recommend for the average colored child the same course of study as for the average white child.

To Benjamin Douglas, March 17, 1926; microfilm reel no. 18, frame no. 696; W.E.B. Du Bois Papers, University of Massachusetts, Amherst.

201. COMPRESSION

If you wish me to speak ten minutes, I will speak exactly ten minutes: Of course, you realize that it will be impossible in ten minutes to treat the [subject of] "Fight for Freedom in Education."

To Howard Selsam, February 4, 1948; microfilm reel no. 62, frame no. 161; W.E.B.
    Du Bois Papers, University of Massachusetts, Amherst.

202. COMPULSORY ILLITERACY

[Blacks are] the most illiterate group in the United States; the group from whom illiteracy was for two centuries compulsory, and a group which by its own efforts, as well as the efforts of friends has done more to reduce its illiteracy than any similar group in the world in the same length of time.

Letter to William J. Cooper, December 18, 1929; *Correspondence*, I, 409.

203. CONSEQUENCES OF DESEGREGATION

In time the Negro schools will be integrated into the one system but much discrimination will be hidden under various subterfuges based on poverty and living districts. Just as now rich suburban districts have excellent public schools while Harlem and the Lower East Side suffer from overcrowding and poor teaching.

"Integration," Aug. 18, 1956; microfilm reel no. 81, frame no. 1025; W.E.B. Du Bois
    Papers, University of Massachusetts, Amherst.

204. COURSE DESCRIPTION

[In] the course, "The Negro in American History".... Reconstruction will be viewed as the struggle between democracy and Big Business in a South dominated by land monopoly and caste.... The development of Capitalism and Imperialism in the twentieth century, covering both World Wars and the Depression, will be considered from the point of view of Negro workers and thinkers.

"The Negro in American History," 1948; microfilm reel no. 62, frame no. 632; W.E.B.
    Du Bois Papers, University of Massachusetts, Amherst.

205. DELIBERATE NONCOMPLIANCE

Using every excuse of neighborhood ghettos, of differences of certification; and variations in ability, the South will enforce racial separation despite the law for many years. The sufferers from this will be the children: the colored children under teachers who despise them; the white children who will expect favoritism, lawlessness which has characterized the South since the emancipation and set it culturally behind the civilized world. Class and caste education will continue. The rich will go to private schools to escape Negroes as the North escaped Jews

and foreigners. The democratic education of the public school will for a long
time not enter the South.

"Race and Integration in the South," ca. 1960; microfilm reel no. 81, frame no. 1405;
    W.E.B. Du Bois Papers, University of Massachusetts, Amherst.

206. DESEGREGATION

Even if by law we could force colored children into the white schools [of the
South], they would not be educated. They would be abused, browbeaten, murdered, kept in something worse than ignorance. What is true in the South is true
in most parts of the border states and in some parts of the North. In some of
these regions where there are mixed schools innocent colored children of tender
years are mercilessly mistreated and discriminated against and practically forced
out of school before they have finished the primary grades. Even in many of the
best Northern states colored pupils while admitted and treated fairly, receive no
inspiration or encouragement.

"The Tragedy of Jim Crow," *Crisis* (Aug. 1922) 169–72; *Selections from* The Crisis,
    vol. 1 (1983) 361.

All this dumping of a black child here or a few black children there into school
with little white devils and vindictive white teachers—can't you see the price
these little victims will pay? They'll drop out of school—or be dropped out—
by the thousands and roam the streets and go to hell!

Worlds of Color (1961) 307.

207. DESEGREGATION DECISION

I have seen the impossible happen. It did happen on May 17, 1954.

National Guardian, May 31, 1954; *Newspaper Columns by W.E.B. Du Bois* (1986) 931.

Manuel Mansart: So, the Supreme Court has spoken and with one voice. They
are wise. They know that if, for another century, we Negroes taught our own
children—in our own bettering schools, with our own trained teachers—we
would never be Americans but another nation with a new culture. . . . Am I glad?
I should be, but I am not. I dreamed too long of a great American Negro race.
Now I can only see a great Human race. It may be bent. I should indeed rejoice.

Worlds of Color (1961) 317–318.

208. DISFRANCHISEMENT AND SCHOOLS

The result and apparently one of the objects of disfranchisement has been to
cut down the Negro school fund, bar out competent teachers, lower the grade
and efficiency of the course of study and employ as teachers in the Negro schools
those willing tools who do not and will not protest or complain.

The Common School and the Negro American (1911) 137.

209. DISHONOR

The Phi Delta Kappa, the leading American educators' national honor frater-
nity, is split over eliminating a clause in its constitution which limits membership
to "white" persons. Sigma chapter at Ohio University admitted a Negro and a
Chinese and had its charter revoked. The fight now goes to the chapters of the
nation, two-thirds of whom must vote in favor before revocation of the restriction
becomes actual.

Phylon 3 (Second Quarter, 1942); *Selections from* Phylon (1980) 419.

210. EARNING A DOCTORATE

In my day a Ph.D. was a sort of proof of brains on the part of colored folk.
Today it is not. It is simply a routine certificate which helps a man who wants
a job as a teacher.

To Yolande Du Bois, February 17, 1928; microfilm reel no. 25, frame no. 370; W.E.B.
    Du Bois Papers, University of Massachusetts, Amherst.

211. EDUCABILITY

The question as to whether American Negroes were capable of education was
no longer a debatable one in 1876. The whole problem was simply one of
opportunity.

Black Reconstruction (1935) 589.

212. EDUCATED

The truly educated man is he who has learned in school how to study and in
life what to study.

"Postgraduate Work in Sociology in Atlanta University" (1900); *in* Aptheker (ed.),
    Against Racism (1985) 67.

213. EDUCATION

We want our children trained as intelligent human beings should be and we
will fight for all time against any proposal to educate black boys and girls simply
as servants and underlings, or simply for the use of other peoples. They have a
right to know, to think, to aspire. (1906)

Autobiography (1968) 251.

All the wealth of the world, save that necessary for sheer decent existence
and for the maintenance of past civilization, is, and of right ought to be, the
property of the children for their education.

Darkwater (1920) 214.

For three hundred years we have denied black Americans an education and now we exploit them before a gaping world: See how ignorant and degraded they are!

Darkwater (1920) 216.

I do not know a thing about education and never had a course in it.

To Helen A. Whiting, May 31, 1941; microfilm reel no. 52, frame no. 537; W.E.B. Du Bois Papers, University of Massachusetts, Amherst.

214. EDUCATIONAL FOUNDATIONS

[Some Northerners developed] a new theory of the solution of race difficulties in the South, sought to build up two competing classes of laborers in the South along racial lines and through this competition to secure industrial peace, and it is not too far fetched to say that the educational movements known as the Southern Education Board and the General Education Board have been primarily based upon the carrying out of this idea. So far as the race question was concerned they were not simply educational movements, they were movements of capitalists designed to settle labor and racial problems in the South along lines chiefly economic.

Statement to United States Commission on Industrial Relations (1915); microfilm reel no. 5, frame no. 209; W.E.B. Du Bois Papers, University of Massachusetts, Amherst.

215. EDUCATIONAL GOALS

The majority of the children of the world are not being systematically fitted for their life work and for life itself. Why? Many seek the reason in the content of the school program. They feverishly argue the relative values of Greek, mathematics, and manual training, but fail with singular unanimity in pointing out the fundamental cause of our failure in human education: That failure is due to the fact that we aim not at the full development of the child, but that the world regards and always has regarded education first as a means of buttressing the established order of things rather than improving it. . . . Instead of seeking to push the coming generation ahead of our pitiful accomplishment, we insist that it march behind. We say, morally, that high character is conformity to present public opinion; we say industrially that the present order is best and that children must be trained to perpetuate it.

Darkwater (1920) 205–206.

We cannot base the education of future citizens on the present inexcusable inequality of wealth nor on physical differences of race. We must seek not to make men carpenters but to make carpenters men.

Darkwater (1920) 210.

216. EDUCATIONAL SEGREGATION

[Present-day] educational segregation involves, as Negroes know all too well, poorer equipment in the schools and poorer teaching than colored children would have if they were admitted to white schools and treated with absolute fairness. . . . With the present attitude of teachers and the public, even if colored students were admitted to white schools they would not in most cases receive decent treatment nor real education. . . . Most Negroes would prefer a good school with properly paid colored teachers for educating their children, to forcing their children into white schools which met them with injustice and humiliation and discouraged their efforts to progress.

Dusk of Dawn (1940) 200, 201.

217. EQUAL SCHOOLING

Negroes are not demanding entrance into "white" schools. They demand entrance into public schools. They know that public free elementary education is the best and simplest path to democracy. . . . The South never established a "Negro" public school system. It set up a separate school system for Negroes, completely dominated by whites. . . . The whites furnished a deliberately inferior system of schools for Negroes and for seventy-five years the federal government permitted this.

"The *National Guardian* Dinner," November 21, 1957; microfilm reel no. 81, frame nos. 1118 and 1119; W.E.B. Du Bois Papers, University of Massachusetts, Amherst.

218. ENSLAVEMENT AND SCHOOLING

The United States of America permitted the enslavement of millions of black folk and then freed them in ignorance and poverty. From that day to this there has been no systematic attempt to give the masses of those people systematic elementary school training. It is time to make such an attempt.

The Common School and the Negro American (1911) 138.

219. FISK UNIVERSITY

At Nashville I stopped . . . to make a speech to the alumni of Fisk University in which I took occasion to tell them that the new endowment of a million dollars which Fisk had almost finished was the least of the things which she needed to make her a university, that she lacked the spirit of freedom, that she was giving the students no chance at self expression and that she was choking the truth by propaganda for the benefit of southern whites, and I insisted that the alumni must have a voice in the running of the institution.

Letter to Joel E. Spingarn, July 16, 1942; *Correspondence*, I, 292.

220. FUTURE INTEGRATED SCHOOLS

There are going to be schools which do not discriminate against colored people and the number is going to increase slowly in the present, but rapidly in the future until long before the year 2000, there will be *no* school segregation on the basis of race. The deficiency in knowledge of Negro history and culture however will remain and this danger must be met or else American Negroes will disappear. Their history and culture will be lost.

"Whither Now and Why?" March 31, 1960; microfilm reel no. 81, frame no. 1299; W.E.B. Du Bois Papers, University of Massachusetts, Amherst.

221. GRADUATE STUDENTS

I do not try to *teach* graduate students. If they are not able to teach themselves I am sorry but this I assume is not my business. I do not regard myself either as a tutor for ignorance or as a wet-nurse for morons. . . . My duty is . . . primarily . . . toward Science, its preservation and further extension.

"What Is Graduate Instruction in Atlanta University?" (January 16, 1940); microfilm reel no. 51, frame no. 126; W.E.B. Du Bois Papers, University of Massachusetts, Amherst (emphasis added).

222. GRADUATE STUDY

It would be grossly unfair to hinder a great man's training because the outlook for his employment is not at present rosy.

To Albert R. Mann, August 18, 1930; microfilm reel no. 31, frame no. 909; W.E.B. Du Bois Papers, University of Massachusetts, Amherst.

223. HAMPTON INSTITUTE

The chief difficulty with Hampton is that its ideals are low. It is . . . deliberately educating a servile class for a servile place. It is substituting the worship of philanthropists like Samuel Armstrong (excellent man though he was) for worship of Manhood. . . . The fact of the matter is, that if the Negro race survives in America and in modern civilization it will be because it assimilates that civilization and develops leaders of large intelligent calibre. The people back of Hampton do not propose that any such thing take place. Consciously or unconsciously they propose to develop the Negro race as a caste of efficient workers, do not expect them to be co-workers in a modern cultured state. It is that underlying falsehood and heresy, the refusing to recognize Negroes as men, which is the real basic criticism of Hampton.

Letter to Paul H. Hanus, May 15, 1916; *Correspondence*, I, 216.

[Hampton is] probably the best center of trade-teaching for Negroes in the United States. . . . We do not feel, at present, that Hampton is our school—on the contrary, we feel that she belongs to the white South and to the reactionary

North, and we fear that she is a center of that underground and silent intrigue which is determined to perpetuate the American Negro as a docile peasant and peon, without political rights or social standing, working for little wage, and heaping up dividends to be doled out in future charity to his children.

"Hampton," *Crisis* 15 (Nov. 1917) 10–12; *Selections from* The Crisis, vol. 1 (1983) 146, 147–48.

224. HARVARD AND GREED

Not even a Harvard School of Business can make greed into a science.

In Battle for Peace (1952) 171.

225. HARVARD CLUB

Your letter of November seventeenth rather astonished me. I have been graduated from Harvard College over fifty years and this is the first time during that period that I have been asked to join a Harvard Club. I have assumed that the reason for this reticence was that I am of Negro descent. Possibly, however, Harvard is learning something from this war for democracy and has changed her attitude. If this is true, I shall be very glad to hear from you and to become a member of the Harvard Club of New York City.

To Dwight P. Robinson, December 16, 1942; microfilm reel no. 53, frame no. 1083; W.E.B. Du Bois Papers, University of Massachusetts, Amherst.

226. HARVARD, FAIR HARVARD

When I was the victim of a ridiculous and utterly untrue accusation [that I was an agent of a foreign principal] it was almost impossible for me to get a single leading lawyer in the United States to take my case. The Civil Liberties Union refused. When I wrote to the dean of the Harvard Law School [Erwin Griswold] for advice I did not even get an answer. It was [Vito] Marcantonio who finally . . . took my case.

"The Political Philosophy of Vito Marcantonio," December 7, 1954; microfilm reel no. 81, frame no. 933; W.E.B. Du Bois Papers, University of Massachusetts, Amherst.

227. HARVARD SEGREGATES

In the last drive for students in the South where both Eliot and Lowell and other Harvard notables have frequently gone, the white South has been encouraged to demand its usual price. And so in the Harvard freshmen dormitories, southern white students must not be forced to live with Negroes.

"Harvard and Democracy" (ca. 1925), Series 3/C, Folder No. 5525, p. 8, *Unpublished Articles*; W.E.B. Du Bois Papers, University of Massachusetts, Amherst.

228. HARVARD UNIVERSITY

Yesterday Harvard received five million dollars to teach that the "American Way" of business was the best in the world; *not*, mind you, to *investigate* business methods in order to find which is best. Few teachers today can hold their job and teach the truth about American industry.

"Address by Dr. W.E.B. Du Bois. . . . ," June 19, 1949; microfilm reel no. 63, frame
    no. 904; W.E.B. Du Bois Papers, University of Massachusetts, Amherst.

Harvard was the goal of my dreams, but my white friends hesitated and my colored friends were silent. Harvard was a mighty conjure-word in that hill town, and even the mill owners' sons had aimed lower.

Darkwater (1920) 12.

I never felt myself a Harvard man as I'd felt myself a Fisk man.

"W.E.B. Du Bois—a Recorded Autobiography" (1961) 1 (Folkways Records).

229. HISTORY TEXTBOOKS

Our historians tend to discuss American slavery so impartially, that in the end nobody seems to have done wrong and everybody was right. Slavery appears to have been thrust upon unwilling helpless America, while the South was blameless in becoming its center. The difference of development, North and South, is explained as a sort of working out of cosmic social and economic law.

Black Reconstruction (1935) 714.

230. HUMILIATION

The irreducible demand of the white South in Negro schools is the teaching and practice of submission to insult—insult of Negroes to make them know their place. This the South insists upon. . . . Talk as we will of the new "interracial" Southern spirit, the white South today stands alone in the civilized world in demanding as a condition of daily intercourse with fellow human beings that they submit to personal humiliation.

"The Dilemma of the Negro," *American Mercury* 3 (October 1924) 179–85; *Writings
    by W.E.B. Du Bois in Periodicals Edited by Others*, vol. 2 (1982) 227.

231. HYSTERIA IN ACADEME

Today scores of professors formerly in leading colleges are without work because of their convictions, even when they have broken no laws. Daily our schools are being deprived of some of our best teachers because those teachers have shown sympathy with socialism or communism; and despite the fact that these beliefs have never interfered with their teaching ability or moral integrity. Our colleges today are filled with students who are afraid to inquire or express their ideas for fear that on graduation they will be denied the right to earn a living.

"To the World Peace Congress at Helsinki," July 1955; microfilm reel no. 81, frame no. 1002; W.E.B. Du Bois Papers, University of Massachusetts, Amherst.

232. IGNORANCE

The degree of ignorance [among rural blacks in Georgia] cannot easily be expressed. We may say, for instance, that nearly two-thirds of them cannot read or write. This but partially expresses the fact. They are ignorant of the world about them, of modern economic organization, of the function of government, of individual worth and possibilities,—of nearly all those things which slavery in self-defense had to keep them from learning.

The Souls of Black Folk (1903) 143.

233. ILLITERACY

At Emancipation . . . illiteracy among the colored population was probably about ninety percent.

The Common School and the Negro American (1911) 16.

234. INDUSTRIAL EDUCATION

The mass of men who preach exclusive industrial education for Negroes are simply welding new shackles for workingmen white and black.

Letter to S. H. Cummings, November 18, 1904; *Correspondence*, I, 80.

235. INFERIOR SEPARATE SCHOOLS

With very few exceptions where there are separate schools the colored teachers receive lower salaries, the buildings for colored children are cheaper, less well-situated and more poorly equipped, and the school funds are much smaller. I do not know of a single case of separate schools where some of these things are not true, and in most cases, all of them are true.

To Clarissa Jester, October 10, 1928; microfilm reel no. 25, frame no. 802; W.E.B. Du Bois Papers, University of Massachusetts, Amherst.

236. INSTITUTIONAL RACISM

[The overall effect of the work of foundations concerned with black schooling in the South has] been a very small result as compared with tremendous disadvantages which have come from the activity of the Southern Education Board and the General Education Board. . . . The men back of these . . . conduct their educational propaganda in the South by a grievous and fatal surrender to dominant southern prejudices. . . . They ended by accepting the attitude not of the advanced

South but of the reactionary South which said, first educate the white people.
The result can easily be seen in the present condition of Negro schools.

Statement to United States Commission on Industrial Relations (1915); microfilm reel
no. 5, frame no. 211; W.E.B. Du Bois Papers, University of Massachusetts,
Amherst.

237.   INTEGRATED SCHOOLS

I am in favor of mixed schools in those communities that are civilized enough
to conduct good schools regardless of the race and color of the students.

To Mary Grayson, December 31, 1930; microfilm reel no. 31, frame no. 366; W.E.B.
Du Bois Papers, University of Massachusetts, Amherst.

238.   JIM CROW

Once I remonstrated with a colored teacher of literature for attending the "Jim
Crow" section of a theater in the top balcony . She answered: "Where else can
I see Shakespeare? I cannot afford to go to New York."

Autobiography (1968) 234.

239.   LACK OF EDUCATION

It is safe to say that today the average Negro child in the United States does
not have a chance to learn to read, write and count accurately and correctly; of
the army recruits, from 18 to 25, one-third of our young American Negroes
could not read and write. This is simply appalling.

Memorandum to Walter White, October 19, 1946; *Correspondence*, III, 121–122.

240.   LARGER WORLD

We should plan to escape the tacit assumption of our academic predecessors
that Europe and America are the only parts of the world that matter. We ought
likewise to make our escape from another tacit assumption, that all history, all
society, all institutions are significant only in relation to the various nations, as
we know them today. As we grow, therefore, let us take the first opportunity
of studying the histories and cultures of Asia, Australia and the early history
and culture of America and let us expand the study we now attempt to make of
the history and culture of Africa; to the end that our work in the social sciences
may present the relevant past, not to minds living in the past, but to the minds
of those who will live in and shape the world of the future.

"What Is Graduate Instruction in the Atlanta University?" January 16, 1940; microfilm
reel no. 51, frame no. 133; W.E.B. Du Bois Papers, University of Massachusetts,
Amherst.

241. LEARN TO READ

The first duty of the public school to its children is to teach them to read; and ... no person ought to be sent out of the elementary school who cannot read.

"Curriculum Revision," ca. 1935; microfilm reel no. 80, frame no. 635; W.E.B. Du
    Bois Papers, University of Massachusetts, Amherst.

242. LEARNING STYLES

The statement that colored children develop differently at certain ages from white children is a silly lie which some persons use to cover up their own prejudice.

To Maggie A. Caldwell, May 22, 1919; microfilm reel no. 28, frame no. 8; W.E.B. Du
    Bois Papers, University of Massachusetts, Amherst.

243. LITERACY CRUSADES

[In response to a federal conference on literacy crusades:] Will you permit me to say ... that if there are any people in the United States who have been more consistently and continuously ... engaged in "illiteracy crusades," more than American Negroes, I should be very much interested to know their names and race. It seems to me little less than outrageous that a Conference on Illiteracy will omit representatives of the most illiterate group in the United States; the group for whom illiteracy was for two centuries compulsory, and a group which by its own efforts, as well as the efforts of friends, has done more to reduce illiteracy than any similar group in the world in the same length of time.

To William John Cooper, December 18, 1929; microfilm reel no. 29, W.E.B. Du Bois
    Papers, University of Massachusetts, Amherst.

244. MAGAZINES

The fundamental difficulty with any periodical in the United States is the surprisingly small number of intelligent people who are willing to take time to read and think. Even those with sufficient intelligence are not willing to pay for thought.

Letter to Lillian E. Smith, January 4, 1938; *Correspondence*, II, 156.

245. MISTREATMENT

There are too many schools in this city [New York City] where Negro children receive such outrageous treatment from teachers as to be thoroughly discouraged in their search of training.

"The Negro in Large Cities," *New York Post*, September 28, 1907, p. 7; *Writings in
    Periodicals Edited by Others*, vol. 1 (1982) 383.

246. MIXED SCHOOLS

There was no doubt that the Negroes in general wanted mixed schools. They wanted the advantage of contact with white children, and they wanted to have this evidence and proof of their equality.

Black Reconstruction (1935) 663.

247. NAMES

Even graduates of Atlanta University teaching in the public schools are still publicly addressed by the superintendent of schools as "Mary" or "Susan." Their names lately, however, are printed with "Miss" in the school reports.

"The Housing of the Negro: VI. The Southern City Negro of the Better Class," *Southern Workman* 3 (February 1902) 65–72; *Writings by W.E.B. Du Bois in Periodicals Edited by Others*, vol. 1 (1982) 138.

248. NATIONAL DEFENSE

West Point and Annapolis have for a long time been virtually closed to Negro cadets, only two or three graduated from West Point and none from Annapolis. . . . There are still a few Negro officers in the army but none in the navy.

"Black America," in Fred J. Ringel (ed.), *America as Americans See It* (New York: Harcourt Brace Jovanovich, 1932) 140–55; *Writings by W.E.B. Du Bois in Periodicals Edited by Others*, vol. 2 (1982) 169.

249. NEGRO CULTURE

The time will come when a course in American Negro culture will be a central study of students of sociology, not only in Negro colleges but in white colleges and universities of the world.

Chicago Defender, September 6, 1947; *Newspaper Columns by W.E.B. Du Bois* (1986) 738.

250. NON-PUBLIC LIBRARY

For a long time no Negroes were admitted at all [to the New York Public Library] and the library branches, even in colored districts, paid just as little attention as possible to the colored constituency. Then, a few colored Assistants were appointed but their promotion has been very slow.

Letter to Ferdinand Q. Morton, February 18, 1930; *Correspondence*, I, 416.

251. OUTDATED EDUCATION

By and large we [members of Sigma Pi Phi fraternity] received our college education in the last century or the first decade of this, when the atom was indivisible; when light always spread in straight lines; when evolution was the survival of the fittest; and when mankind consisted of five indestructible races and socialism was a fool's dream.

Fragment (1958?); microfilm reel no. 80, frame no. 1117; W.E.B. Du Bois Papers, University of Massachusetts, Amherst.

252. OVERLOOKED

The President of Yale University, in talking to his students, pictures a community in which the standards of international conduct are those to which we have pledged loyalty in our private lives and as citizens; one that fosters honesty, kindliness, service to others, a respect for the life of others, a recognition of a general law that will serve in behalf of the weak as well as the strong. He perhaps forgot that the United States includes Georgia.

Phylon 2 (Fourth Quarter 1941); *Selections from* Phylon (1980) 150.

253. PARENTS

In the North with mixed schools unless colored patrons take intelligent, continuous and organized interest in the schools which their children attend, the children will be neglected, treated unjustly, discouraged and balked of their natural self-expression and ambition. Do not allow this. Supervise your children's schools.

In the South unless the patrons know and visit the schools and keep up continuous intelligent agitation, the teachers will be sycophants, the studies designed to make servant girls, and the funds stolen by the white trustees.

"Education," *Crisis* 24 (October 1922) 252; *Writings in Periodicals Edited by W.E.B. Du Bois*, vol. 1 (1983) 342.

254. PHILANTHROPY

The Southern Education Board, designed first for Negro education, then for all education, ended by working "for white people only" with the cheerful assent of its Northern promoters. The General Education Board, under Wallace Buttrick, as soon as it was sure of its millions, began to disabuse the minds of black folk of any assumption they may have had that the board had the slightest interest in them or intended to help except in the most casual and niggardly way.

June 1914; *Book Reviews by W.E.B. Du Bois* (1977) 34.

255. POVERTY AND IGNORANCE

We Negroes are today, in large degree, poor and ignorant through the crime of the nation.

"The Suffrage Fight in Georgia" (1899); *Writings by W.E.B. Du Bois in Periodicals Edited by Others*, vol. 1 (1982) 65.

256. PREFERENTIAL TREATMENT

A city may establish high schools and colleges for white people or Irishmen or French-Canadians, and at the same time refuse these privileges to Negroes or Swedes or Germans, because as the Supreme Court wisely remarks "the establishment of a white high school does not harm the Negroes."

"The Georgia Negro Again" (1900), Series 3/C, Folder 5505, *Unpublished Articles*; W.E.B. Du Bois Papers, University of Massachusetts, Amherst.

257. PREMATURE DESEGREGATION

No law today passed by the Federal government or by state governments in the South could do away with separation by race in the public school system. And that not because racial separation is right but because the pattern of racial separation is so thoroughly ground into the Southern mind that it is too soon for law to change it.

Amsterdam News, December 19, 1942; *Newspaper Columns by W.E.B. Du Bois* (1986) 490.

258. PRINCETON UNIVERSITY

Princeton University is the only northern college that has never admitted Negro students; also though repeatedly approached, it has never had the courage to explain its attitude.

Letter to Elmer Adler, May 4, 1944; *Correspondence*, II, 389.

I am . . . just back from a lecture at Princeton. I think that probably this is the first time that Princeton University ever had a Negro lecturer.

To Marshall Bidwell, December 18, 1947; microfilm reel no. 59, frame no. 1057; W.E.B. Du Bois Papers, University of Massachusetts, Amherst.

259. PRIVILEGE AND CONTROL

[The present educational system is] largely determined by that very economic inequality which it seeks to solve; and the power to administer the system lies all too largely in hands interested in privilege rather than in justice, in class advantage rather than in democratic control.

"The Future of the Negro State University," January 12, 1941; microfilm reel no. 80, frame no. 807; W.E.B. Du Bois Papers, University of Massachusetts, Amherst.

260. PUBLIC EDUCATION

The first great mass movement for public education at the expense of the state, in the South, came from Negroes. . . . Public education for all at public expense, was, in the South a Negro idea.

Black Reconstruction (1935) 638.

261. QUOTAS

At Harvard and Columbia only a certain number of Negroes are admitted. At Yale the limit is even lower than at other colleges. This applies not only to Negroes but to Jews and some other "undesirables." The policy which Butler [College in Indianapolis] is adopting is the policy used by Czarist Russia and now in use in Hungary and possibly in Poland against the Jews.

To Alva W. Taylor, November 16, 1927; microfilm reel no. 23, frame no. 257; W.E.B.
    Du Bois Papers, University of Massachusetts, Amherst.

262. RIGHT TO LEARN

Of all the civil rights for which the world has struggled and fought for five thousand years, the right to learn is undoubtedly the most fundamental. If a people has preserved this right, then no matter how far it goes astray, no matter how many mistakes it makes, in the long run, in the unfolding of generations, it is going to come back to the right. But if at any time, or for any long period, people are prevented from thinking, children are indoctrinated with dogma, and they are made to learn not what is necessarily true, but what the dominant forces in their world want them to think is true, then there is no aberration from truth and progress of which such a people may not be guilty.

"The Freedom to Learn," *Midwest Journal* 2 (Winter 1949) 9–11; *Writings by W.E.B.
    Du Bois in Periodicals Edited by Others*, vol. 4 (1982) 134.

263. SCHOOL AND SOCIETY

The school has but one way to cure the ills of society, and that is by making men intelligent.

"Curriculum Revision," ca. 1935; microfilm reel no. 80, frame no. 636; W.E.B. Du
    Bois Papers, University of Massachusetts, Amherst.

264. SCHOOLING

If American Negroes had had half the chance of the Russians to learn to read, write and count, there would be no Negro question today.

In Battle for Peace (1952) 163–164.

265. SCIENCE

Science today is a matter chiefly for endowed fellowships and college chairs. Negroes have small chance here because of race exclusion.

The Gift of Black Folk (1924) 316.

266. SCIENTIFIC IDIOCY

I am returning this personal rating scale. Of course, no one except a teacher or a parent could fill out any such idiotic schedule as this. I have written saying that I think Henrietta Shivery is a bright, energetic capable girl.

To the Registrar, Fisk University, September 15, 1930; microfilm reel no. 31, frame no. 285; W.E.B. Du Bois Papers, University of Massachusetts, Amherst.

267. SEGREGATED SCHOOLS

A "Jim Crow" school system is the greatest possible menace to democracy and the single greatest hindrance to our advance in the United States. At the same time, we have separate schools in the South and in some cases in the North and these schools have done [and] are doing excellent work. The teachers in them in most cases have been capable, self-sacrificing persons. I believe in these schools in the sense that without them we could not have gotten our present education. I should be sorry and alarmed to see their number increased and I look forward to the time when all separate institutions based simply upon race will disappear.

Letter to J. A. Walden, July 25, 1923, *Correspondence*, I, 273.

If Negroes have done well in certain separate Negro schools, two speculations arise: how much more might Negroes have done if all their separate schools had been adequately equipped and taught; and further what might not the Negro pupil have done if without hurt or hindrance the whole educational opportunity of America had been open to him, without discrimination.

"Pechstein and Pecksniff," *Crisis* 36 (September 1929) 313–4; *Selections from* The Crisis, vol. 2 (1983) 559.

There should never be an opposition to segregation pure and simple unless that segregation . . . involve[s] discrimination. . . . But if the existence of . . . [an all-black] school is made reason and cause for giving it worse housing, poorer facilities, poorer equipment and poorer teachers, then we do object, and objection is not against the color of the pupils' or teachers' skins, but against the discrimination.

"Segregation," *Crisis* 41 (January 1934) 20; *Selections from* The Crisis, vol. 2 (1983) 727.

Even in the North in a city like Chicago, you have segregated schools, Du Sable High School, for example. Instead of neglecting or criticizing such a school because it is separate, make it the best high school in Chicago. That is the only practical way to attack segregation today. Attack it by accepting it and making the best of it and at the same time stating the fact that the principle underlying such segregation is idiotic.

Letter to Sherman Briscol, February 11, 1941; *Correspondence*, II, 276.

If you segregate the disadvantaged part of a community, not only in its own schools but in its own semi-slum districts, you are retarding the rate of uplift for the whole community. You are giving that part of the community which already has the advantage, extra privileges but in the long run they will pay a bitter and exaggerated price in crime and disease which will affect the whole community and not simply Negroes.

Chicago Defender, October 13, 1945; *Newspaper Columns by W.E.B. Du Bois* (1986) 658–59.

268. SEGREGATION OR INTEGRATION?

Theoretically, the Negro needs neither segregated schools nor mixed schools. What he needs is Education. What he must remember is that there is no magic, either in mixed schools or in segregated schools. A mixed school with poor unsympathetic teachers, with hostile public opinion, and no teaching of truth concerning black folks, is bad. A segregated school with ignorant placeholders, inadequate equipment, poor salaries, and wretched housing, is equally bad. Other things being equal, the mixed school is the broader, more natural basis for the education of all youth. It gives wider contacts; it inspires greater self-confidence; and suppresses the inferiority complex. But other things seldom are equal, and in that case, Sympathy, Knowledge, and the Truth, outweigh all that the mixed school can offer.

"Does the Negro Need Separate Schools?" *Journal of Negro Education* 4 (July 1935) 328–35; *Writings by W.E.B. Du Bois in Periodicals Edited by Others*, vol. 3 (1982) 14.

269. SOCIAL SPACE

In all things that degrade and drag down there is in Atlanta little argument as to the color line; that facilities for drinking, gambling, and carousing are as wide open for black boys as for whites, and that, while the city has not seats enough in her schoolhouses for half her black children, she has ample provision for them in her jails.

"The Opening of the Library," *Independent* 54 (April 3, 1902) 809–10; *Writings by W.E.B. Du Bois in Periodicals Edited by Others*, vol. 1 (1982) 147.

270. SPENDING AND SCHOOLING

Negro education cannot function until you spend money on Negro education. It is idle to measure and discuss the way in which it falls behind other educational effort until this is done. Here in Atlanta, we have a Negro High School built for 1400, which now has over 4000 and double sessions, that is all the students going on half time. A series of measurements could easily show how woefully these students fall below standards, but why waste time on measurements? The one fact stands out that Atlanta is not adequately supporting her Negro schools.

To Ina Corinne Brown, March 6, 1944; microfilm reel no. 55, frame no. 1000; W.E.B. Du Bois Papers, University of Massachusetts, Amherst.

271. STUDENT FINANCIAL AID

I was brought up in a day and state where education beyond the grammar school, beyond elementary reading, writing and arithmetic was considered to be a private matter. If a child was to be educated in the high school and college and for the professions, this was a matter to which the private individual and private fortunes should attend. This was the New England counterpart of the English idea of education which lasted there down almost to our day. There grew up consequently in New England endowed high schools and private colleges which have become the best known in the nation and which long prided themselves on giving training not simply to the rich and well-to-do but even to talented children of all classes and races. I can remember that the first catalogue of Harvard University which I ever saw had in it a statement that the experience of the university warrants the statement that no student of ability need leave the institution because of lack of funds. This situation gradually changed. The demand for high school and college training on the part of the mass of youth in the United States rapidly outran the facilities which private institutions supported by private endowments could furnish, and there arose the public town and city high school and the state university.

"The Future of the Negro State University," January 12, 1941; microfilm reel no. 80, frame no. 807; W.E.B. Du Bois Papers, University of Massachusetts, Amherst.

272. TALENT

We know in America how to discourage, choke, and murder ability when it so far forgets itself as to choose a dark skin.

Darkwater (1920) 199.

273. TWO LONG MOVEMENTS

What is needed . . . is two long movements moving toward the same end: the increase in the endowment and efficiency of the colored college until it becomes the equal in facilities and teaching to the white college; the broadening and cultural liberation of the white college so that it can come to the place where a black student can be really welcomed and trained.

"A Philosophy of Race Segregation," October 1935; microfilm reel no. 80, frame no. 631; W.E.B. Du Bois Papers, University of Massachusetts, Amherst.

274. UNEQUAL SCHOOLING

Thirty-four City Superintendents, from all the Southern States, sent in reports. In only three cases did the cities reporting maintain colored high schools, although nearly all had white high schools.

The Negro Common School (1901) 105.

275. UNIVERSITIES

Not one of the 12 colored Ph.D.'s of last year, trained by highest American and European standards, is going to get a job in any white university.

"Segregation in the North," *Crisis* 41 (April 1934) 115–17; *Selections from* The Crisis, vol. 2 (1983) 746.

There are today on the faculties of the leading universities of the North seventy Negro instructors, ranging from a full professor at the University of Chicago to associate professors and instructors in other institutions.

"The Negro Since 1900: A Progress Report," *New York Times Magazine*, Nov. 21, 1948; *Writings by W.E.B. Du Bois in Periodicals Edited by Others*, vol. 4 (1982) 91.

No American university (except Negro institutions in understandable self-defense) has ever recognized that I had any claim to scholarship.

Autobiography (1968) 25.

276. UNIVERSITY OF CHICAGO

There has been for years in the University of Chicago in certain departments a strong anti-Negro bias. There has been among its students, drawn largely as they are from the middle South, a pro-Southern attitude which zealots like [historian] Avery Craven have striven bitterly to fasten upon the institution. Certain departments have absolutely refused to give degrees to Negroes despite their accomplishment, and it is intimated that in the case of Allison Davis his appointment came in spite of President Hutchins and not with his approval. But be this as it may, no institution in the United States needs more the broadening social outlook of a proven Negro scholar than the University of Chicago.

Amsterdam News, June 27, 1942: *Newspaper Columns by W.E.B. Du Bois* (1986) 444.

The department of history . . . is noted as having a good deal of anti-Negro prejudice.

To Rufus E. Clement, August 3, 1939; microfilm reel no. 49, frame no. 1024; W.E.B. Du Bois Papers, University of Massachusetts, Amherst.

Even the History Department of Chicago University could not continue to deny the Ph.D. degree, by unfair marking, although it tried desperately for years, and supported a department of white Southern race philosophy.

Worlds of Color (1961) 17.

277. UNIVERSITY OF NORTH CAROLINA

No study of lynching in the United States, backed by adequate funds, has been made. The University of North Carolina . . . has plenty of money to study matters which are of interest and favorable to the white race, but for nothing else.

To A. N. der Hollander, August 19, 1932; microfilm reel no. 36, frame no. 1061; W.E.B. Du Bois Papers, University of Massachusetts, Amherst.

278. UNIVERSITY OF PENNSYLVANIA

Within the memory of living men the University of Pennsylvania not only refused to admit Negroes as students, but even as listeners in the lecture halls.

The Philadelphia Negro (1899) 88.

279. VESTED INTERESTS

I believe thoroughly that the United States Government should give aid to the education of Negroes in the South [and I] should not care whether the Southern whites objected or not. This . . . seems to me a rather curious proviso; it is as though we should say that Child Labor should be stopped in factories providing all the stockholders agreed. Or that labor should be granted decent wages on request of capitalists.

Letter to Alfred Vollum, October 24, 1907; *Correspondence*, I, 135.

280. VOCATIONAL EDUCATION

Negro youth are being taught the technique of a rapidly disappearing age of hand work. The training has undoubtedly good physical and mental results but if used as a means of livelihood it will command the poor and decreasing wages of tinkers and repairers; and those who follow these methods will be completely shut out of modern machine industry.

The Negro American Artisan (1912) 121.

281. VOCATIONAL GUIDANCE

Very few Negroes would get a chance to go to college if white vocational guidance had the last word.

To Mildred Scott Olmsted, January 11, 1922; microfilm reel no. 11, frame no. 211; W.E.B. Du Bois Papers, University of Massachusetts, Amherst.

282. VOCATIONAL TRAINING

We believe in vocational training, but we also believe that the vocation of a man in a modern civilized land includes not only the technique of his actual work but intelligent comprehension of his elementary duties as a father, citizen, and maker of public opinion, as a possible voter, a conservor of the public health, an intelligent follower of moral customs, and one who can at least appreciate if not partake something of the higher spiritual life of the world.

"Politics and Industry," May 31, 1909; microfilm reel no. 80, frame no. 187; W.E.B. Du Bois Papers, University of Massachusetts, Amherst.

283. WILBERFORCE UNIVERSITY

Wilberforce was a small colored denominational college married to a state normal school [in Ohio]. The church was too poor to run the college; the state tolerated the normal school so as to keep Negroes out of other state schools.

Autobiography (1968) 185–186.

284. WOODSON, CARTER G.

No white university ever recognized his work; no white scientific society ever honored him. Perhaps this was his greatest award.

Chicago Globe, April 29, 1950; *Newspaper Columns by W.E.B. Du Bois* (1986) 1048.

285. YALE UNIVERSITY

Mr. Johnson, the new dean of Yale . . . is a Southerner, and recently told a colored applicant that Yale did not want "Chinese, Jews or Negroes." The ideal of such folk would be a world inhabited by flaxenhaired wax dolls with or without brains.

"Politics," *Crisis* 4 (August 1912) 180–81; *Selections from* The Crisis, vol. 1 (1983) 40.

Judging from the experience at Yale, it will be at least fifty years before a black professor appears.

"The Social Significance of These Three Cases" (1951); *Against Racism* (1985) 281.

5

Racism

286. AMERICA'S BELGIUM

What is the black man but America's Belgium, and how could America condemn in Germany that which she commits, just as brutally, within her own borders?

Darkwater (1920) 34.

287. ANCIENT HISTORY

I want to get a line on the more important references to Negroes and black folk in Greek and Latin literature. . . . I have a theory that the Greeks who knew Negroes before Christ thought them quite the equals of any men.

To Frank M. Snowden, Jr., May 17, 1945; microfilm reel no. 57, frame no. 1281; W.E.B. Du Bois Papers, University of Massachusetts, Amherst.

288. ANCIENT SLAVERY

Greece and Rome had their chief supplies of slaves from Europe and Asia. Egypt enslaved races of all colors, and if there were more blacks than others among her slaves, there were also more blacks among her nobles and Pharaohs, and both facts are explained by her racial origin and geographical position.

The Negro (1915) 86.

289. AUDIENCES

I am going to tell this story as though Negroes were ordinary human beings, realizing that this attitude will from the first seriously curtail my audience.

Black Reconstruction (1935), "To the Reader."

290. BEING JIM CROWED

If an obviously colored person goes to make a reservation on one of the through reclining coach trains, he may be assigned to coach No. 1. This is not a "Jim Crow" coach, but on leaving Washington, no white person is seated there and all colored persons are segregated there. The same thing happens in Chicago, on through trains South. On the other hand, if the colored person secures an assignment to some other coach till he comes to the Mason and Dixon line; even then, on many occasions, he is not disturbed. On other occasions, he is asked to move, but not compelled if he does not want to; and in still other cases he is forcibly removed or even arrested and fined.

To Carl Murphy, December 17, 1948; microfilm reel no. 62, frame no. 387; W.E.B. Du Bois Papers, University of Massachusetts, Amherst.

291. BELIEF AND ACTION

[Most Americans] have made up their minds that it is impossible for colored people to be human and free in the same sense as the citizens of modern white countries. If this were simply a belief no great harm would be done, but immediately such people start out to make their belief come true. They seek to educate colored children as inferiors, they lay out inferior careers for colored men, they open up limited opportunities for colored youth and when colored folk chafe under these limitations they regard them as fighting against fate.

Letter to C. G. Kidder, April 20, 1914; *Correspondence*, I, 194.

292. BLACK FACES

[In *Crisis* magazine] I portrayed the faces and features of colored folk. One cannot realize today how rare that was in 1910. The colored papers carried few or no illustrations; the white papers none. In many great periodicals, it was the standing rule that no Negro portrait was to appear and that rule still holds in some American periodicals.

Dusk of Dawn (1940) 271.

293. BLACKNESS

No black people ever considered their color unusual or unbeautiful until they were taught to through others and then could only be taught this through physical force. Not only this, but people of other colors did not consider black as degraded or a curse in earlier days.

To Zora Neale Hurston, June 23, 1926; microfilm reel no. 18; W.E.B. Du Bois Papers, University of Massachusetts, Amherst.

294. BLOODY PROGRESS

It is only in the current series [of anti-black race riots] that the organized Negro-Hater is in hiding, clandestine, and absolutely without open defenders.

In every previous outbreak, the killers were aggressive, open, loud-mouthed and truculent. This is progress, even though it is through blood.

Amsterdam News, July 17, 1943; *Newspaper Columns by W.E.B. Du Bois* (1986) 538.

295. BOOK REVIEW

[Thomas Pearce Bailey's work] *Race Orthodoxy in the South* is a calamity rather than a book.

Book Reviews by W.E.B. Du Bois (1977) 49.

296. CLEOPATRA

I do not know whether . . . Cleopatra was dark enough to be called "nigger," but if she had been . . . she would not have minded it a bit; she would have probably smiled graciously.

To Lewis Gannett, February 3, 1947; microfilm reel no. 60, frame no. 462; W.E.B. Du Bois Papers, University of Massachusetts, Amherst.

297. COLOR AND CONQUEST

Ever have men striven to conceive of their victims as different from the victors, endlessly different, in soul and blood, strength and cunning, race and lineage. It has been left, however, to Europe and to modern days to discover the eternal world-wide work of meanness,—color!

Darkwater (1920) 42.

298. COLOR LINE

In many respects the Negro question—the greater Negro question—the whole problem of the color line is peculiarly the child of the 19th and 20th centuries, and yet we may trace its elements, may trace the same social questions under different garbs back through centuries of European history.

"The Present Outlook for the Dark Races of Mankind," *Church Review* 17 (October 1900); *Writings by W.E.B. Du Bois in Periodicals Edited by Others*, vol. 1 (1982) 79.

The problem of the twentieth century is the problem of the color-line,—the relation of the darker to the lighter races of men in Asia and Africa, in America and the islands of the sea.

The Souls of Black Folk (1903) 13.

To draw a color line does not free the situation of race prejudice. It impacts more prejudice into the situation.

To William Mason, December 25, 1928; microfilm reel no. 25, frame no. 1004; W.E.B. Du Bois Papers, University of Massachusetts, Amherst.

The one thing that unites . . . [the colored peoples of the colonies] in the world's thought is their poverty, ignorance, and disease, which renders them all in different degrees, unresisting victims of modern capitalistic exploitation. On this foundation the modern "Color Line" has been built, with all its superstitions and pseudo-science. And it is this complex today which more than anything else excuses the suppression of democracy not only in Asia and Africa, but in Europe and the Americas. But it is left to the greatest modern democracy, the United States, to defend human slavery and caste, and even defeat democratic government in its own boundaries, ostensibly because of an inferior race, but really in order to make profits out of cheap labor, both black and white.

Color and Democracy (1945) 85.

The color line as it is practiced in the United States today is a modern institution; beginning with the cotton kingdom in 1820, solidifying about 1850 and becoming widespread since the Civil War.

To editor of *New York Times*, 1947; microfilm reel no. 60, frame no. 467; W.E.B. Du
    Bois Papers, University of Massachusetts, Amherst.

I still think today as yesterday that the color line is a great problem of this century. But today I see more clearly than yesterday that back of the problem of race and color, lies a greater problem which both obscures and implements it: and that is the fact that so many civilized persons are willing to live in comfort even if the price of this is poverty, ignorance and disease of the majority of their fellowmen; that to maintain this privilege men have waged war until today war tends to become universal and continuous, and the excuse for this war continues largely to be color and race.

"Fifty Years After," in *The Souls of Black Folk*, xi. These words were written fifty years
    after the book's first publication in 1903.

299.   COLOR PREJUDICE

Such curious kinks of the human mind exist and must be reckoned with soberly. . . . They must not be encouraged by being let alone. They must be recognized as facts, but unpleasant facts; things that stand in the way of civilization and religion and common decency. They can be met in but one way—by the breadth and broadening of human reason, by catholicity of taste and culture.

The Souls of Black Folk (1903) 90.

Undoubtedly color prejudice in the modern world is the child of the American slave trade and the Cotton Kingdom. Before American slavery became the foundation of a new and world-wide economic development, the trend of human thought was toward recognizing the essential equality of all men, despite obvious differences. Beginning, however, with the second quarter of the nineteenth century and with the recognition of the value of black slave labor, came a determined, even though partially unconscious, effort to prove scientifically the essential inferiority of Africans.

Black Folk Then and Now (1939) 119.

300. COST OF PREJUDICE

[A very great cost of prejudice] is the distinct retrogression today in the spirit of humanity. A careful observer may see it everywhere: he may view it in the appalling increase of unpunished murder, in the recrudescence of delight in public torture; in the careless contemplation of human suffering and in the widespread and noticeable hilarity over the systematic humiliation of human beings. We would have to go back many hundred years to match the present low ebb of the feeling of human brotherhood in certain broad fields and this is due mainly to the increase and nourishing of unreasoning and unreasonable prejudices against certain human beings solely because of race.

"Race Prejudice," March 5, 1910; microfilm reel no. 80, frame no. 232; W.E.B. Du Bois Papers, University of Massachusetts, Amherst.

301. DEFINING RACE

It is easy to see that scientific definition of race is impossible; it is easy to prove that physical characteristics are not so inherited as to make it possible to divide the world into races; that ability is the monopoly of no known aristocracy; that the possibilities of human development cannot be circumscribed by color, nationality, or any conceivable definition of race; all this has nothing to do with the plain fact that throughout the world today organized groups of men by monopoly of economic and physical power, legal enactment and intellectual training are limiting with determination and unflagging zeal the development of other groups; and that the concentration particularly of economic power today puts the majority of mankind into a slavery to the rest.

Dusk of Dawn (1940) 137–138.

302. ECONOMIC STANDARDS

I still believe in fighting race prejudice and segregation, but knowing that we cannot fight successfully unless we have jobs and income, and since our position in this respect is worse than it was in 1910 when the NAACP began, I believe today . . . not that we should fight discrimination less; but that we should seek economic safety more.

To S. Henry Grillo, March 11, 1936; microfilm reel no. 45, frame no. 979; W.E.B. Du Bois Papers, University of Massachusetts, Amherst.

303. ECONOMICS OF RACISM

At the bottom of race prejudice is the great economic cause. But I do not believe that this is the sole cause of race prejudice, particularly in a country like the United States. On the other hand, it would be a great deal easier to do away with race prejudice if we had economic justice.

"Basic Philosophy and Policies for Negro Life in the North," March 25, 1936; microfilm reel no. 80, frame no. 653; W.E.B. Du Bois Papers, University of Massachusetts, Amherst.

304. EVOLUTION

It has been quite usual in museums of natural history to illustrate the development of man by showing monkeys, baboons and Negroes as intermediate steps in the development of animal life to its highest accomplishment, the white man.

Phylon 2 (Fourth Quarter, 1941); *Selections from* Phylon (1980) 135.

305. EXPENSE OF EQUALITY

The NAACP feels if it had One Million Dollars for every dollar that it possesses, it could not take up the causes of injustice against the twelve million Negroes in the United States.

To Eldridge J. Baker, March 11, 1926; microfilm reel no. 18, frame no. 186; W.E.B. Du Bois Papers, University of Massachusetts, Amherst.

306. HISTORY OF RACE

The medieval world had no real race problem. The human problems were those of nationality and culture and religion, and it was mainly as the new economy of an expanding population demanded a laboring class that this class tended here and there to be composed of alien races.

"Interracial Implications of the Ethiopian Crisis: A Negro View," *Foreign Affairs* 14 (October 1935) 89–92; *Writings by W.E.B. Du Bois in Periodicals Edited by Others*, vol. 3 (1982) 16.

307. IMMIGRANTS

[America] . . . trains her immigrants to this despising of "niggers" from the day of their landing, and they carry and send the news back to the submerged classes in the fatherlands.

Darkwater (1920) 51.

308. INTERMARRIAGE

You have a right to choose your own wives but you have no right to choose mine.

"Black Social Equals" (undated), Series 3/C, Folder no. 7, *Unpublished Articles*, p. 10; W.E.B. Du Bois Papers, University of Massachusetts, Amherst.

309. INTERRACIAL LOVE

Would an American audience listen to an opera which was based on the love of a black man for a white woman? Of course in this case the love affair never comes to consummation and there are no love scenes, but you know American prejudice only too well.

To Roland Hayes, January 23, 1926; microfilm reel no. 18, frame no. 1037; W.E.B. Du Bois Papers, University of Massachusetts, Amherst.

310. LABOR AND RACE

Questions of labor, caste, ignorance and race were bound to arise in America; they were simply complicated here and intensified there by the present of the Negro.

"The Study of the Negro Problems" (1898); *Writings by W.E.B. Du Bois in Periodicals Edited by Others*, vol. 1 (1982) 43.

311. LAND

Agitation to prevent the selling of land to Negroes has for a long time been evident over large districts of the South and is still spreading.

The Negro American Artisan (1912) 130.

312. LOOPHOLES

The [Richmond] *Times-Dispatch* gnashes its teeth and orders the [Virginia] Legislature to pass a law defining a colored person as one having "any ascertainable amount of Negro blood." But this surely is not enough. Does the *Times-Dispatch* want its sister to marry a man who has an *un*ascertainable amount of Negro blood? My God! What a loophole!

"Virginia," *Crisis* 37 (May 1930) 172; *Writings in Periodicals Edited by W.E.B. Du Bois. Selections from* The Crisis, vol. 2 (1983) 580 (emphasis added).

313. NATIONAL CRIME

It is wrong to aid and abet a national crime simply because it is unpopular not to do so.

The Souls of Black Folk (1903) 55.

314. NO BLACK ZION

Negroes have no Zion. There is no place where they can go today and not be subject to worse caste and greater disabilities from the dominant white imperialistic world than they suffer here today.

Dusk of Dawn (1940) 306.

315.   OBJECTIONABLE WORDS

When the word "nigger" or "darky" is used by a contemporary, it is a matter to be resented. When, however, as in "Old Folks at Home" it is embalmed in literature and tradition, it would be foolish to object to it. We have no right to correct the text, because that is the way the thing was written, and certainly we would not want to lose a beautiful piece of music because some of the words are at present objectionable. In the case of a theme of no importance like the "Shoemaker's Dance," it was quite right to have the word "nigger" changed. I think it is also perfectly justifiable to let the authorities know that the present use of those terms is not at all proper.

Memorandum to James Weldon Johnson, March 11, 1925; microfilm reel no. 15; frame
    no. 1228; W.E.B. Du Bois Papers, University of Massachusetts, Amherst.

316.   PAN-AFRICANISM

I do not believe that it is possible to settle the Negro problem in America until the color problems of the world are well on the way toward settlement. I do not believe that the descendants of Africans are going to be received as American citizens so long as the peoples of Africa are kept by white civilization in semi-slavery, serfdom and economic exploitation.

Pittsburgh Courier, April 25, 1936; *Newspaper Columns by W.E.B. Du Bois* (1986) 66.

317.   PERSISTENCE

[The country] loved Negroes no better after emancipation than it did before and it had no more respect for them. It was just as willing in 1870 that Negroes should be slaves as in 1860; so long as they did not endanger the white man's income.

"The Problem of Problems," *Intercollegiate Socialist* 6 (December-January 1917–1918)
    5–9; *Writings by W.E.B. Du Bois in Periodicals Edited by Others*, vol. 2 (1982)
    116.

318.   PREDICTION

The South is on the threshold of doing away not only with hindrances to voting by the use of the poll tax and other enactments, but is also beginning to see that the white primary must go and that the mass of Negroes and poor whites must be allowed to vote. A Federal anti-poll tax law . . . is quite possible.

Amsterdam News, December 19, 1942; *Newspaper Columns by W.E.B. Du Bois* (1986)
    489.

It is fairly certain that by 1965 the American Negro will have a fair chance to earn a living at decent wages. There will still be discrimination in work and wages but the mass of Negroes will have begun their economic emancipation. . . . There will still be separate schools in the South, but separation in education in the lower parts of the North and even in some border states will have ceased. . . . Segregation in home and residential areas will for the most part have disappeared and race segregation by covenant will be illegal. The Negro will be voting effectively both in the North and in the South. . . . It is highly possible that in the next twenty years this discovery of [black] talent will go on at increased tempo and will be the most outstanding development in race relations.

"Can the Negro Expect Freedom by 1965?" *Negro Digest* 5 (April 1947) 4–9; *Writings by W.E.B. Du Bois in Periodicals Edited by Others*, vol. 4 (1982) 33–34.

319. PRESIDENTS

[Abraham] Lincoln came to know Negroes personally. He came to recognize their manhood. He praised them generously as soldiers, and suggested that they be admitted to the ballot. [Andrew] Johnson, on the contrary, could never regard Negroes as men.

Black Reconstruction (1935) 248.

320. RACE COMPARISONS

The fundamental and logical difficulty with all racial comparisons is that there is no way of determining just what a race is: how far the characteristics of a given group are inherited; how far they are due to social and physical environment and what biological mixtures have taken place.

Black Folk Then and Now (1939) 120.

321. RACE CONCEPT

The ancient world knew no races; only families, clans, nations; and degrees and contrasts of culture. The medieval world evolved an ideal of personal worth and freedom for wide groups of men and a dawning belief in humanity as such. . . . The new thing in the Renaissance was not simply freedom of spirit and body, but a new freedom to destroy freedom; freedom for eager merchants to exploit labor; freedom for white men to make black slaves. . . . The cry for the freedom of man's spirit became a shriek for freedom in trade and profit.

Black Folk Then and Now (1939) 126–127.

322. RACE IN ANTIQUITY

In ancient and medieval days the color of a man's skin was usually not stressed or even mentioned unless it had cultural significance; that is, if a group of black folk had a particular cultural pattern, then reference to the skin color of an individual belonging to that group fixed his cultural status. On the other hand, a man might be black and not belong to a black cultural group; in that case his skin color would not be mentioned at all.

The World and Africa (1947, 1965) 224.

323. RACE PREJUDICE

Without education or deliberate propaganda there is no race feeling at all. Children have no race prejudice. Race feeling and race repulsion only come because of persisted teaching and because scoundrels can profit by it.

Material appended to letter to Lester A. Walton, May 7, 1917; microfilm reel no. 23, frame no. 439; W.E.B. Du Bois Papers, University of Massachusetts, Amherst.

324. RACES

There is no race so homogeneous in attainment and heredity and education that you can speak of them in a lump, and predicate any far revealing truth concerning them.

To A. G. Thurman, February 25, 1908; microfilm reel no. 3, frame no. 327; W.E.B. Du Bois Papers, University of Massachusetts, Amherst.

325. RACISM AND REVOLUTION

The chief difference between us is this. You believe quite sincerely that a realization on the part of white workers of their class interest as opposed to white capital is going to make them rise above racial antipathy. I do not believe it. I believe that race hate will persist in the United States even when the lines of the class struggle are closely defined.

To Will Herberg, September 23, 1931; microfilm reel no. 35, frame no. 714; W.E.B. Du Bois Papers, University of Massachusetts, Amherst.

326. RACIST CONCEPTIONS

To the Northern masses the Negro was a curiosity, a sub-human minstrel, willingly and naturally a slave, and treated as well as he deserved to be. . . . Negroes on the whole were considered cowards and inferior beings whose very presence in America was unfortunate.

Black Reconstruction (1935) 56.

327. RACIST DOGMA

No history is accurate and no "political science" scientific that starts with the gratuitous assumption that the Negro race has been proven incapable of modern civilization. Such a dogma is simply the modern and American residue of a universal belief that most men are subnormal and that civilization is the gift of the Chosen Few.

Black Reconstruction (1935) 382.

328. RACIST TEACHERS

Teachers and officials whose racial prejudices influence their work have no place in colleges. I sympathize with all lawful effort to get rid of them.

Telegram to David Tyson, April 12, 1949; microfilm reel no. 64, frame no. 374; W.E.B.
Du Bois Papers, University of Massachusetts, Amherst.

329. RELIGION OF HATE

For two or more centuries America has marched proudly in the van of human
hatred,—making bonfires of human flesh and laughing at them hideously, and
making the insulting of millions more than a matter of dislike,—rather a great
religion, a world war cry: Up white, down black; to your tents, O white folk,
and world war with black and part-colored mongrel beasts!

Darkwater (1920) 50.

330. A RIGGED CONTEST

The race problem was not . . . a matter of clear, fair competition, for which I
was ready and eager. It was rather a matter of segregation, of hindrance and
inhibitions.

Dusk of Dawn (1940) 130.

331. SELECTIVE SILENCE

The public have in later years come to be impatient of hearing about prejudice.
They call it dwelling on the unpleasant side. They ask social students and
observers to be optimistic and to dwell simply upon the shortcomings of the
Negroes.

"Violations of Property Rights," March 30, 1911; microfilm reel no. 80, frame no. 292;
W.E.B. Du Bois Papers, University of Massachusetts, Amherst.

332. SPEAK OUT

What can one do in great causes and in particular places depends on so many
variables that the perfect answer is only possible for the person involved at the
particular time and in the particular place. Generalities are only meaningless but
I may say this: what is conspicuously lacking in race relations is courage in
particular persons who have the right ideas to express themselves clearly when
occasions occur. I do not mean speeches or harangues but I do mean that there
come specific times when it is the duty of a person to say clearly: I believe in
race equality; I do not subscribe to the color line; I think the conduct just
mentioned was wrong and contemptible.

Letter to Johanna Griggs, March 13, 1945; *Correspondence*, III, 31.

333. STANDARDS

I despise men and nations which judge human beings by their color, religious
beliefs or income.

In Battle for Peace (1952) 164.

334. SUPREME COURT

Living men may yet see a Supreme Court with guts and common decency to throw out the window the whole body of legal color-caste in the South and elsewhere as both unconstitutional and uncivilized.

The World and Africa (1947, 1965) 254.

335. TANGLED GROWTH

Historical evidence . . . tends to prove that there was at first comparatively little race prejudice between whites and blacks in early colonial times, and that the prejudice only appeared after a long period of artificial fostering by the laws of the land.

"Contributions to the Negro Problems" (1891); *in* Aptheker (ed.), *Against Racism* (1985) 21.

336. TEACHING RACE CONSCIOUSNESS

It was wrong to introduce the child to race consciousness prematurely; it is dangerous to let that consciousness grow spontaneously without intelligent guidance. With every step of dawning intelligence, explanation—frank, free, guiding explanation—must come. The day will dawn when mother must explain gently but clearly why the little girls next door do not want to play with "niggers"; what the real cause is of the teachers' unsympathetic attitude; and how people may ride in the back of street cars and the smoker end of trains and still be people, honest highminded souls.

Darkwater (1920) 204.

337. TRIVIAL BUT COSMIC

It is strange what small things determine the course of human lives. My life, for instance, has been conditioned by the color of my skin. This fact, trivial of itself, was of cosmic importance in the eyes of the world at the time I was born.

"The Life of W.E.B. Du Bois, 1868–1953," June 1953; microfilm reel no. 81, frame no. 678; W.E.B. Du Bois Papers, University of Massachusetts, Amherst.

6

Working Class

338. A.F. of L.

The A.F. of L. has discriminated against Jews, Italians, Slovaks and Negroes, and it has discriminated against white Americans, whenever chance or opportunity came; high wage for the few even if that involved aiding in the exploitation of common labor and being bribed by employers to keep labor peace when the mass of laborers is receiving less than the living wage and indecent treatment.

"The A.F. of L.," *Crisis* 40 (December 1933) 292; *Selections from* The Crisis, vol. 2 (1983) 724.

339. ANGELS' TEARS

[In the North, before the Civil War] the common white workingman and particularly the new English, Scotch and Irish immigrants entirely misconceived the writhing of the black man. These white laborers, themselves so near slavery, did not recognize the struggle of the black slave as part of their own struggle; rather they felt the sting of economic rivalry and underbidding for home and job; they easily absorbed hatred and contempt for Negroes as their first American lesson and were flattered by the white capitalists, slave owners and sympathizers with slavery into lynching and clubbing their dark fellow victims back into the pit whence they sought to crawl. It was a scene for angels' tears.

The Gift of Black Folk (1924) 160–161.

340. ANTI-RACISM

Probably the greatest and most effective effort toward interracial understanding among the working masses has come about through the trade unions. The organization of the CIO in 1935 was an attempt to bring the mass of workers into the union movement as contrasted with the AFL effort to unionize only the skilled workers of industry. As a result, numbers of men like those in the steel and automotive industries have been thrown together, black and white as fellow workers striving for the same objects. There has been on this account an astonishing spread of interracial tolerance and understanding. Probably no movement in the last 30 years has been so successful in softening race prejudice among the masses.

"Race Relations in the United States: 1917–1947," *Phylon* 9 (3rd Quarter 1948) 234–47; *Writings by W.E.B. Du Bois in Periodicals Edited by Others*, vol. 4 (1982) 68.

341. BLACK AND WHITE

If we could count on the cooperation of the white working classes nothing could stop the advance of both. We cannot count upon that. The mass of the white workers are our deliberate enemies.

To Dr. Brawn, January 23, 1926; microfilm reel no. 18, frame no. 326; W.E.B. Du Bois Papers, University of Massachusetts, Amherst.

342. BLACK LABOR

The Negro as a common laborer belonged . . . not in but beneath the white American labor movement.

Black Reconstruction (1935) 596.

Black folk made up half of the total labor force at the birth of the nation and from a third to a fourth until emancipation. In the southern United States they formed from 2/3 to the total group of laborers.

"Gift of Black Folk," February 11, 1955; microfilm reel no. 81, frame no. 946; W.E.B. Du Bois Papers, University of Massachusetts, Amherst.

343. BLACK UNION

The organization of the Pullman Porters is the most significant economic step taken by American Negroes in the last decade.

To Benjamin Stolberg, November 9, 1926; microfilm reel no. 19, frame no. 1060; W.E.B. Du Bois Papers, University of Massachusetts, Amherst.

344. BLACKS AND UNIONS

The labor movement was imported into the United States by immigrant laborers, and these laborers from the earliest times found the Negro slave and freedman as a competitor and tool in the hands of the capitalist. Instead, however, of taking the part of the Negro and helping him toward physical and economic freedom, the American labor movement from the beginning has tried to achieve freedom at the expense of the Negro.

"The Socialist Party and the Negro," February 12, 1929; microfilm reel no. 80, frame
no. 368; W.E.B. Du Bois Papers, University of Massachusetts, Amherst.

345. BLACK-WHITE CLASS

I am convinced that there can be no real and fundamental labor movement in
the United States that does not gather itself around the Negro labor group as a
nucleus and thus expand into a whole Negro-White labor class. This is logical
because unless labor consciousness begins with the most exploited and lower
class of labor, it becomes petty bourgeois and capitalist, which is exactly the
history of the American Federation of Labor. So long as American labor is more
conscious of color and race than it is of the fundamental economic needs of the
whole laboring class, just so long the development of labor solidarity in the
United States is impossible.

Pittsburgh Courier, June 5, 1937; *Newspaper Columns by W.E.B. Du Bois* (1986) 207.

346. CASTE SYSTEM

So long as white labor must compete with black labor, it must approximate
black labor conditions—long hours, small wages, child labor, labor of women,
and even peonage. Moreover it can raise itself above black labor only by a
legalized caste system which will cut off competition and this is what the South
is straining every nerve to create.

"The Economic Revolution in the South," in Booker T. Washington and Du Bois, *The
Negro in the South* (Philadelphia, Penn.: Geo. W. Jacobs Co., 1907) 77–122;
Writings by W.E.B. Du Bois in Periodicals Edited by Others, vol. 2 (1982) 69.

347. COMMUNIST PARTY

One result of Communistic agitation among Negroes was . . . far-reaching; and
that was to impress the younger intellectuals with the fact that American Negroes
were overwhelmingly workers, and that their first duty was to associate themselves with the white labor movement, and thus seek to bridge the gap of color,
and eradicate the deep-seated racial instincts.

Dusk of Dawn (1940) 206.

348. CONTRIVED CONFLICT

There is . . . a provable correlation between the migration of Northern capital
to the South for industry and industrial education. Indeed, the pioneer of this
phase was the late William N. Baldwin, President of the Long Island Railroad.
. . . Baldwin openly states that his plan was to train in the South two sets of
workers, equally skilled, black and white, who could be used to offset each
other and break the power of the trade unions.

To Merle E. Curti, December 9, 1932; microfilm reel no. 36, frame no. 1047; W.E.B.
Du Bois Papers, University of Massachusetts, Amherst. (See, also, letter of December 15 by Du Bois to Curti.)

349. FELLOW WORKERS

In America colored and white people cannot work in the same office and at
the same tasks except when one is in authority over the other. Since there must
be some center of authority that center must be white or colored. If the head is
colored, the whites gradually leave. . . . If the head is white, the colored people
gradually drop out of the inner circle of authority and initiative and become
clerks—mere helpers of white philanthropists working "for your people."

Letter to Joel E. Spingarn, October 28, 1914, *Correspondence*, I, 206–207.

350. HUNGER AND HATRED

If the white workingmen of East St. Louis felt sure that Negro workers would
not and could not take the bread and cake from their mouths, their race hatred
would never have been translated into murder. If the black workingmen of the
South could earn a decent living under decent circumstances at home, they would
not be compelled to underbid their white fellows. Thus, the shadow of hunger,
in a world which never needs to be hungry, drives us to war and murder and
hate.

Darkwater (1920) 99.

351. INDUSTRIAL FREEDOM

The Negro must have industrial freedom. Between the peonage of the rural
South, the oppression of shrewd capitalists and the jealousy of certain trade
unions, the Negro laborer is the most exploited class in the country, giving more
hard toil for less than any other American and has less voice in the conditions
of his labor.

"The Immediate Program of the American Negro," *Crisis* 9 (April 1915) 310–12; *Selections from* The Crisis, vol. 1 (1983) 94.

352. LABOR COMPETITION

So long as union labor fights for humanity, its mission is divine; but when it
fights for a clique of Americans, Irish or German monopolists who have cornered
or are trying to corner the market on a certain type of service, and are seeking
to sell that service at a premium, while other competent workmen starve, they
deserve themselves the starvation which they plan for their darker and poorer
fellows.

"Organized Labor," *Crisis* 4 (July 1912) 131; *Selections from* The Crisis, vol. 1 (1983)
38.

The difficulty always with Negro labor is that even in prosperous times it is not distributed according to ability or desert and in times of depression some of the best workers find themselves in needless competition with the worst of all races.

Letter to John W. Davis, September 21, 1931, *Correspondence*, I, 422.

[Before the Civil War, white labor] failed to comprehend . . . that the black man enslaved was an even more formidable and fatal competitor than the black man free.

Black Reconstruction (1935) 20.

The wages of both classes could be kept low, the whites fearing to be supplemented by Negro labor, the Negroes always being threatened by the substitution of white labor.

Black Reconstruction (1935) 701.

Before the twentieth century no white man would admit that he might not become a rich employer, exploiting Negroes of course, and white workers who would be naturally of the upper laboring class. But now in the twentieth century it was becoming clear that a considerable class of white people were always going to be laborers; that they must look forward to their children earning wages, and that if they did not take care, those children were going to be dragged down to the level of Negro labor. They must therefore organize and fight and use their political power to see that a privilege[d] class of laborers was established, with better wages, better treatment, and above all, political power.

The Ordeal of Mansart (1957) 300.

John Baldwin: The reason we are going to educate the Negroes is to make them rivals to the white workers and keep down wages.

Mansart Builds a School (1959) 150.

[Governor Eugene] Talmadge explained elaborately. White union labor must not get out of control in Georgia. If once they raised wages unreasonably, the employers would hire Negroes. That would drag wages down permanently. This repression of the unreasonable demands of white labor was simply guarding them against themselves.

Mansart Builds a School (1959) 328.

The Bishop: Have you ever thought that while you are excluding Negro labor from the factories of Springfield [Mass.] these mills may one day go to Mississippi where there are no unions, and where, if unions come, black scabs will stand ready to displace white workers? Think that over my sons. Consider if it might not be wisdom to admit one black man now and here rather than face a national competition which will drive your sons into war or poverty.

Worlds of Color (1961) 129.

353.   LABOR MOVEMENT

The importance of the Negro as a laboring group is going to advance by leaps and bounds in the next twenty-five years, partly on account of increasing intelligence, partly on account of the restriction of . . . [immigration], and for other reasons. If the Negro does not embrace the doctrine of socialism his advance will increase difficulties of the labor movement.

To Algernon Lee, February 15, 1929; microfilm reel no. 29, frame no. 83; W.E.B. Du
    Bois Papers, University of Massachusetts, Amherst.

354.   LABOR, NOT RACE PROBLEM

The degradation of Negro workers is a labor problem. Slavery in the United States was a labor problem and not a Negro problem. As long as the supply of cheap white labor satisfied the plantations, white labor [in the form of indentured servitude] was enslaved. When black labor became cheaper and more plentiful, Negro slavery ensued. . . . Slowly but surely the Labor movement in the United States is beginning to realize that when workers of a nation condone segregation, discrimination and disfranchisement, low wages forced on one tenth of their number, they are cutting their own throats.

"Labor Unions and Negroes," February 11, 1948; microfilm reel no. 80, frame no.
    1081; W.E.B. Du Bois Papers, University of Massachusetts, Amherst.

355.   LABOR REVOLUTION

A "National Assembly of North America" was held at Louisville, Kentucky, in 1864, and passed resolutions concerning working men and labor conditions; but it said nothing of the greatest revolution in labor that had happened in America for a hundred years—the emancipation of slaves.

Black Reconstruction (1935) 217.

356.   LABOR UNIONS

Fully half of the trade unions in the United States, counted by numerical strength, exclude Negroes from membership and thus usually prevent them from working at the trade. . . . In only a few unions, mostly unskilled, is the Negro welcomed, as in the case of the miners.

The Negro American Artisan (1912) 129.

357.   LINKED DEGRADATION

I can remember as a boy that the most fearsome thing in life were the yells, sneers, and fists of the German and Irish factory children of my birthplace [of Great Barrington, Mass.]. Their squalid homes, dirt and ignorance, were all in my child mind but part of their deep hatred and enmity toward me. It has taken some determined mental readjustments in my mature years to make me realize a common cause to their degradation and mine. No such metamorphosis has taken place today among the mass of thinking Negroes. White labor to them is the group that steals their jobs, keeps them out of work, denies them property, hounds them out of decent living quarters, and swells the mobs.

"What the New Negro Is Thinking," December 27, 1931; microfilm reel no. 80, frame no. 464; W.E.B. Du Bois Papers, University of Massachusetts, Amherst.

358. NEGROES AND LABOR

If in America Negroes were leaders in the labor movement, and the labor movement accomplished a revolutionary change in industry, then Negroes might see anti-Negro prejudice disappear with the new regime. But Negroes have always been excluded from the main labor movement in the United States and consequently a triumph of labor would not necessarily mean a lessening of race prejudice.

"Basic Philosophy and Policies for Negro Life in the North," March 25, 1936; microfilm reel no. 80, frame no. 652; W.E.B. Du Bois Papers, University of Massachusetts, Amherst.

359. NEW SOUTH

[After the mid-1870s] the South was [regarded by some as] a field which could be exploited if peaceful conditions could be reached and the laboring class made sufficiently content and submissive. It was the business then of the "New" South to show to the northern capitalists that by uniting the economic interests of both, they could exploit the Negro laborer and the white laborer—pitting the two classes against each other, keeping out labor unions and building a new industrial South which would pay tremendous returns. This was the program which began with the withdrawal of Northern troops in 1876 and was carried on up to 1890 when it gained political sanction by open laws disfranchising the Negro.

The Gift of Black Folk (1924) 254–255.

360. PINEAPPLES

I do not like Mr. Dole and I am suspicious of his pineapple. Too much sweat and labor of the poor have gone into his coffers and cans.

To Lurlani Smith, September 7, 1937; microfilm reel no. 48, frame no. 147; W.E.B. Du Bois Papers, University of Massachusetts, Amherst.

361. PROLETARIAT

Theoretically we are a part of the world proletariat in the sense that we are mainly an exploited class of cheap laborers; but practically we are not a part of the white proletariat and are not recognized by that proletariat to any great extent. We are the victims of their physical oppression, social ostracism, economic exclusion and personal hatred, and when in self defense we seek sheer subsistence we are howled down as "scabs."

"The Class Struggle," *Crisis* 22 (June 1921) 55–56; *Selections from* The Crisis, vol. 1 (1983) 303.

The mass of Negroes in the United States belong distinctly to the working proletariat. Of every thousand working Negroes less than a hundred and fifty belong to any class that could be considered bourgeois. And even this more educated and prosperous class has but small connections with the exploiters of wage and labor. Nevertheless, this black proletariat is not part of the white proletariat. Black and white work together in many cases, and influence each other's rate of wages. They have similar complaints against capitalists, save that the grievances of the Negro worker are more fundamental and indefensible, ranging as they do, since the day of Karl Marx, from chattel slavery, to the worst paid, sweated, mobbed and cheated labor in any civilized land.

"Marxism and the Negro Problem," *Crisis* 40 (May 1933) 103–04, 118; *Selections from* The Crisis, vol. 2 (1983) 695.

362. RACE AND CLASS

The fact that black men must face is that there is not in the United States, and never has been, any solidarity of labor across the color line; race prejudice has been more potent than class consciousness.

Pittsburgh Courier, May 29, 1937; *Newspaper Columns by W.E.B. Du Bois* (1986) 206.

363. RACIAL PREROGATIVES

White labor saw in every advance of Negroes a threat to their racial prerogatives, so that in many districts [of the South], Negroes were afraid to build decent homes or dress well, or own carriages, bicycles or automobiles, because of possible retaliation on the part of the whites.

Black Reconstruction (1935) 701.

364. RACISM AND LABOR

So long as the Southern white laborers could be induced to prefer poverty to equality with the Negro, just so long was a labor movement in the South made impossible.

Black Reconstruction (1935) 680.

365. RACIST STRIKES

Between 1881 and 1900, fifty strikes occurred in the United States against the employment of Negroes, and probably twice that number really against

Negroes, but ostensibly against non-union men, when in reality the Negro was not permitted to join the union.

"A Field for Socialists," *New Review* (January 11, 1913) 54–57; *Writings by W.E.B. Du Bois in Periodicals Edited by Others*, vol. 1 (1982) 83.

366. RECONSTRUCTION

It was a vast labor movement of ignorant, earnest, and bewildered black men whose faces had been ground in the mud by their three awful centuries of degradation and who now staggered forward blindly in blood and tears amid petty division, hate and hurt, and surrounded by every disaster of war and industrial upheaval. Reconstruction was a vast labor movement of ignorant, muddled and bewildered white men who had been disinherited of land and labor and fought a long battle with sheer subsistence, hanging on the edge of poverty, eating clay and chasing slaves and now lurching up to manhood. Reconstruction was the turn of white northern migration southward to new and sudden economic opportunity which followed the disaster and dislocation of war, and an attempt to organize capital and labor on a new pattern and build a new economy. Finally Reconstruction was a desperate effort of a dislodged, maimed, impoverished and ruined oligarchy and monopoly to restore an anachronism in economic organization by force, fraud and slander, in defiance of law and order, and in the face of a great labor movement of white and black, and in bitter strife with a new capitalism a new political framework.

Black Construction (1935) 346–347.

367. SLAVERY AND LABOR

The middle of the nineteenth century saw the beginning of the rise of the modern working class. By means of political power the laborers slowly but surely began to demand a large share in the profiting industry. In the United States their demand bade fair to be halted by the competition of slave labor.

The Negro (1915) 140.

368. THE ULTIMATE EXPLOITED

The black worker was the ultimate exploited; he formed that mass of labor which had neither wish nor power to escape from the labor status, in order to directly exploit other laborers, or indirectly, by alliance with capital, to share in their exploitation.

Black Reconstruction (1935) 15.

369. WORKERS

The first group of persons who came to America specifically as workers were Negroes.

"The American Negro and the Labor Movement," ca. 1945; microfilm reel no. 80, frame no. 895; W.E.B. Du Bois Papers, University of Massachusetts, Amherst.

370. WORKERS' COUNCILS

We believe that Negro workers should join the labor movement and affiliate with such trade unions as welcome them and treat them fairly. We believe that workers' councils organized by Negroes for interracial understanding should strive to fight race prejudice in the working class.

Pittsburgh Courier, June 20, 1936; *Newspaper Columns by W.E.B. Du Bois* (1986) 82.

7

Forced Labor

371. ADRIFT

Physical emancipation came in 1863, but economic emancipation is still far off. The great majority of Negroes are still serfs bound to the soil or house-servants. The nation which robbed them of the fruits of their labor for two and a half centuries, finally set them adrift penniless.

The Negro in Business (1899) 5.

372. BLACK LABOR

In the United States the efforts of the slaves to free themselves stand in the same class as the labor unions among whites. The Negroes' efforts fall into two categories: First, a series of revolts from 1800 to the Civil War, and secondly and more important, the organized running away of slaves from the South to the mountains, swamps, the northern states and Canada.

"Gift of Black Folk," February 11, 1955; microfilm reel no. 81, frame no. 949; W.E.B. Du Bois Papers, University of Massachusetts, Amherst.

373. CONVICT-LEASING

The first and greatest cause of Negro crime in the South is the convict-lease system. States which use their criminals as sources of revenue in the hands of irresponsible speculators, who herd girls, boys, men and women promiscuously together without distinction or protection, who parade chained convicts in public, guarded by staves and pistols, and then plunge into this abyss of degradation the ignorant little black boy who steals a chicken or a handful of peanuts—what can such States expect but a harvest of criminals and prostitutes?

"The Negro and Crime" (1899); *Writings by W.E.B. Du Bois in Periodicals Edited by Others*, vol. 1 (1982) 58.

The sentences inflicted are cruel and excessive: 25 percent of the convicts are condemned for life and 60 percent for ten years and more. . . . These slaves of the state are then sold body and soul to private capitalists for the sake of gain, without the shadow of an attempt at reformation, and are thrown into relentless competition with free Negro laborers.

"Address of the First Annual Meeting of the Georgia Equal Rights Convention," *Voice of the Negro* 3 (March 1906) 175–77; *Writings by W.E.B. Du Bois in Periodicals Edited by Others*, vol. 1 (1982) 324.

374. DISTINCTIVENESS

America could not have been America, without the African slave trade and African slavery.

"The Future of Africa in America" (1941); Series 3/C, Folder no. 5552, p. 9, *Unpublished Articles*; W.E.B. Du Bois Papers, University of Massachusetts, Amherst.

375. DRAMA OF HISTORY

The most magnificent drama in the last thousand years of human history is the transportation of ten million human beings out of the dark beauty of their mother continent into the new-found Eldorado of the West. They descended into Hell; and in the third century they arose from the dead, in the finest effort to achieve democracy for the working millions which this world has ever seen.

Black Reconstruction (1935) 727.

376. ENSLAVED LABOR

This nation had to fight a Civil War to prevent all American labor from becoming half enslaved. Thus, from 1620 when the Puritans landed until 1865 when slavery was abolished, there was no complete democracy in the United States. This was not only because a large part of the laboring class was enslaved, but also because white labor was in competition with slaves and thus itself not really free.

"The Negro and Socialism," in Helen Alfred (ed.), *Toward a Socialist America* (New York: Peace Publications, 1958) 179–91; *Writings by W.E.B. Du Bois in Non-Periodical Literature Edited by Others* (1982) 286.

377. FARM TENANCY

For every man whom the system [of southern farm tenancy] has helped into independence it has pushed ten back into virtual slavery.

The Negro American Artisan (1912) 138.

378. FORCED LABOR

[In Dougherty County, Georgia] the black folks say that only colored boys
are sent to jail, and they are not because they are guilty, but because the State
needs criminals to eke out its income by their forced labor.

The Souls of Black Folk (1903) 126.

379. FREEDOM AND SLAVERY

One cannot study the Negro in freedom and come to general conclusions about
his destiny without knowing his history in slavery.

"The Study of the Negro Problems" (1898); *Writings by W.E.B. Du Bois in Periodicals
Edited by Others*, vol. 1 (1982) 46.

380. GREAT EXPERIMENT

The greatest experiment in Negro slavery as the base of a modern industrial
system was made on the mainland of North America and in the confines of the
present United States.

Black Folk Then and Now (1939) 196.

381. HONOR AND PROPERTY

There was one part of the world which his code of honor did not cover. . . .
The uninitiated cannot easily picture to himself the mental attitude of a former
slaveholder toward property in the hands of a Negro. Such property belonged
of right to the master, if the master needed it; and since ridiculous laws safe-
guarded the property, it was perfectly permissible to circumvent such laws. No
Negro starved on the Cresswell place, neither did any accumulate property.
Colonel Cresswell saw to both matters.

The Quest of the Silver Fleece (1911) 364.

382. HUMAN DEGRADATION

Never in modern times has a large section of a nation so used its combined
energies to the degradation [as in the United States during the 1840s and 1850s].
The hurt to the Negro in this era was not only his treatment in slavery; it was
the wound dealt to his reputation as a human being. Nothing was left; nothing
was sacred.

Black Reconstruction (1935) 39.

383. MODERN SLAVERY

Modern African slavery was the beginning of the modern labor problem and
must be looked at and interpreted from that point of view. Unless we lose
ourselves in an altogether false analogy. Modern world commerce, modern

imperialism, the modern factory system and the modern labor problem began with the African slave trade. The first modern method of securing labor on a wide commercial scale and primarily for profit was inaugurated in the middle of the fifteenth century and in the commerce between Africa. . . . The survivors of this wholesale rape became a great international laboring force in America on which the modern capitalistic movement has been built and out of which modern labor problems have arisen.

"The Negro's Fatherland," *Survey* 39 (November 10, 1917) 141; *Writings by W.E.B. Du Bois in Periodicals Edited by Others*, vol. 2 (1982) 112.

384. A NEW NAME

[After the Civil War] slavery persisted, only we called it the plantation system and supported it by vagrancy laws, the convict lease system and lynching. Labor unions carefully guarded against Negro competition in the decently-paid trades, while on the other hand the price of common labor in the North was kept a notch above Southern wages by world migration.

"The Problem of Problems," *Intercollegiate Socialist* 6 (December-January 1917–1918) 5–9; *Writings by W.E.B. Du Bois in Periodicals Edited by Others*, vol. 2 (1982) 116.

385. NORTHERN MONEYMAKING

The North was not Abolitionist. It was overwhelmingly in favor of Negro slavery, so long as this did not interfere with Northern moneymaking.

Black Reconstruction (1935) 83.

386. POLYGAMY

Broadly speaking, the greatest social effect of American slavery was to substitute for the polygamous Negro home a new polygamy less guarded, less effective, and less civilized [than in Africa].

The Negro Church (1903) 4.

387. POWER MONOPOLY

Any system of free labor where the returns of the laborer, the settlement of all disputes, the drawing of the contract, the determination of the rent, the expenditures of the employers, the prices they pay for living, the character of the house they live in, and their movements during and after work—any system of free labor where all these things are left practically to the unquestionable power of one man who owns the land and profits by the labor and is in the exercise of his power practically unrestrained by public opinion or the courts and has no fear of ballots in the hands of the laborers or of their friends—any such system is inherently wrong.

"The Economic Future of the Negro," *Publications of the American Economic Association*, Series 3, 7 (1906) 219–42; *Writings by W.E.B. Du Bois in Periodicals Edited by Others*, vol. 1 (1982) 355.

388. SLAVE TRADE

No university in New York City and few in the United States give a single semester course of study to the subject of the African slave trade.

"The African Slave Trade," October 31, 1947; microfilm reel no. 80, frame no. 1001; W.E.B. Du Bois Papers, University of Massachusetts, Amherst.

On the whole, these acts [to suppress the African slave trade after 1807] were poorly conceived, loosely drawn, and wretchedly enforced. . . . The carnival of lawlessness that succeeded the Act of 1807, and that which preceded final suppression in 1861, were glaring examples of the failure of the efforts to suppress the slave-trade by mere law.

The Suppression of the African Slave Trade (1896) 197.

For four hundred years white Europe was the chief support of that trade in human beings which first and last robbed black Africa of a hundred million human beings, transformed the face of her social life, overthrew organized government, distorted ancient industry, and snuffed out the lights of cultural development.

Darkwater (1920) 58.

389. SLAVERY

[The freed slave] . . . had emerged from . . . a slavery that had here and there something of kindliness, fidelity, and happiness—but withal slavery, which, as far as human aspiration and desert were concerned, classed the black man and the ox together.

The Souls of Black Folk (1903) 28.

There never was a time in the history of America where the [slave] system had a slighter economic, political, and moral justification than in 1787 [the year the Constitution was written]; and yet with this real, existent, growing evil before their eyes, a bargain largely of dollars and cents was allowed to open the highway that led straight to the Civil War.

The Suppression of the African Slave Trade (1896) 198.

There is always a certain glamour about the idea of a nation rising to crush an evil simply because it is wrong. Unfortunately, this can seldom be realized in real life; for the very existence of the evil usually argues a moral weakness in the very place where extraordinary moral strength is called for. . . . An appeal to moral rectitude was unheard in Carolina when rice had become a great crop, and in Massachusetts when the rum-slave-traffic was paying a profit of

100%. . . . As years rolled by, it was found well-nigh impossible to rouse the moral sense of the nation.

The Suppression of the African Slave Trade (1896) 195–196.

Throughout colonial history, in spite of many honest attempts to stop the further pursuit of the slave-trade, we notice back of nearly all such attempts a certain moral apathy, an indisposition to attack the evil with the sharp weapons which its nature demanded.

The Suppression of the African Slave Trade (1896) 195.

For at least a century, in the West Indies and the southern United States, agriculture flourished, trade increased, and English manufacturers were nourished, in just such proportion as Americans stole Negroes and worked them to death.

The Suppression of the African Slave Trade (1896) 194.

Once degrade the laborer so that he cannot assert his own rights, and there is but one limit below which his price cannot be reduced. That limit is not his physical well-being, for it may be, and in the Gulf it was, cheaper to work him rapidly to death; the limit is simply the cost of procuring him and keeping him alive a profitable length of time. . . . When a community has once been debauched by slavery, its moral sense offers little resistance to economic demand.

The Suppression of the African Slave Trade (1896) 169.

With all the instances of kindness and affection (and there were hundreds of such instances) the net result of any such system was, and was bound to be oppression, cruelty, concubinage, and moral retrogression.

Book review of Thomas N. Page, *The Negro: The Southerner's Problem* (1905); in *Dial*, May 1, 1905; *in* Aptheker (ed.), *Book Reviews by W.E.B. Du Bois* (1977) 11.

Few West Indian masters—fewer Spanish or Dutch were callous enough to sell their own children into slavery. Not so with English and Americans. With a harshness and indecency seldom paralleled in the civilized world white masters on the mainland sold their mulatto children, half-brothers and half-sisters, and their own wives in all but name, into life-slavery by the hundreds and thousands. They originated a special branch of slave-trading for this trade.

Darkwater (1920) 114.

Slavery was a cruel, dirty, costly and inexcusable anachronism, which nearly ruined the world's greatest experiment in democracy.

Black Reconstruction (1935) 715.

[Ulrich B. Phillips' *American Negro Slavery*, 1918] is a defense of American slavery—a defense of an institution which was at best a mistake and at worst a crime—made in a day when we need sharp and implacable judgment against collective wrongdoing by cultured and courteous men.

Aptheker (ed.), *Book Reviews by W.E.B. Du Bois* (1977) 60.

390. STATE SLAVERY

[In some areas of the South] emancipation gave rise to an attempt to substitute state slavery for the individual slavery that had been abolished. The machinery of the state judiciary was, in many cases, after the withdrawal of the Freedmen's Bureau, used to place Negroes under the control of the state. "Vagrancy," theft, loitering, "impudence" and assault were the easily proven charges which forced large number of Negroes into penal servitude. The next step was to hire the labor of these persons to private contractors: thus was born the Convict Lease System. Many large planters conducted their plantations with such labor, and erected for them "barracks" and "stockades"—i.e., large enclosed quarters, guarded by high fences and crowded with inmates.

"The Problem of Housing the Negro: III. The Home of the Country Freedman," *Southern Workman* 30 (October 1901) 535–46; *Writings by W.E.B. Du Bois in Periodicals Edited by Others*, vol. 1 (1982) 117.

391. UNPAID TOIL

The present industrial development of America is built on the blood and brawn of unpaid Negro toil in the 17th, 18th and 19th centuries.

"Caste and Class in the United States," *Boston Post*, February 12, 1904; *Writings by W.E.B. Du Bois in Periodicals Edited by Others*, vol. 1 (1982) 196.

392. URBAN FREEDOM

The country life of the Negro still savours of slavery and often the only way to escape peonage is to run away to town.

"The City Negro," ca. 1910; microfilm reel no. 80, frame no. 276; W.E.B. Du Bois Papers, University of Massachusetts, Amherst.

393. WHITE SLAVES

In the seventeenth century the African slave trade to America expanded. It was not yet however a trade which made the word synonymous with Negro or black: during these years the Mohammedan rulers of Egypt were buying white slaves by the tens of thousands in Europe and Asia and bringing them to Syria, Palestine, and the Valley of the Nile.

The World and Africa (1947, 1965) 51–52.

394. WITHHELD WAGES

It is a conservative estimate to say that three-fourths of the stipulated wages and shares of crops which the Negro has earned on the farm since emancipation has been illegally withheld from him by the white landlords, either on the plea that this was for his own good or without any plea.

"The Economic Future of the Negro," *Publications of the American Economic Association*, Series 3, 7 (1906) 219–42; *Writings by W.E.B. Du Bois in Periodicals Edited by Others*, vol. 1 (1982) 353.

8

Ruling and Other Classes

395. ALLIANCE

[During the mid-1870s] the South sensed the willingness of Big Business, threatened by liberal revolt, labor upheaval and state interference, to make new alliance with organized Southern capital if assured that the tariff, banks and national debt, and above all the new freedom of corporations, would not be subjected to mass attack. Such a double bargain was more than agreeable to Southern leaders.

Black Reconstruction (1935) 686.

396. BARGAIN OF 1876

The bargain of 1876 was essentially an understanding by which the Federal Government ceased to sustain the right to vote of half of the laboring population of the South, and left capital as represented by the old planter class, the new Northern capitalist, and the capitalist that began to arise out of the poor whites, with a control of labor greater than in any modern industrial state in civilized lands.

Black Reconstruction (1935) 630.

397. BELIEF

I am convinced of the essential truth of the Marxian Philosophy and believe that eventually land, machines and materials must belong to the state; that private profit must be abolished; that the system of exploiting labor must disappear; that people who work must have essentially equal income; and that in their hands the political rulership of the state must eventually rest.

"Social Planning for the Negro Past and Present," *Journal of Negro Education* 5 (January
    1936) 110–25; *Writings by W.E.B. Du Bois in Periodicals Edited by Others*
    (1982) 38.

398. BIG BUSINESS

[Late in the 19th century] new and integrated world industry arose called "Big
Business"—a misleading misnomer. Its significance lay not simply in its size.
It was not just little shops grown larger. It was an organized super-government
of mankind in matters of work and wages, directed with science and skill for
the private profit of individuals. It could not be controlled by popular vote unless
that vote was intelligent, experienced, and cast by persons essentially equal in
income and power. The overwhelming majority of mankind was still ignorant,
sick and poverty stricken.

"The Negro and Socialism," *in* Helen Alfred (ed.), *Toward a Socialist America* (New
    York: Peace Publications, 1958) 179–91; *Writings by W.E.B. Du Bois in Non-
    Periodical Literature Edited by Others* (1982) 285.

399. BLACK CAPITALISM

The main danger and the central question of the capitalistic development
through which the Negro American group is forced to go is the question of the
ultimate control of the capital which they must raise and use. If this capital is,
going to be controlled by a few men for their own benefit, then we are destined
to suffer from our own capitalists exactly what we are suffering from white
capitalists today. And while this is not a pleasant prospect, it is certainly no
worse than the present actuality. If, on the other hand, because of our more
democratic organization and our widespread interclass sympathy we can introduce a more democratic control, taking advantage of what the white world is
itself doing to introduce industrial democracy, then we may not only escape our
present economic slavery but even guide and lead a distrait economic world.

"The Class Struggle," *Crisis* 22 (June 1921) 55–56; *Writings in Periodicals Edited by
    W.E.B. Du Bois. Selections from* The Crisis, vol. 1 (1983) 304.

Inside the Negro race there is a tendency to build up a race capitalism which
it is difficult to oppose always; since some of the thriftiest and most intelligent
are the new capitalists. But many of us see the danger here and are giving
attention to it. At present this tendency has not gone far, so that we have no
millionaires, and there is greater equality of wealth in our group than in any
other American group.

"An Answer to the Memorandum on the Bettering of the Position of the Colored People
    in America," 1926; microfilm reel no. 77, frame no. 422; W.E.B. Du Bois Papers,
    University of Massachusetts, Amherst.

There is . . . only one real opening and real plan in the restoration of complete
capitalism for the Negro and that is the old plan which seeks to admit to the

ranks of capitalists enough of the Negro bourgeoisie to enable them to share in the exploitation chiefly of Negro labor and to some extent of white labor. So far as the attitude of white capitalists is concerned, it is very doubtful if they will be more minded tomorrow than today to admit the Negro capitalists, save to small, outlying fields where the chances of success are very small.

"The Negro and Social Reconstruction" (1936); in Aptheker (ed.), *Against Racism* (1985)
    139.

400. BLACK CLASS DEVELOPMENT

Things have changed. . . . Differences of income within the Negro race have become large and important. Larger and larger numbers of Negroes are living on the use and exploitation of the labor of other Negroes and . . . we are building up within the American Negro group, the same kind of economic hierarchy which you can see in larger and more developed forms of England, France, the former Germany, Italy and Spain.

"The Talented Tenth. The Re-examination of a Concept," 1948; microfilm reel no. 80,
    frame no. 1111; W.E.B. Du Bois Papers, University of Massachusetts, Amherst.

401. BLACKS AS COLONY

Negroes are in a quasi-colonial status. They belong to the lower class of the world. These classes are, have been, and are going to be for a long time exploited by the more powerful groups and nations in the world for the benefit of those groups. The real problem before the United States is whether we are really beginning to reason about this world-wide feeling of class dominance with its resultant wars: wars for rivalry for the sharing of the spoils of exploitation, and wars against exploitation.

"Race Relations in the United States: 1917–1947," *Phylon* 9 (3rd Quarter 1948) 234–
    47; *Writings by W.E.B. Du Bois in Periodicals Edited by Others*, vol. 4 (1982)
    75.

402. CADILLACS

Let us not be too optimistic about the Negro's efforts to get rich, American style. Our survival will not depend on the number of Cadillacs we own.

"On Negro America," *Sunday Compass*, July 10, 1949, 4–5; *Writings by W.E.B. Du
    Bois in Periodicals Edited by Others*, vol. 4 (1982) 120.

403. CAPITAL

The Abolitionists were not enemies of capital.

Black Reconstruction (1935) 327.

404. CASTE

No sooner does the virus of caste distinction penetrate a nation's vitals than good and evil in that nation come to be judged from the point of view of the privileged classes alone.

"The Negro Question as a Class Question," *Boston Transcript*, February 21, 1904;
  Writings by W.E.B. Du Bois in Periodicals Edited by Others, vol. 1 (1982) 198.

The result of a caste system is in the long run simply to enthrone over the destinies of the nation that particular form of immorality most prevalent among the ruling classes of the land.

"Caste: That Is the Root of Trouble," *Des Moines Register Leader*, October 19, 1904;
  Writings by W.E.B. Du Bois in Periodicals Edited by Others, vol. 1 (1982) 231.

405. CASTE AND CLASS

The Negro problem is but the sign of growing class privileges and caste distinction in America, and not as some fondly imagine, the cause of it.

"Caste and Class in the United States," *Boston Post*, February 12, 1904; *Writings by*
  W.E.B. Du Bois in Periodicals Edited by Others, vol. 1, (1982) 196.

406. CASTE AND CORPORATE POWER

The power of private corporate wealth in the United States has throttled democracy and this was made possible by the color caste which followed Reconstruction after the Civil War. When the Negro was disfranchised in the South, the white South was and is owned increasingly by the industrial North. Thus, caste which deprived the mass of Negroes of political and civil rights and compelled them to accept the lowest wage, lay underneath the vast industrial profits of the years 1890 to 1900 when the greatest combinations of capital took place.

Autobiography (1968) 354.

407. CASTE AND POWER

We have an industrial system by which it is easy and common for the earnings of thrift, efficiency and genius to be seized and appropriated by the strong, the crafty and the impudent. . . . And with this widespread moral degeneration staring us in the face, we are faced by unmistakable signs of the growth of caste and class privilege, of greater social and political power concentrated in the hands of the already powerful. . . . The strong and influential groups are coming to view with impatience any sort of education for the young which is not calculated to perpetuate our present social and economic order.

"Caste: That Is the Root of Trouble," *Des Moines Register Leader*, October 19, 1904;
  Writings by W.E.B. Du Bois in Periodicals Edited by Others, vol. 1 (1982)
  231–32.

408. CLASS CONFLICT

Most Negroes are employed by white capitalists and Negro capital is often invested in white business. The main labor problem, therefore, is the relation of capital owned by white folk and the mass of white and colored laborers. . . . Besides retail business, Negroes have invested in farms, newspapers, banking and insurance, barber shops and boarding houses; but in all these cases, the group of capitalists, as distinct from workers, is small. What we have here is not capitalists and workers, but workers with some capital and with a few exceptions this is a characteristic development of Negro business.

"Colored Capital and Labor" (ca. 1936); Series 3/C, Folder no. 5544, pp. 7, 9, *Unpublished Articles*; W.E.B. Du Bois Papers, University of Massachusetts, Amherst.

409. CLASS STRUCTURE

Wide variations in antecedents, wealth, intelligence and general efficiency have already been differentiated within this group. These differences are not, to be sure, so great or so patent as those among the whites of today, and yet they undoubtedly equal the difference among the masses of the people in certain sections of the land fifty or one hundred years ago.

The Philadelphia Negro (1899) 309–310.

Public opinion today, for the first time, is coming to recognize classes among Negroes, and to suspect any discussion that puts the colored civil service clerks of Washington and the plantation peons of Mississippi under one head. Men are beginning to see that there are Negroes representing all degrees of training, ability, and wealth, and that differentiation is rapidly progressing.

"Hopeful Signs for the Negro," *Advance* 44 (October 2, 1902) 327–28; *Writings by W.E.B. Du Bois in Periodicals Edited by Others*, vol. 1 (1982) 151.

The colored group is not yet divided into capitalists and laborers. There are only the beginnings of such a division. In one hundred years if we develop along conventional lines we would have such fully separated classes, but today to a very large extent our laborers are our capitalists and our capitalists are our laborers. Our small class of well-to-do men have come to affluence largely through manual toil and have never been physically or mentally separated from the toilers. Our professional classes are sons and daughters of porters, washer-women and laborers.

"The Class Struggle," *Crisis* 22 (June 1921) 55–56; *Selections from* The Crisis, vol. 1 (1983) 303.

Negro capital consists mainly of small individual savings invested in homes, and in insurance, in lands for direct cultivation and individually used tools and machines. . . . Much of the retail business is done in small stores with small stocks of goods, where the owner works side by side with one or two helpers, and makes a personal profit less than a normal American wage. . . . There are few colored manufacturers of material who speculate on the products of hired labor. Nine-tenths of the hired Negro labor is under the control of white capitalists. . . . Emancipation will not come . . . from an internal readjustment and ousting of exploiters; rather it will come from a wholesale emancipation from the grip of the white exploiters without.

"The Negro and Communism," *Crisis* 38 (September 1931) 313–15, 318, 320; *Selections from* The Crisis, vol. 2 (1983), 636.

We have no rich or poor as yet. We have some who are better off than others; but after all you cannot say that the class struggle, the economic struggle, has shown itself inside the Negro race. But this is partially hidden by the fact that we are living in a great country where most of our employment comes from the white capitalists. But if the things keep on and our thinking keeps clear as in the past we are going to have this division, a real economic class.

"What Is Wrong with the NAACP?" May 18, 1932; microfilm reel no. 80, frame no. 496; W.E.B. Du Bois Papers, University of Massachusetts, Amherst.

We cannot follow the class structure of America; we do not have the economic or political power, the ownership of machines and materials, the power to direct the processes of industry, the monopoly of capital and credit simply to be the victims of exploitation and social exclusion.

Dusk of Dawn (1940) 192.

This dichotomy in the Negro group, this development of class structure, was to be expected, and will be more manifest in the future, as discrimination against Negroes as such decreases. There will gradually arise among American Negroes a separation according to their attitudes toward labor, wealth and work.

In Battle for Peace (1952) 76.

The outstanding fact about the Negro group in America . . . is that it is flying apart into opposing economic classes. . . . The American Negro is . . . developing a distinct bourgeoisie bound to and aping American acquisitive society and developing an employing and a laboring class. This division is only in embryo, but it can be sensed. . . . Negro businessmen . . . today form the most powerful class among Negroes and dominate their thought and action. . . . Class differentiation in Negro organizations is developing more slowly than in general life. . . . Opposite the small Negro bourgeoisie is the great mass of black labor. It is at present only vaguely aware of its conflict of interest with the Negro businessman.

National Guardian, January 23, 1956; *Newspaper Columns by W.E.B. Du Bois* (1986) 953–54.

In the new NAACP [of 1909 there] was no real representation of the Negro worker. It did not enter the thought of the teachers, professional men and social workers that they did not represent and speak for the black laboring classes. They were, to be sure, nearer to black workers than similar classes of whites were to their workers. The Negro proletariat was not yet quite differentiated from the petty bourgeois[ie]. In the same black family might often be servants and laborers, clerks in stores and students studying for professions. This meant a unity and sympathy that few white families showed.

The Ordeal of Mansart (1957) 291.

A class structure began to arise within the Negro group which produced haves and have nots, and tended to encourage more successful Negroes to join the forces of monopoly and exploitation, and help victimize their own lower class.

"Socialism and the American Negro" (1960); *Against Racism* (1985) 303.

410. CLASSES

As long as one man is lazy, and another industrious, you will, you must have social classes.

"Does Education Pay?" (1891); *Writings by W.E.B. Du Bois in Periodicals Edited by Others*, vol. 1 (1982) 10.

411. CORPORATIONS

These corporations having neither bodies to be kicked nor souls to be damned, for the most part do as they please, and no one can be held responsible for their actions or failure to act.

Fragment, undated; microfilm reel no. 83, frame no. 1065; W.E.B. Du Bois Papers, University of Massachusetts, Amherst.

412. DICTATORSHIP OF PROPERTY

[On the eve of the Civil War] the North had yielded to democracy, but only because democracy was curbed by a dictatorship of property and investment which left in the hands of the leaders of industry such economic power as insured their mastery and their profits.

Black Reconstruction (1935) 46.

413. ECONOMICS OF HATE

It is usual for the stranger in Georgia to think of race prejudice and race hatred as being the great, the central, the inalterable fact and to go off into general considerations as to race differences and the eternal likes and dislikes of mankind. But that line leads one astray. The central thing is not race hatred in Georgia; it is successful industry and commercial investment in race hatred for the purpose of profit. All the time behind the scenes in whispered tones and in secret conference, Georgia is feeding the flame of race hatred with economic fuel. And while this is not the conscious and deliberate action of all, it is so with some and subconscious with many others.

"Georgia: Invisible Empire State," in Ernest Gruening (ed.), *These United States*, II (New York: Boni and Liveright, 1924) 322–45; *Writings by W.E.B. Du Bois in Periodicals Edited by Others*, vol. 2 (1982) 139.

414. EXPLOITATION

The Negro is exploited to a degree that means poverty, crime, delinquency and indigence. And that exploitation comes not from a black capitalistic class but from the white capitalists and equally from the white proletariat. His only defense is such internal organization as will protect him from both parties, and such practical economic insight as will prevent inside the race group any large development of capitalistic exploitation.

"Marxism and the Negro Problem," *Crisis* 40 (May 1933) 103–04, 118; *Selections from The Crisis*, vol. 2 (1983) 699.

Manuel Mansart: We black folk will make a great mistake if we continue to ape white folk, whose wealth and power is based on taking from workers most of what the workers earn, and using it to amass untold power and luxury for parasites who have no right to it.

Worlds of Color (1961) 340.

415. FINANCE

The difficulty with purely colored financial institutions is that you cannot segregate business and credit [,] and without sharing the great credit facilities of organized finance in this country and in the world, colored institutions are going to be pitifully weak.

To W. P. Dabney, July 17, 1925; microfilm reel no. 15, frame no. 162; W.E.B. Du Bois Papers, University of Massachusetts, Amherst.

416. FRIENDS

Our natural friends are not the rich but the poor, not the great but the masses, not the employers but the employees.

"Over-Look," *Horizon* 1 (February 1907) 3–4, 6–10; *Selections from* The Horizon (1985) 6.

417. FOLLOWING WHITE EXAMPLE

In Charleston, South Carolina, a well-to-do and well educated Negro physician pointed out to me the tenement houses which he was renting to poor workers at huge profit. In Atlanta I have seen an insurance society bought by a Negro group from whites, which was cheating and stealing from the workers with exactly the same methods that the white company used, and piling up fortunes for young colored men. In fact, the more widely and successfully colored businessmen follow the methods of white businessmen, the more many of us regard them as unusually successful.

"On the Future of the American Negro," May 18, 1952; microfilm reel no. 81, frame nos. 405–406; W.E.B. Du Bois Papers, University of Massachusetts, Amherst.

418. GETTING RICH

If I wished to paint the picture of a consummate idiot, I would paint a man who had spent his life in getting rich, and then had no project in life other than to get richer.

"Does Education Pay?" (1891); *Writings by W.E.B. Du Bois in Periodicals Edited by Others*, vol. 1 (1982) 7.

419. HANDICAP

Can anyone . . . [accept] under modern competitive industry that a class of workers could survive without the defense of a vote? Are Negroes, handicapped by the past and discriminated against in the present, to accomplish what German, French, and English workingmen could scarce do with law, order, and universal suffrage?

"The Case for the Negro," undated, Series 3/C, Folder no. 5507, p. 4, *Unpublished Articles*; W.E.B. Du Bois Papers, University of Massachusetts, Amherst.

420. HARDSHIPS

To be a poor man is hard, but to be a poor race in a land of dollars is the very bottom of hardships.

The Souls of Black Folk (1903) 8.

421. HENRY GRADY

[Grady] believed in capitalist exploitation as he believed in God.

The Ordeal of Mansart (1957) 140.

422. HIDDEN HANDS

To curtail the [economic] function of government does not mean that human freedom is increased, it means simply that the real control of human freedom lies in hidden hands: the hands of the wealthy, the privileged, the monopolists; and not in the hands of a government in which the governed have voice.

Pittsburgh Courier, February 22, 1936; *Newspaper Columns by W.E.B. Du Bois* (1986) 32.

423. INVESTMENT OF CAPITAL

There is considerable Negro capital invested in enterprises conducted by whites. Of the wealthy Negroes in one northern city only a fifth invested their capital in purely Negro enterprises. So, too, in the South, Negro business ventures have not yet begun to attract the bulk of Negro savings.

The Negro in Business (1899) 20.

424. LAND AND DEMOCRACY

To have given each one of the million Negro free families a forty-acre freehold would have made a basis of real democracy in the United States that might easily have transformed the modern world.

Black Reconstruction (1935) 602.

425. MONEY AND CONSCIENCE

I had to remember, as both of us from time to time are compelled to, the enemy has the money and they are going to use it. Our choice then is not how that money could be used best, from our point of view, but how far without great sacrifice of principle, we can keep it from being misused.

To Carter G. Woodson, January 29, 1932; microfilm reel no. 37, frame no. 820; W.E.B. Du Bois Papers, University of Massachusetts, Amherst.

426. NEGRO JOBS

From the time of Emancipation down until the [First] World War, the Negro had a monopoly on certain jobs in the South that were poorly paid and involved menial service. . . . These so-called Negro jobs were the jobs of servants and laborers, but they were fairly permanent and the workers received certain perquisites in food, in clothes and had personal relations with employers that gave them a degree of legal and social protection. The money which built homes and churches for Negroes, educated Negro children and saved sums for capital investment, came largely out of this wage.

"The Negro and Social Reconstruction" (1936); *in* Aptheker (ed.), *Against Racism* (1985) 128.

427. NEGRO LAWYERS

Failure of most Negro lawyers is not in all cases due to lack of ability and push on their part. Its principal cause is that the Negroes furnish little lucrative law business, and a Negro lawyer will seldom be employed by whites. Moreover, while the work of a physician is largely private, depending on individual skill, a lawyer must have cooperation from fellow lawyers and respect and influence in court; thus prejudice or discrimination of any kind is especially felt in this profession. For these reasons Negro lawyers are for the most part confined to petty criminal practice and seldom get a chance to show their ability.

The Philadelphia Negro (1899) 114–115.

428. NEW HIERARCHIES

Liberal thought and violent revolution in the eighteenth and early nineteenth centuries shook the foundations of a social hierarchy in Europe based on unchangeable class distinctions. But in the nineteenth and early twentieth centuries the Color Line was drawn as at least partial substitute for this stratification. Granting that all white men were born free and equal was it not manifest . . . that Africans and Asians were born slaves, serfs or inferiors?

"The Realities in Africa: European Profit or Negro Development?" *Foreign Affairs* 21 (July 1943) 721–32; *Writings by W.E.B. Du Bois in Periodicals Edited by Others*, vol. 3 (1982) 173.

429. OLIGARCHY

This nation has become a country ruled by an oligarchy of less than 1,000 persons, controlling the largest pool of natural resources, processed goods and finance capital the world ever saw; and devoted today to making the world believe that its greatest danger is Communism and the Soviet Union.

In Battle for Peace (1952) 174.

430. OLIGARCHY AND CORRUPTION

Before the [Civil] war, the South was ruled by an oligarchy and the functions of the state carried on largely by individuals. This meant that the state had little to do, and its expenses were small. The oligarchic state does not need to resort to corruption of the government. Its leaders, having the right to exploit labor to the limit, receive an income which makes them conspicuously independent of any income from the government. The government revenues are kept purposely small and the salaries low so that poor men cannot afford to enter into government service.

Black Reconstruction (1935) 617.

431. OPPRESSOR'S IMAGINATION

That there is a general fear of the Negroes, not only in the Black Belt but everywhere is certain but it is the fear the oppressor has of the oppressed; the fear of the man who is always looking for insurrection from beneath because he knows that the lower class has been wronged, that same fear existed during slavery time, that same vague apprehension that some insurrection might take place.

Du Bois to Ray Stannard Baker, "Memorandum for Mr. Ray Stannard Baker on his article on The Country Negro," 1907; microfilm reel no. 1, frame no. 307; W.E.B. Du Bois Papers, University of Massachusetts, Amherst.

432. THE POOR

The ideal of the poor in America is usually to become rich and ride on the necks of the poorer.

Color and Democracy (1945) 72.

433. POOR WHITE SOUTH

It was the drear destiny of the Poor White South that, deserting its economic class and itself, it became the instrument by which democracy in the nation was done to death, race provincialism deified, and the world delivered to plutocracy.

Black Reconstruction (1935) 241.

434. POOR WHITES

The poor white clung frantically to the planter and his ideals; and although ignorant and impoverished, maimed and discouraged, victims of a war fought largely by the poor white for the benefit of the rich planter, they sought redress by demanding unity of white against black, and not unity of poor against rich, or of worker against exploiter.

Black Reconstruction (1935) 130.

435. PRESSING QUESTIONS

Back of all our discussion of present problems, of war and communism; of wages, prices and housing; of political power and law and order, stands one pressing question which we fear to touch; and that is the ethics of property, wealth and income. How far it is right or wrong for us to receive the income which we are receiving or to support the methods by which wealth today is accumulated and distributed. . . . The question before the people of the United States and of the World today is that curbing of the power of wealth, the compulsory distribution of income in accordance with need and social plan, the vesting of natural resources in the ownership of the people, the practice of democracy in industry as well as government.

"A Sermon for the Churchman" (1948); Series 3/C, Folder no. 5557, pp. 1, 4, *Unpublished Articles*; W.E.B. Du Bois Papers, University of Massachusetts, Amherst.

436. PRIVATE OWNERSHIP

Private ownership of land, tools, and raw materials may at one stage of economic development be a method of stimulating production and one which does not greatly interfere with equitable distribution. When, however, the intricacy and length of technical production is increased, the ownership of these things becomes a monopoly, which easily makes the rich richer and the poor poorer.

Dark Water (1920) 100.

437. PROPERTY

Society creates property and loans it to the individual for the good of all.

Amsterdam News, May 30, 1942; *Newspaper Columns by W.E.B. Du Bois* (1986) 437.

438. RACES AND CLASSES

The world today consists, not of races, but of the imperial commercial group of master capitalists, international and predominantly white; the national middle classes of the several nations, white, yellow, and brown, with strong blood bonds, common languages, and common history; the international laboring class of all colors; the backward, oppressed groups of nature-folk, predominantly yellow, brown, and black.

Darkwater (1920) 98.

439. RACIAL EQUALITY

The fight for racial equality continues, only it cannot longer be called this. It must hereafter be regarded, if not actually called, the problem of the colored and black working classes, and the burden of its effort must not be to prove biological and cultural sameness; this science has already proved. But it must be to insist on the identity of the Negro problem and the Yellow Peril and the "menace" of the lower classes; and the identity of all these problems with the labor problems of the world, and with the whole question of the education, political power, and economic position of the mass of men.

Pittsburgh Courier, November 14, 1936; *Newspaper Columns by W.E.B. Du Bois* (1986) 136.

440. RICH AND POOR

The chief and repeated accusations against the [constitutional] convention and succeeding legislatures [in both South Carolina in 1868 and after] was that they were composed of poor men, white and black. . . . Since the great majority of the white people of the state had been kept in ignorance and poverty, and practically all of the Negroes were slaves whose education was a penal offense, one would hardly expect universal suffrage to put rich men in the legislature.

Black Reconstruction (1935) 390, 391.

441. SALVATION

Not by the development of upper classes to exploit the workers, nor by the escape of individual genius into the white world, can we effect the salvation of our group in America. And the salvation of this group carries with it the emancipation, not only of the darker races of men who make the vast majority of mankind but of all men of all races.

Pittsburgh Courier, April 11, 1936; *Newspaper Columns by W.E.B. Du Bois* (1986) 59.

442. STATUS

It was not always the actual hunger and dire want that frightened this [small southern] town as much as the fear of loss of status among the few who were on the edge of security, among the well-to-do who were striving between riches and poverty, and among the rich who realized that their wealth was in continuous danger. . . . The first part of status was color of skin, and the second was land.

The Ordeal of Mansart (1957) 199.

443. STOCK MARKET

In the long run stock market speculation does not distribute goods in the most valuable and beneficent way. It distributes power, on the other hand, where it never ought to rest.

Chicago Defender, February 28, 1948; *Newspaper Columns by W.E.B. Du Bois* (1986) 766.

444. SURRENDER AND SILENCE

The world will not give a decent living to the persons who are out to reform it. . . . Those persons who control income are not going to yield any part of that income to the people who propose to disturb their power. . . . How long can you get the necessary bread and butter by speaking out frankly and plainly? When you can no longer do this, what compromises can you make in unessentials that will allow you to save your soul? Beyond that, is oblivion. The oblivion of complete surrender or of complete silence. The object of life is to avoid either of these.

Letter to Leonard C. Cartwright, October 4, 1928, *Correspondence*, I, 381–382.

445. SURVIVAL OF FITTEST

Those who desired large income through ownership of capital used Darwin's doctrine to excuse the growing reduction of the majority of the world's laborers to the cheap use of their toil and land for the increasing profit of capitalism.

John Brown (1909 and 1962) 399. [John Brown was executed in 1859, the year of publication of *Origin and Species* by Darwin.]

446. USE AND ABUSE

Most Americans used the Negro to defend their own economic interests and, refusing him adequate land and real education and even common justice, deserted him shamelessly as soon as their selfish interests were safe. Nor does this for a moment deny that unselfish and far-seeing Americans, poor as well as rich, by supplying public schools when the Negroes demanded them and establishing higher schools to train teachers, saved the Negro from being entirely reenslaved or exterminated in an unequal and cowardly renewal of war.

Black Reconstruction (1935) 378–379.

447. BOOKER T. WASHINGTON

He did not take the side of the employer against the employee because he did not sense any real opposition. The employer was of course right and normal. The only recognizable ambition of an employee was to become an employer or to serve humbly as a worker.

To Karl R. Wallace, January 21, 1938; microfilm reel no. 49, frame no. 799; W.E.B.
    Du Bois Papers, University of Massachusetts, Amherst.

448. WEALTH

Wealth was God. Everywhere men sought wealth and especially in America there was extravagant living; everywhere the poor planned to be rich and the rich planned to be richer; everywhere wider, bigger, higher, better things were set down as inevitable.

Dusk of Dawn (1940) 26–27. [Du Bois was referring to the year 1885 and thereabouts.]

449. WEALTH AND INCOME

It is quite possible that long before the end of the twentieth century, the deliberate distribution of property and income by the state on an equitable and logical basis will be looked upon as the state's prime function.

Black Reconstruction (1935) 591.

The freedman sought eagerly, after the war, property and income. He believed that his condition was not his own fault but due to theft on a mighty scale. He demanded reimbursement and redress sufficient for a decent livelihood.

Black Reconstruction (1935) 599.

It would astonish most persons to learn how little we know about wealth and income. Our ignorance is nothing less than shameful. We do not know accurately the income of the individuals and families who compose our populations. We have made no accurate studies of this matter and law will not permit us to do it.

Amsterdam News, September 19, 1942; *Newspaper Columns by W.E.B. Du Bois* (1986) 468.

9

Women

450. BLACK MAMMY

Above all looms the figure of the Black Mammy, one of the most pitiful of the world's Christs. Whether drab or dirty drudge or dark and gentle lady she played her part in the uplift of the South. She was an embodied Sorrow, an anomaly crucified on the cross of her own neglected children for the sake of the children of masters who bought and sold her as they bought and sold cattle.

The Gift of Black Folk (1924) 337–338.

451. BLACK WOMANLINESS

No other woman on earth could have emerged from the hell of force and temptation which once engulfed and still surrounds black women in America with half the modesty and womanliness that they retain.

Darkwater (1920) 186.

452. BLACK WOMEN WORKERS

There were in 1910 two and a half million Negro homes in the United States. Out of these homes walked daily to work two million women and girls over ten years of age,—over half of the colored female population as against a fifth in the case of white women. These, then, are a group of workers, fighting for their daily bread like men; independent and approaching economic freedom! They furnished a million farm laborers, 80,000 farmers, 22,000 teachers, 600,000 servants and washerwomen, and 50,000 in trades and merchandizing.

Darkwater (1920) 179–180.

453.   COLORED WOMEN

If they were pretty and comely they must marry early and even then their husbands had a hard time protecting them from white men. If they did not marry they were fair prey for both white and colored men. If they went into house service they were fairly certain to become concubines, and in a few cases colored women were supported openly in the town and everyone knew what white man was their master. Sometimes the colored women fought furiously to ward off white men even to maiming and murder. In other cases they flaunted their sex attraction for white men in the very faces of white women, who could but helplessly hate, and hate they did.

The Ordeal of Mansart (1957) 201–202.

454.   MARRIAGE

Very few of our colored men want to marry women with brains; I don't know whether it is modesty or fear!

To Mr. and Mrs. Eugene Davidson, November 28, 1950; microfilm reel no. 64, frame no. 1201; W.E.B. Du Bois Papers, University of Massachusetts, Amherst.

455.   PATIENCE

A civilization that required nineteen centuries to recognize the Rights of Women can confidently be expected some day to abolish the Color Line.

"Triumph," *Crisis* 20 (October 1920) 261; *Selections from* The Crisis, vol. 1 (1983) 275.

456.   SEX RATIO

From the beginning the industrial opportunities of Negro women in cities have been far greater than those of men, through their large employment in domestic service. At the same time the restriction of employments open to Negroes, which perhaps reached a climax in 1830–1840, and which still plays a great part, has served to limit the number of men. The proportion, therefore, of men to women is a rough index of the industrial opportunities of the Negro. . . . Its effects are seen in a large percent of illegitimate births.

The Philadelphia Negro (1899) 55.

457.   SEXISM ON WHEELS

Any time a member of the female sex, or anyone else in fact, thinks that after a month's tutelage she can drive a car, she is due a session in the hospital.

To Shirley Graham, February 26, 1942; microfilm reel no. 53, frame no. 1043; W.E.B. Du Bois Papers, University of Massachusetts, Amherst.

458. WOMAN SUFFRAGE

Every argument for Negro suffrage is an argument for woman's suffrage; every argument for woman suffrage is an argument for Negro suffrage; both are great movements in democracy.

"Woman Suffrage," *Crisis* 9 (April 1915) 285; *Selections from* The Crisis, vol. 1 (1983) 92.

459. WOMANHOOD

The meaning of the twentieth century is the freeing of the individual soul; the soul longest in slavery and still in the most disgusting and indefensible slavery is the soul of womanhood.

"Woman Suffrage," *Crisis* II (November 1915) 29–30; *Selections from* The Crisis, vol. 1 (1983) 112.

The future woman must have a life work and economic independence. She must have knowledge. She must have the right of motherhood at her own discretion.

Darkwater (1920) 164–165.

460. WOMEN

[Kathie] has written me and with a woman's usual care, has forgotten to put in her address while I have forgotten her last name.

To J. Samuel Belboder, April 14, 1930; microfilm reel no. 30, frame no. 935; W.E.B. Du Bois Papers, University of Massachusetts, Amherst.

461. WOMEN VOTERS

There is not the slightest reason for supposing that white American women under ordinary circumstances are going to be any more intelligent, liberal or humane toward the black, the poor and unfortunate than white men are. On the contrary, considering what the subjection of a race, a class or a sex must mean, there will undoubtedly manifest itself among women voters at first more prejudice and petty meanness toward Negroes than we have now. It is the awful penalty of injustice and oppression to breed in the oppressed the desire to oppress others.

"Votes for Women," *Crisis* 8 (August 1914) 170–80; *Selections from* The Crisis, vol. 1 (1983) 79.

462. WOMEN'S RIGHTS

Women do need the ballot. They need it to right the balance of a world sadly awry because of its brutal neglect of the rights of women and children. With the best will and knowledge, no man can know women's wants as well as women themselves. To disfranchise women is deliberately to turn from knowledge and grope in ignorance.

Darkwater (1920) 146.

10

Ideals and Realities

463. ADMINISTRATORS AND AUTHORS

I am always sorry to have an author go into administrative work, and yet it is almost inevitable. For how can the world's work get done except by the help of those who know what the world is, and especially in times like the present.

To Barrows Dunham, May 2, 1961; microfilm reel no. 75, frame no. 134; W.E.B. Du Bois Papers, University of Massachusetts, Amherst.

464. ADVOCACY

No man today has a right to describe himself as liberal or radical who refuses to face the problem of black folk and colored people; who proposes to reform the world for the benefit of white people on the tacit assumption that other folk are not human in the same sense that white people are human.

"Liberals, Radicals and the Negro" (ca. 1930), Series 3/C, Folder no. 5532, p. 8, *Unpublished Articles*; W.E.B. Du Bois Papers, University of Massachusetts, Amherst.

465. BANKS

On that morning when I arrived in New York [in 1933], the banks were on their knees. They were not talking about free enterprise or individual initiative. They were not complaining of the power of the Federal Government. They were begging the Federal Government for God's sake to give them law and money in order to keep from collapse, not only their own institutions but the economic and industrial organization of their country.

"Roosevelt," January 30, 1948; microfilm reel no. 80, frame no. 1077; W.E.B. Du Bois Papers, University of Massachusetts, Amherst.

466.   BURDENS OF SUFFRAGE

Negro and white labor ought to have had the right to vote; . . . they ought to have tried to change the basis of property and redistribute income; and . . . their failure to do this was a disaster to democratic government in the United States.

Black Reconstruction (1935) 591.

467.   COMMERCE WITH THE STARS

It would not do to concenter all effort on economic well-being and forget freedom and manhood and equality. Rather Negroes must live and eat and strive, and still hold unfaltering commerce with the stars.

Dusk of Dawn (1940) 7.

468.   COMPARATIVE EMANCIPATION

To emancipate four million laborers whose labor has been owned, and separate them from the land upon which they had worked for nearly two and half centuries, was an operation such as no modern country had for a moment attempted or contemplated. The German and English and French serf, the Italian and Russian serf, were, on emancipation, given definite rights in the land. Only the American Negro slave was emancipated without such rights and in the end this spelled for him the continuation of slavery.

Black Reconstruction (1935) 611.

469.   COMPROMISING MORAL WRONG

How far in a State can a recognized moral wrong safely be compromised? And although this chapter of history can give us no definite answer to the ever varying aspect of political life, yet it would seem to warn any nation from allowing, through carelessness and moral cowardice, any social evil to grow. No persons would have seen the Civil War with more surprise and horror than the Revolutionists of 1776; yet from the small and apparently dying institution of their day arose the walled and castled Slave Power. From this we may conclude that it behooves nations as well as men to do things at the very moment when they ought to be done.

The Suppression of the African Slave Trade (1896) 199.

470.   CRY ALOUD AND SPARE NOT

Humanity is progressing toward an ideal; but not, please God, solely by help of men who sit in cloistered ease, hesitate from action and seek sweetness and light; rather we progress today, as in the past, by the soul-torn strength of those who can never sit still and silent while the disinherited and the damned clog our gutters and gasp their lives out on our front porches. These are the men who go down in the blood and dust of battle. They say ugly things to an ugly world. They spew the lukewarm fence straddlers out of their mouths, like God of old; they cry aloud and spare not; they shout from the housetops, and they make this world so damned uncomfortable with its nasty burden of evil that it tries to get good and does get better.

"The Philosophy of Mr. Dole," *Crisis* 8 (May 1914) 24–26; *Selections from* The Crisis, vol. 1 (1983) 76.

471. DEMOCRACY

To call that government a democracy which makes majority votes an excuse for crushing ideas and individuality and self-development, is manifestly a peculiarly dangerous perversion of the real democratic ideal.

Darkwater (1920) 152.

You can say that the United States is a democracy. You know it is not. When the United States makes a failure in democracy, immediately you put it down to democracy. You should on the contrary put it down to the credit of those who are ruling the United States.

"Democracy in America," ca. 1928; microfilm reel no. 80, frame no. 362; W.E.B. Du Bois Papers, University of Massachusetts, Amherst.

Democracy is not merely a distribution of power among a vast number of individuals. It is not merely majority rule based on the fact that the majority has the physical force to prevail. It is something far more fundamental than this: It rests upon the fact, that when we have proven knowledge, interpreted through the experience of a large number of individuals, it is possible through this pooled knowledge and experience to come to decisions much more fundamental and much more far-reaching than can be had in any other way. . . . The people participating effectively in this pool of democracy must be alive and well, they must know the world which they are interpreting and they must know themselves.

"Human Rights for All Minorities," April 29, 1947; microfilm reel no. 80, frame no. 981; W.E.B. Du Bois Papers, University of Massachusetts, Amherst.

Over most of our history, democracy has been strictly limited, now by religion and status, now by race, now by ownership of property, later by the slave system, then by legal disfranchisement, and today by the power of corporate wealth.

In Battle for Peace (1952) 166.

Of course our democracy [in Great Barrington] was not full and free. Certain well-known and well-to-do citizens were always elected to office—not the richest or most noted but just as surely not the poorest or the Irish Catholics.

Autobiography (1968) 93.

Democracy is a method of realizing the broadest measure of justice to all human beings.

Darkwater (1920) 142.

Democracy to the world first meant simply the transfer of privilege and opportunity from waning to waxing power, from the well-born to the rich, from the nobility to the merchants.

The Gift of Black Folk (1924) 136.

The democracy established in America in the eighteenth century was not, and was not designed to be, a democracy of the masses of men and it was thus singularly easy for people to fail to see the incongruity of democracy and slavery. It was the Negro himself who forced the consideration of this incongruity, who made emancipation inevitable and made the modern world at least consider if not wholly accept the idea of a democracy including men of all races and colors.

The Gift of Black Folk (1924) 139.

It is as clear as day that the failure of democracy lies in the fact that it has not been tried in precisely those activities of life where it is most important. The democratic selection of more or less irresponsible [government] officials means nothing so long as we have autocracy and aristocracy in industry.

Statement to Harry W. Laidler, December 9, 1925; microfilm reel no. 15, frame no. 922; W.E.B. Du Bois Papers, University of Massachusetts, Amherst.

The greatest fact in the world is that the colored world is fighting for democracy.

"Democracy in America," ca. 1928; microfilm reel no. 80, frame no. 366; W.E.B. Du Bois Papers, University of Massachusetts, Amherst.

Democracy has failed because so many fear it. They believe that wealth and happiness are so limited that a world full of intelligent, healthy, and free people is impossible, if not undesirable.

Color and Democracy (1945) 99.

Democracy is not simply the self-defense of the competent; it is the unloosing of the energies and the capabilities of the depressed.

Color and Democracy (1945) 116.

The great contribution of the United States to democracy was proof that the most unlikely classes and races of people could be made fit for self-government, if they were given opportunity for education and for remunerative work. It must be remembered that before the American experiment, it was common belief among Europeans, that democratic government was only possible for a selected class of citizens.

"No Second Class Citizens," November 28, 1947; microfilm reel no. 80, frame no. 1046; W.E.B. Du Bois Papers, University of Massachusetts, Amherst.

Whenever and wherever the democratic method threatens to invade the inner citadels of real social power then we may expect prolonged effort to curtail democracy and limit it to such areas as will be . . . least dangerous to the current rulers.

"Vito Marcantonio/Benjamin J. Davis Election Speech," October 27, 1949; microfilm
reel no. 80, frame no. 1257; W.E.B. Du Bois Papers, University of Massachusetts,
Amherst.

Democracy is not perfect. It only promises that by continuous appeal to the experience and commonsense of the mass of people in any case, but particularly if these people be increasingly educated you get the closest approach to universal wisdom that human beings can hope for. When you deny this process even with a few people and in a limited region you begin to ruin it for the whole nation.
. . . The beginnings of the present failure of democracy in America was the repudiation of the democratic process in the case of Black American citizens in the South.

"Democracy Fails in America," June 1954; microfilm reel no. 81, frame no. 899; W.E.B.
Du Bois Papers, University of Massachusetts, Amherst.

No nation in the world has in the past made a greater effort toward democracy even though today democracy does not function in this nation.

"Our American Heritage," July 4, 1954; microfilm reel no. 81, frame no. 909; W.E.B.
Du Bois Papers, University of Massachusetts, Amherst.

We have done more to make it possible for people of diverse race and culture to live together than any other nation. But we have not done enough, and the problems of human conduct which remain even in America are dangerous. But especially in the matters of democracy and distribution of wealth we have not only ceased to move forward toward making these gifts greater and more effective, we have actually begun to retreat. There is less effective democratic government in the United States than there was a century ago, and the most threatening trend is the movement toward fascist dictatorship instead of toward the rule of public opinion.

"Our American Heritage," July 4, 1954; microfilm reel no. 81, frame no. 910; W.E.B.
Du Bois Papers, University of Massachusetts, Amherst.

472. ECONOMIC GROWTH

It is historically unprovable that the advance of undeveloped peoples has been helped by wholesale exploitation at the hands of their richer, stronger, and more unscrupulous neighbors. This idea is a legend of the long exploded doctrine of inevitable economic harmonies in all business life.

John Brown (1909, 1962) 394.

473. ECONOMIC SELF-INTEREST

One of the great postulates of the science of economics—that men will seek their economic advantage—is in this case untrue, because in many cases men will not do this if it involves association, even in a casual and business way, with Negroes. And this fact must be taken account of in all judgments as to the Negro's economic progress.

The Philadelphia Negro (1899) 146.

474. FREE SILENCE

The greatest lack of freedom of discussion of present American problems comes not in problems which you are not allowed to discuss but rather in those which you are free to discuss but afraid of. I know and you know that the conspiracy of silence that surrounds the Negro problem in the United States arises because you do not dare, you are without the moral courage to discuss it freely.

"The Problem of Problems," *Intercollegiate Socialist* 6 (December-January 1917–1918) 5–9; *Writings by W.E.B. Du Bois in Periodicals Edited by Others*, vol. 2 (1982) 117.

475. HUMAN RIGHTS

What is wrong about human rights is not the lack of pious statements, but the question as to what application is made of them and what is to be done when human rights are denied in the face of law and declarations.

To Walter White, November 24, 1947; microfilm reel no. 60, frame no. 615; W.E.B. Du Bois Papers, University of Massachusetts, Amherst.

476. INDUSTRIAL DEMOCRACY

The failure of modern democracy comes from no false premises touching the right of the governed to a voice in government; but rather is due to the fact that in the widest and most important realm of human action—that is in industry—democracy has never been tried, and that there tyrannous and selfish monarchy is not only the rule, but almost the only dreamed-of possibility or refuge. And that is the reason today why the attempt to apply intelligence to the industrial maladjustment in this land and throughout the world, is so difficult and bootless.

"Curriculum Revision," ca. 1935; microfilm reel no. 80, frame no. 634; W.E.B. Du Bois Papers, University of Massachusetts, Amherst.

477. LOCAL CONTROL

How much longer [can] the United States . . . in deference to its Manchester economics, leave the great question of the education of its citizens entirely to local control, and thus increase and intensify present evils by giving the worst schools to the poorest and most ignorant communities [?].

"The Afro-American" (ca. 1894–1896), Series 3/C, Folder no. 5502, *Unpublished Articles*; W.E.B. Du Bois Papers, University of Massachusetts, Amherst.

478. PARIAH IDEALS

In the boast of having risen far above the narrowness of this class conception no land has equalled or approached ours. And yet of all great modern nations not a single one has more resolutely or doggedly persisted in denying the attribute of manhood to a large proportion of its inhabitants, and persisted in making for these pariah ideals of living and aspiration far different from those of the rest of their fellow-men.

"The Negro Ideals of Life," *Christian Register* 84 (October 25, 1905) 1197–99; *Writings by W.E.B. Du Bois in Periodicals Edited by Others*, vol. 1 (1982) 268.

479. RACE PREJUDICE

In the years from 1896 to the [first world] war, I expected that race prejudice in the United States was going gradually to crumble before scientific fact and agitation. I think now that we made some progress and inroads, but I am satisfied that we expected too rapid a solution, and . . . it does not seem to me that any person now living is going to see essential change in the attitude of whites toward Negroes. Some change there will be, but race prejudice is going to persist for a long time in the United States. If, now, we had reasonable economic independence, we could just wait, even though the waiting took a few generations. But, our economic situation is such that while we are continuing to hammer at the false logic of race prejudice and continuing to bring forward scientific fact, we have got to live and earn a living, and therefore the immediate problem is how to do that?

Letter to George Streator, April 24, 1935; *Correspondence*, II, 90–91.

480. RULE BY WEALTH

The United States is not a Democracy; it is ruled by wealth.

To Tertius Chandler, July 20, 1959; microfilm reel no. 73, frame no. 613; W.E.B. Du Bois Papers, University of Massachusetts, Amherst.

481. SOCIALIST PARTY

I know the record of the Socialist party toward the Negro very well. On the whole it has been exceptionally good as I have said from time to time. But for the most part its theoretical attitude has never been put to a practical test. . . . On the other hand, the question of segregated Locals in the South is of tremendous practical importance and it is here that the Party is wavering and, I am afraid, failing to stand up to its ideals.

To Frank Crosswaith, July 10, 1923; microfilm reel no. 11, frame no. 788; W.E.B. Du Bois Papers, University of Massachusetts, Amherst.

482. SWEEPING DISFRANCHISEMENT

[After the 1890s] the disfranchisement of Negroes in the South became nearly complete. In no other civilized and modern land has so great a group of people, most of whom were able to read and write, been allowed so small a voice in their own government.

Black Reconstruction (1935) 694.

483. TALKING DEMOCRACY

We can't open our mouths today without saying something about democracy, but we never say anything about democracy in Africa, and we don't say much about democracy in the South. We're taught democracy among those people who have the power, who have had the power and who propose to keep the power.

"General Social Background of the Present Situation," January 23, 1941; microfilm reel no. 80, frame no. 839; W.E.B. Du Bois Papers, University of Massachusetts, Amherst.

484. TOUGH TIMES

Liberal and Radical white Southerners and liberal and radical Negroes are having a pretty tough time these days; especially the white Southerner who talks a liberal creed with one side of his mouth and contradicts it with the other and does nothing with his hands; and also the colored man, who because he is liberal so far as his own shoe pinches, is quite willing to be reactionary in all other social matters.

To Harold Preece, August 12, 1947; microfilm reel no. 60, frame no. 756; W.E.B. Du Bois Papers, University of Massachusetts, Amherst.

11

Literature

485. AUTHENTICITY AND AUDIENCE

No authentic group literature can rise save at the demand and with the support of the group which is calling for self-expression. The depression of industry, which came with a crash in 1929, was foreshadowed in the Negro group several years before, despite the apparent industrial boom. The circulation of the *Crisis* went down, the contributions to the National Association [for the Advancement of Colored People] were curtailed and the new Negro literature was forced to place its dependence almost entirely upon a white audience and that audience had its own distinct patterns and preferences for Negro writing.

Dusk of Dawn (1940) 270–271.

486. AUTOBIOGRAPHY

[An autobiography] cannot be entirely frank and totally revealing. . . . Partly it may be due to fear of hurting others; partly to reluctance to tell the world all about yourself. But chiefly, I suppose, it is because we really do not know nearly as much about ourselves as we think we do or as we would like to. The ego never really stands aside and reveals itself as a third person. Mixed up in the attempt is what you think you are, what you wish you were, what you've been told you are, and so forth and so on. . . . Perhaps if one's believing wife collaborated with one's best enemy, the result, if a result were reached, would be of great value.

"Forward [Foreword] to proposed biography of Du Bois, to be written by Shirley Graham Du Bois," February 23, 1955; microfilm reel no. 87, frame no. 129; W.E.B. Du Bois Papers, University of Massachusetts, Amherst.

487. BLACK ART

With a vast wealth of human material about us, our own writers and artists fear to paint the truth lest they criticize their own and be in turn criticized for it. They fail to see the Eternal Beauty that shines through all Truth, and try to portray a world of stilted artificial black folk such as never were on land or sea.

"Negro Art," *Crisis* 22 (June 1921) 55–56; *Selections from* The Crisis, vol. 1 (1983) 301.

488. BLACK LITERATURE

Scarcely a history of American literature used in the public schools today mentions a single Negro writer; even Dunbar, Chesnutt and Cullen are systematically omitted. It would be too bad for us to have to wait for the growth of a buying audience among Negroes before we could have a development of Negro literature for such literature is of significance not merely to Negroes, not even mainly to Negroes; it is of significance to America.

To Dorothy M. Eller, June 2, 1938; microfilm reel no. 48, frame no. 971; W.E.B. Du Bois Papers, University of Massachusetts, Amherst.

We have three or more Church Publishing Houses printing from year to year nonsensical Sunday School literature. They should be publishing Negro history and biography.... Without a large and continuing Negro demand for Negro literature, this literature will die, or worse than that, never be born.

To Arthur Huff Fauset, June 30, 1958; microfilm reel no. 73, frame no. 132; W.E.B. Du Bois Papers, University of Massachusetts, Amherst.

489. BLACK RECONSTRUCTION

I think I have a book of unusual importance. Of course, it will not sell widely; it will not pay, but in the long run, it can never be ignored.

To F. P. Keppel, November 17, 1934; microfilm reel no. 41, frame no. 1133; W.E.B. Du Bois Papers, University of Massachusetts, Amherst.

490. BOOK REVIEWER

I have read it. I think I had rather not write a review of it. There is a great deal in it that is valuable but much that I should criticize unfavorably, and I hesitate to do this in the case of these young authors who are beginning a career in a good cause.

To Elmer A. Carter, September 27, 1937; microfilm reel no. 47, frame no. 944; W.E.B. Du Bois Papers, University of Massachusetts, Amherst.

491. COMPRESSION

No human being could, in a twenty-minute paper, treat the Thirteenth, Fourteenth and Fifteenth Amendments and "add general comment upon the situation which we now have with respect to the rights of the Negro People.'' After all, I am just a writer, not a magician.

To Robert J. Silberstein, February 10, 1949; microfilm reel no. 64, frame no. 127; W.E.B. Du Bois Papers, University of Massachusetts, Amherst.

492. GROUP AND INDIVIDUAL

[After election as a member of the American Institute of Arts and Letters:] If I were an individual I might with much joy, join Upton Sinclair and others [in rejecting membership] and tell the Institute that since we have lived more than seventy years without them, we would tread on the rest of the way alone, but I am not an individual, I am a group; and the group must say yes very humbly.

To Ridgely Torrence, December 29, 1943; microfilm reel no. 55, frame no. 757; W.E.B. Du Bois Papers, University of Massachusetts, Amherst.

493. LITERATURE

As a normal human being reacting humanly to human problems the Negro has never appeared in the fiction or the science of white writers, with a bare half dozen exceptions.

The Gift of Black Folk (1924) 295.

494. MAKING LITERATURE

Much of my life has been devoted to writing. I am not entirely satisfied with it, because so much of it has been hurried hack writings, ill-conceived and ill-digested. I would wish to correct that by eliminating haste and impatience and stressing more the carefully digested and more perfectly finished book. The immediate result may not have differed greatly, but in the long run, I might have made literature.

"If I Were Young Again: Reading, Writings and Real Estate,'' *Negro Digest* 1 (October 1943) 63–65; *Writings in Periodicals Edited by Others*, vol. 3 (1982) 180.

495. NEGRO BOOK CLUB

Mr. James W. Johnson and myself together with the editors of Viking Press and representatives of the Book of the Month Club went pretty thoroughly into the matter of a Negro Book of the Month Club some twenty years ago. Our conclusion then was that there did not seem to be the prospect of collecting enough revenue to operate such a group successfully. How far in the last two decades this condition has changed, I am not sure. The circulation of Negro weekly newspapers has greatly increased. With that Negroes buy more books but still not very many. My own books have been sold to Negroes in very small numbers.

To Luther R. White, January 23, 1945; microfilm reel no. 58, frame no. 215; W.E.B.
Du Bois Papers, University of Massachusetts, Amherst.

496. NO BUSINESS

I have been very much surprised to the comparatively small number of writers
who seem to be interested in Negro business. We [in *Crisis* magazine] get a
flood of poetry and fiction. We have had some excellent essays and cover
drawings, but young black America doesn't know what American Negroes are
doing in insurance and banking, in retail business, in manufacturing, and the
like. They must be induced to learn.

To G. W. Buckner, October 27, 1927; microfilm reel no. 22, frame no. 1234; W.E.B.
Du Bois Papers, University of Massachusetts, Amherst.

497. NON-BEST SELLERS

I do not think that any . . . [publishing] firms have lost money on my works
but my work has not sold largely because I have insisted on writing on a subject
which is unpopular: the relation of the Negro to the United States.

To Frank E. Taylor, March 29, 1943; microfilm reel no. 55, frame no. 650; W.E.B. Du
Bois Papers, University of Massachusetts, Amherst.

498. NON-BUYING LIBRARIES

I have never thought it was exactly fair for libraries to ask authors not only
to write books but to buy them and give them to libraries.

To Jacob Hodnefiled, March 10, 1927; microfilm reel no. 22, frame no. 804; W.E.B.
Du Bois Papers, University of Massachusetts, Amherst.

499. NON-PUBLIC LIBRARY

[A year after the Carnegie library for whites opened in Atlanta a committee
of blacks met with trustees of the library.] I demanded . . . the same rights to
use the library as were accorded white citizens. I pointed out that the discrimination was unfair; that although my own books were in the library, I could not
take them out; and that this sort of discrimination was not democracy. Some of
the trustees were quite angry at the demand and showed it in their faces and by
what they said. The result of the visit was that we not only got no rights in the
Central Library but for 10 years no branch library was established.

Letter to Virginia Lacy Jones, December 19, 1950; *Correspondence*, III, 302.

500. NON-READING MATERIAL

The 40 or more volumes of the CRISIS, which I edited from 1910 to 1934,
can hardly be found outside of New York. The Atlanta Studies of the Negro
Problem from 1896 to 1914 are also out of print. Then I have written and

published some 16 different volumes, and all of them except the last two or three are out of print.

To Wolfgang Saur, July 21, 1950; microfilm reel no. 65, frame no. 620; W.E.B. Du Bois Papers, University of Massachusetts, Amherst. [Today virtually all his works are back in print.]

501. PIVOT

The most dramatic group of people in the history of the United States is the American Negro. It would be very easy for a great artist so to interpret the history of our country as to make the plot turn entirely upon the black man.

"The Negro and the American Stage," *Crisis* 28 (June 1924) 56–57; *Selections from The Crisis*, vol. 1 (1983) 404.

502. PLAGIARISM

I have had so much of my work calmly annexed by others that I have gotten used to it and almost stopped complaining.

To Helen Boardman, March 29, 1943; microfilm reel no. 55, frame no. 95; W.E.B. Du Bois Papers, University of Massachusetts, Amherst.

503. POETRY

My poetry has been simply a part of my urge to express myself, and has been written quite unconscious of any accepted form. In fact I have given no attention to the form of poetic expression.

To John Francis McDermott, June 3, 1930; microfilm reel no. 31, frame no. 900; W.E.B. Du Bois Papers, University of Massachusetts, Amherst.

504. POETRY AND POVERTY

There is no chance to sell poetry while people are so desperately in need of bread, but selling is the least part of poetry.

To Barbara Wheaton, August 11, 1932; microfilm reel no. 37, frame no. 747; W.E.B. Du Bois Papers, University of Massachusetts, Amherst.

505. PRODUCING PLAYS

[White publishers of plays] do not usually accept plays with colored casts or on the Negro problem, because they do not think that the public will attend such plays. Nevertheless, there is no market for any play . . . [except] the producers of plays, and there are very few Negroes who produce plays.

To S. W. Jennings, November 14, 1931; microfilm reel no. 34, frame no. 1233; W.E.B. Du Bois Papers, University of Massachusetts, Amherst.

506. PROPAGANDA AND ART

I stand in utter shamelessness and say that whatever art I have for writing has been used always for propaganda for gaining the right of black folk to love and enjoy. I do not care a damn for any art that is not used for propaganda. But I do care when propaganda is confined to one side while the other is stripped and silent.

"Criteria of Negro Art," *Crisis* 32 (October 1926) 290–97; *Selections from* The Crisis, vol. 2 (1983) 448.

507. REGENCY

You show a naive faith in assuming that the best work in any line of literature has been done in the last fifteen years.

To Catherine R. Nichols, January 31, 1945; microfilm reel no. 57, frame no. 724; W.E.B. Du Bois Papers, University of Massachusetts, Amherst.

508. SALEABILITY

The themes on which Negro writers naturally write best, with deepest knowledge and clearest understanding, are precisely the themes most editors do not want treated. . . . White Americans are willing to read about Negroes, but they prefer to read about Negroes who are fools, clowns, prostitutes, or at any rate, in despair and contemplating suicide. Other sorts of Negroes do not interest them because, as they say, they are "just like white folks." But their interest in white folks, we notice, continues.

"Mencken," *Crisis* 34 (October 1927) 276; *Selections from* The Crisis, vol. 2 (1983) 486.

509. SELF-ADMIRATION

Do not worry too much about the way in which a manuscript sounds after first writing it. If you let it lie awhile you may be surprised at how good it is and see clearly just how it can be made better.

To Rachel Davis Du Bois, February 26, 1936; microfilm reel no. 45, frame no. 831; W.E.B. Du Bois Papers, University of Massachusetts, Amherst.

510. VIEWPOINT

It goes without saying that anything I write is pro-Negro. Naturally it is going to defend the poor black and ignorant against prejudice and power.

To Raymond B. Fosdick, November 18, 1927; microfilm reel no. 22, frame no. 1323; W.E.B. Du Bois Papers, University of Massachusetts, Amherst.

511. WRITER'S WAGES

You are a good and even brilliant writer and for just that reason you have small chance to earn a living today unless you are willing to write convincingly of what you do not believe and sell your writings to those who happen to have money. Personally I have long insisted on writing what I believed and I would have starved to death if I had depended upon the income from this writing.

To Almena Lomax, September 19, 1960; microfilm reel no. 74, frame no. 492; W.E.B. Du Bois Papers, University of Massachusetts, Amherst.

512. WRITING

[My writings] have wavered between literature and statistics, propaganda and impression.

Untitled memorandum, undated [1933?]; microfilm reel no. 40, frame no. 411; W.E.B. Du Bois Papers, University of Massachusetts, Amherst.

513. WRITING AND MONEY

The money consideration is the least thing I have in mind in writing.

To W. T. Couch, September 24, 1940; microfilm reel no. 51, frame no. 979; W.E.B. Du Bois Papers, University of Massachusetts, Amherst.

514. WRITING AS PROPERTY

My writing is the most valuable form of my property and I have always asked respect for it.

To John H. H. Sengstacke, December 30, 1946; microfilm reel no. 58, frame no. 674; W.E.B. Du Bois Papers, University of Massachusetts, Amherst.

515. WRITING INTRODUCTIONS

By far the worst thing for a young author is to face the public on his own responsibility. I do not believe that introductions [written by others] help much or that many people read them. If you have got something to say, say it on your own responsibility and get full credit for it.

To J. Neal Hughley, August 29, 1935; microfilm reel no. 44, frame no. 386; W.E.B. Du Bois Papers, University of Massachusetts, Amherst.

12

Reform, Radicalism, and Revolution

516. PEDRO ALBIZU CAMPOS

During a recent trip to Cuba I heard of Pedro Albizu Campos of Puerto Rico whom I believe is incarcerated in your institution [Atlanta Federal Penitentiary]. I should like very much to have permission to talk with him under such regulations as are usual. He is, I understand, a colored man and a graduate of Harvard which is my alma mater.

To the warden, July 7, 1941; microfilm reel no. 52, frame no. 431; W.E.B. Du Bois Papers, University of Massachusetts, Amherst. [Albizu Campos was a revolutionary independence leader in Puerto Rico.]

517. AMERICAN CAPITALISM

The . . . land and resources of America . . . became in part a gift to the landless poor of Europe and a gateway to freedom of speech, freedom of belief, and freedom from want and fear. But the presence of Indians and Negroes as low paid labor depressed by slavery and caste, also made this continent a boon to producers of basic material in the world-wide demand, which were exchanged into capital goods and became the foundation of a new capitalism out of which the swiftly growing technique developed an Industrial Revolution. Thus both individual freedom and exploitation of labor developed side by side in America and were confused in world thought, as differing aspects of the same expanding culture.

Russia and America: An Interpretation (1950, unpublished); microfilm reel no. 85, frame no. 479; W.E.B. Du Bois Papers, University of Massachusetts, Amherst.

518. ANTICOMMUNISM

Today in this country it is becoming standard reaction to call anything "communist" and therefore subversive and unpatriotic, which anybody for any reason dislikes. We feel strongly that this tactic has already gone too far; that it is not sufficient today to trace a proposal to a communist source in order to dismiss it with contempt.

Letter to Dean Acheson, July 14, 1950; *Correspondence*, III, 305.

519. BELIEFS

I am a socialist and a great admirer of Russia but do not accept the whole communist doctrine although sympathetic to part of it.

To Marvel Cooke, October 20, 1944; microfilm reel no. 56, frame no. 558; W.E.B. Du Bois Papers, University of Massachusetts, Amherst.

520. BIG BUSINESS

In general big business in the United States has recently become desperately afraid that Negroes in the United States would turn to the left and consequently it has been taking many steps to appease them.

To Dorothy Sterling, December 19, 1949; microfilm reel no. 64, frame no. 339; W.E.B. Du Bois Papers, University of Massachusetts, Amherst.

521. BLACK AND NATIONAL PROBLEMS

I think that Dr. [John] Dewey and Mr. [Howard Y.] Williams are both generally interested in the Negro and mean to include him in their plan and action. The trouble is however, that they do not integrate the Negro problem as part of the general labor and social problem. It is to them an outside and incidental thing. We do not ask for Negro enfranchisement, because the Negro is disfranchised, but because the disfranchisement of one-tenth of any nation, be they white, black, green, means the failure of democracy to function for the whole nation. It is just so in all specific social problems.

To Mabel Stuart Lewis, March 18, 1932; microfilm reel no. 37, frame no. 169; W.E.B. Du Bois Papers, University of Massachusetts, Amherst.

522. BOYCOTT

The colored people have a right, after ascertaining the facts, to agree among themselves not to trade with certain stores until they either get better treatment or until the stores hire colored clerks, or until other changes in policy are made.

"The Boycott," *Crisis* 37 (March 1930) 102; *Selections from* The Crisis, vol. 2 (1983) 578.

523. CAMPAIGN FOR EQUALITY

There is no way in which the American Negro can force this nation to treat him as equal until the unconscious cerebration and folkways of the nation, as well as its rational deliberate thought among the majority of whites, are willing to grant equality.

Dusk of Dawn (1940) 194.

524. CENSORS AND PERSECUTORS

Your exchange with the McCarran Committee was most illuminating. It shows the abysmal ignorance of our censors and the effort of the Government and Big Business to keep the public ignorant. We are lurching around in a fog of misunderstanding, and when anyone ventures to state the simple truth, our persecutors are simply amazed that anybody knows more than they do or that there is anything to know.

To William Mandel, November 15, 1952; microfilm reel no. 79, frame no. 1045; W.E.B. Du Bois Papers, University of Massachusetts, Amherst.

525. CENTER OF PROBLEM

Negroes who have grown in intelligence and awareness of their handicaps . . . have begun to fight back by the use of the boycott and passive resistance. The experience in Montgomery [Alabama], the extraordinary uprising of the students all over the South and beginning in the North, shows an awareness of our situation which is most encouraging. But it still does not reach the center of the problem. And that center is not simply the right of Americans to spend their money as they wish and according to law, but the chance for American Negroes to have money to spend because of employment in which they can make a decent wage. What then is the next step? It is for American Negroes in increasing numbers and more and more widely to insist upon the legal rights which are already theirs and to add to that increasingly a socialistic form of government.

"Socialism and the American Negro," April 9, 1960; microfilm reel no. 81, frame no. 1323; W.E.B. Du Bois Papers, University of Massachusetts, Amherst.

526. CITIZENSHIP

The Fourteenth Amendment . . . made Negroes citizens of the United States and sought to insure their civil rights. But it did a great deal more than this. It established for all Americans a national citizenship as distinct from state citizenship: before the Fourteenth Amendment a man might be a citizen of Mississippi or of New York but there was legally no such thing as a citizen of the United States.

To Emilie Hapgood, October 9, 1917; microfilm reel no. 5, frame no. 934; W.E.B. Du Bois Papers, University of Massachusetts, Amherst.

527. CIVIL RIGHTS AND SOCIALISM

[On the NAACP's] Board of Directors in 1913, there were 4 members of the Socialist Party, 6 who were advanced liberals and sympathized with Socialism, and 5 who were strong capitalists. This was out of a total Board of 30 members.

To Oakley Johnson, [February ?] 1961; microfilm reel no. 75, frame no. 339; W.E.B. Du Bois Papers, University of Massachusetts, Amherst.

528. COMMUNISM

Communism is a "pain in the neck."

Afro-American, February 15, 1936.

I am not a communist but I appreciate what the communists are trying to do and endeavor always in my classes and elsewhere to give a fair and balanced judgment concerning them.

Letter to George W. Cook, November 7, 1938; *Correspondence*, II, 170.

I believe in communism. I mean by communism, a planned way of life in the production of wealth and work designed for building a state whose object is the highest welfare of its people and not merely the profit of a part.

Autobiography (1968) 57.

529. COMMUNIST PARTY

One of the worst things that Negroes could do today would be to join the American Communist Party or any of its many branches. The Communists of America have become dogmatic exponents of the inspired word of Karl Marx as they read it. They believe, apparently in immediate, violent and bloody revolution, and they are willing to try any and all means of raising hell anywhere and under any circumstances. This is a silly program even for white men. For American colored men, it is suicide.

"Social Planning for the Negro, Past and Present," *Journal of Negro Education* 5 (January 1936) 110–25; *Writings by W.E.B. Du Bois in Periodicals Edited by Others*, vol. 3 (1982) 38.

So far as I am concerned, I am not a member of the Communist Party and I never have been. I have stated that under oath, on several occasions when, as a witness, the question was asked in the course of trial procedure.

To Kwame Nkrumah, February 12, 1958; microfilm reel no. 73, frame no. 330; W.E.B. Du Bois Papers, University of Massachusetts, Amherst.

On this first day of October, 1961, I am applying for admission to membership in the Communist Party of the United States. I have been long and slow in coming to this conclusion, but at last my mind is settled. . . . Today I have reached a firm conclusion: Capitalism cannot reform itself; it is doomed to self-destruction. No universal selfishness can bring social good to all. Communism—the effort to give all men what they need and to ask of each the best they can contribute—this is the only way of human life.

Letter to Gus Hall, October 1, 1961; *Correspondence*, III, 439, 440.

530. CULTURE OF EQUALS

We are definitely approaching now a time when the American Negro will become in law equal in citizenship to other Americans. . . . When we become equal American citizens what will be our aims and ideals and what will we have to do with selecting these aims and ideals? Are we to assume that we will simply adopt the ideals of Americans and become what they are or want to be; and that we will have in this process no ideals of our own? . . . What I have been fighting for and am still fighting for is the possibility of black folk and black cultural patterns existing in America without discrimination; and on terms of equality.

"Whither Now and Why," March 31, 1960; microfilm reel no. 81, frame no. 1298; W.E.B. Du Bois Papers, University of Massachusetts, Amherst.

531. DO SOMETHING

You and I can never be satisfied with sitting down before a great human problem and saying nothing can be done. We must do something. That is the reason we are on Earth.

Letter to William D. Hooper, October 11, 1909; *Correspondence*, I, 153.

532. ECONOMIC CONFINEMENT

The one hope of American Negroes is Socialism. Otherwise, under the corporate rule of monopolized wealth, they will be confined to the lowest wage group as long as Wealth rules.

"American Negroes and Socialism," undated; microfilm reel no. 81, frame no. 1470; W.E.B. Du Bois Papers, University of Massachusetts, Amherst.

533. EQUALITY

Equality of income is rational and based on essential equality of human needs. There is no equality of human accomplishment and no demand for it and no need for it.

To E. J. Van Lennep, May 26, 1941; microfilm reel no. 53, frame no. 525; W.E.B. Du Bois Papers, University of Massachusetts, Amherst.

534. EXTERMINATION OR EQUALITY

This the American black man knows; his fight here is a fight to the finish. Either he dies or wins. If he wins it will be by no subterfuge or evasion of amalgamation. He will enter modern civilization here in America as a black man on terms of perfect and unlimited equality with any white man, or he will not enter at all. Either extermination root and branch, or absolute equality. There can be no compromise. This is the last great battle of the West.

Black Reconstruction (1935) 703.

535.   FELLOW TRAVELER

I am a fellow-traveler with communists in so far as they believe the great ideals of socialism as laid down by the world's great thinkers since the 17th century. I believe in the abolition of poverty. I believe in curbing the social and political power of wealth, I believe in planned industry and more just distribution of wealth.

Testimony before the House Committee on Foreign Relations, August 8, 1949; microfilm reel no. 63, frame no. 917; W.E.B. Du Bois Papers, University of Massachusetts, Amherst.

536.   FELLOW-TRAVELING

It is more than stupid to refuse cooperation because other men's aims are not all yours. The man who works for peace is my brother; the woman who works for Africa and against colonialism is your sister. . . . So long as he walks toward the truth as I see it, I will be fellow traveler with communist or capitalist, with white man or black and I will proclaim as a fool the man who lays down a goal and then refuses himself to follow it because somebody he does not like walks to the same great end.

"Address by Dr. W.E.B. Du Bois," June 19, 1949; microfilm reel no. 80, frame no. 1235; W.E.B. Du Bois Papers, University of Massachusetts, Amherst.

537.   GENERAL STRIKE

Whenever Northern armies appeared, Negro laborers came. . . . It was a general strike [of slaves] that involved directly in the end perhaps a half million people. They wanted to stop the economy of the plantation system, and to do that they left the plantations.

Black Reconstruction (1935) 66, 67.

538.   GOALS

[In beginning *Phylon* magazine early in 1940] we shall strive to abolish the present economic illiteracy and paralysis; and openly hold up to frank criticism that widespread assumption that the industrial organization of the nineteenth century was something permanent and sacred and furnished a final word which estops the twentieth century from facing the problem of abolishing poverty as a first step toward real freedom, democracy and art among men, through the use of industrial technique and planned economy.

Phylon 1 (First Quarter 1940); *Selections from* Phylon (1980) 6.

539. HUMAN PROBLEMS

The trouble with us is not that the problems fronting us are insoluble but that we are unwilling to pay the cost.

"William Lloyd Garrison," October 16, 1909; microfilm reel no. 80, frame no. 198; W.E.B. Du Bois Papers, University of Massachusetts, Amherst.

540. HUMAN RELATIONS

I do not believe that the only relations between men or groups of men are the relation of master and serf, ruler and ruled.

Letter to Bernice E. Brand, November 16, 1927; *Correspondence*, I, 365.

541. MAGNIFYING PROGRESS

I am willing, nay eager, to accept every small concession, every inch of advance and be thankful for it, but I will not pay for it with the lying assertion that it's all I want.

"The Forward Movement," October 1910; microfilm reel no. 80, frame no. 272; W.E.B. Du Bois Papers, University of Massachusetts, Amherst.

542. KARL MARX

I have been re-reading Marx recently as everyone must these days. . . . Send me a list of four or five best books which the perfect Marxist must know.

To Abram L. Harris, January 6, 1933; microfilm reel no. 40, frame no. 66; W.E.B. Du Bois Papers, University of Massachusetts, Amherst.

543. MIGRATION NORTHWARDS

The Negro is not a fool and when he is treated like a dog he knows it and he acts accordingly. He gets out of the way or, if cornered, he fights. To put down the migration of the Negro to the credit of the boll weevil is silly. The reason the Negro is leaving the South is because the South does not treat him like a man.

To J. H. Wagner, September 15, 1924; microfilm reel no. 14, frame no. 297; W.E.B. Du Bois Papers, University of Massachusetts, Amherst.

544. MONTGOMERY—WHAT NEXT?

In Montgomery . . . [the black] church found intelligent leaders and staged an unusually successful strike [against segregated buses]. The question is where does it go from here? This is not clear. It is now taking uncertain refuge in prayer meetings and following Gandhi's techniques. It should emphasize the right to register and vote and get better jobs at higher wages for ordinary Negro workers who began this fight and bore the brunt of its burden. This requires an understanding of socialism and its need among Negro workers. Cooperative farming and consumers cooperation are basic necessities for black workers in the South and they cannot exist under uncurbed private capitalism.

"The New Negro Liberation Movements," ca. 1956; microfilm reel no. 81, frame no. 1037; W.E.B. Du Bois Papers, University of Massachusetts, Amherst.

545. MOUND BAYOU

The black folk under Isaiah Montgomery began a singular experiment in race segregation as an answer to the Negro problem. They founded the Negro city of Mound Bayou [Miss.], and dreamed of furthering such experiments. The enterprise was widely hailed and publicized by the white world, but Negroes were not so unanimous. They whispered: what can a black town do in a white state where the blacks have no vote?

Worlds of Color (1961) 15.

546. MULTICULTURAL STATE

The object toward which the far-sighted American Negro must aim is not a racial Negro state inhabited by Negroes and run by Negroes for Negroes but a cultural movement or movements localized or more or less united based on Negro experience and history carried on by such Negroes as so desire not by those who do not but welcoming to cooperation any folk of any race who want to join. This cultural program would include making a living, taking part in a democratic state, spreading knowledge and creating art. It would not countenance electing Negroes to office because they are Negroes any more than electing white men because they are white. It would *not* permit segregation by race in any place or activity, knowing such procedure is leading back to a world of antagonistic hating nations instead of *forward* to *one world* of men agreeing on all the essentials of life.

Untitled, undated; microfilm reel no. 81, frame no. 1509; W.E.B. Du Bois Papers, University of Massachusetts, Amherst.

547. NAACP

It is a mistake for anyone to assume that this organization [NAACP] awaits popular applause before action. We are not spineless appeasers. When we see wrong or persistence in wrong we protest. We have done this for forty years and we shall continue this program.

The Editor, *Morgantown Post*, October 27, 1947; microfilm reel no. 60, frame no. 324; W.E.B. Du Bois Papers, University of Massachusetts, Amherst.

548. NEGRO GROUP SOCIALISM

In my book "Dusk of Dawn" [1940] I was trying to answer the question as to how the American Negro would survive if color caste continued for two or three generations as I thought it would. I advocated a Negro group socialism to furnish work, encourage surroundings, and advance literature and art among Negroes. I did not advocate increase of segregation, but use of such segregation as was inevitable to preserve American Negroes for future integration into American and world culture. . . . This philosophy of group socialism was not out of keeping with my earlier or later ideas, and was guided by Marxian philosophy.

To Clemmon King, January 29, 1958; microfilm reel no. 73, frame no. 225; W.E.B. Du Bois Papers, University of Massachusetts, Amherst.

549. NEW DEAL

The basic problem of the New Deal was whether to make its objective an effort to "restore" former "prosperity" or some more fundamental change in the essential economic structure of the nation to bring greater stability and economic justice. If it was the first, there was not much hope for the Negro. He simply could look forward to being "restored" to situations in which his prospects for economic development were growing less and less.

Mansart Builds a School (1959) 344.

550. OUTSIDER ON THE INSIDE

I can . . . at once look on the United States as an outsider and continuous visitor, unintegrated into its culture and yet knowing and sharing it. I can see as few others can, the way in which the presence of a depressed class of human beings has distorted and still distorts our social development. My emotional sympathy with this group will doubtless exaggerate its influence, and for this margin of error the reader must make allowance.

Russia and America: An Interpretation (1950, unpublished); microfilm reel no. 85, frame no. 478; W.E.B. Du Bois Papers, University of Massachusetts, Amherst.

551. PASSIVE RESISTANCE

Passive resistance is not the end of action, but the beginning. After refusing to fight, there is the question how to live.

"The Negro and Socialism," *in* Helen Alfred (ed.), *Toward a Socialist America* (New York: Peace Publications, 1958) 179–91; *Writings by W.E.B. Du Bois in Non-Periodical Literature Edited by Others* (1982) 292.

552. PRINCIPLE

The thing that we have got to face is that when for the sake of principle we take a radical position, we have got to pay for it. There is no use of either you or I expecting any position in an interracial movement until . . . such a movement moves much further toward the Left than it has yet.

To William N. Jones, December 21, 1933; microfilm reel no. 40, frame no. 270; W.E.B. Du Bois Papers, University of Massachusetts, Amherst.

553. PROFESSIONAL LIBERALS

John Temple Graves II . . . Virginius Dabney . . . [and] Ralph McGill . . . are professional liberals . . . who are not willing to stand up for principles. Until the South gets and keeps at home a group willing to suffer for the right, it will never become a great section.

To Charles T. Dixon, June 21, 1945; microfilm reel no. 57, frame no. 48; W.E.B. Du Bois Papers, University of Massachusetts, Amherst.

554. RADICALISM

The pressure from those who dislike to have anything radical said is strengthening every day, and they call anything radical which asserts the full manhood rights of Negroes as American citizens, or which demands that they be judged by the same criterion as other men.

To Frances Haggan, April 2, 1910; microfilm reel no. 2, frame no. 143; W.E.B. Du Bois Papers, University of Massachusetts, Amherst.

As long as our voices are low and do not carry far, we may advocate tremendous changes and even revolution; but when it comes to reaching the real audience of the thinking world, we find that the newspapers are acting, like the *New York Times*, in the case of Russia and the British [general] strike, deliberately spreading misinformation concerning the facts and the causes. . . . The man who worships present conditions—holds to them, defends them with life and property is rewarded and be-medaled, knighted and made rich and powerful. The radical who looks backward may gain small following but he is not feared: we know or think we know the past. We entrust its advocate and defender with toleration and vast pity.

"The Radical" (1926?), Series 3/C, Folder no. 5529, pp. 2, 4; *Unpublished Articles*; W.E.B. Du Bois Papers, University of Massachusetts, Amherst.

555. THE REAL SOULS

[John Brown was] the man who of all Americans has perhaps come nearest to touching the real souls of black folk.

John Brown (1909, 1962) 8.

556. REJECTING INFERIORITY

Does any race accept the doctrine of their inferiority to another race?
Never. They accept only the outward humiliations until they are able to rebel against them.

"Race Relations," undated; microfilm reel no. 85; W.E.B. Du Bois Papers, University of Massachusetts, Amherst.

557. REVOLUTION

American Negroes do not propose to be the shock troops of the Communist Revolution, driven out in front to death, cruelty and humiliation in order to win victories for white workers. They are picking no chestnuts from the fire, neither for capital nor white labor. Negroes know perfectly well that whenever they try to lead revolution in America, the nation will unite as one fist to crush them alone. There is no conceivable idea that seems to the present overwhelming majority of Americans higher than keeping Negroes "in their place." Negroes perceive clearly that the real interests of the white worker are identical with the interest of the black worker, but until the white worker recognizes this, the black worker is compelled in sheer self-defense to refuse to be made the sacrificial goat.

"The Negro and Communism," *Crisis* 38 (September 1931), 313–15, 318, 320; *Selections from* The Crisis, vol. 2 (1983) 639.

There is not at present the slightest indication that a Marxian revolution based on a united class-conscious proletariat is anywhere on the American far horizon. Rather race antagonism and labor group rivalry is still undisturbed by world catastrophe. In the hearts of black laborers alone, therefore, lie these ideals of democracy in politics and industry which may in time make the workers of the world effective dictators of civilization.

"Marxism and the Negro Problem," *Crisis* 40 (May 1933) 103–04, 118; *Selections from* The Crisis, vol. 2 (1983) 699.

In any real social revolution, every step that saves violence is to the glory of the great end. We should not forget that revolution is not the objective of socialism or communism rightly conceived; the real objective is social justice, and if haply the world can find that justice without blood, the world is the infinite gainer. . . . The first duty of workers is not to fight but to convince themselves that union of workers, class solidarity, is better than force and a substitute for it. The real problem, then, is this concert of the workers. The real emphasis today should not be on revolution but on class consciousness, and labor's uplift. This is the job of socialism, and the first proof of conversion is the abolition of color and race prejudice among the laboring class.

"The Negro and Social Reconstruction" (1936); *Against Racism* (1985) 142–43.

What ensued in the South after emancipation was not at all the classical bourgeois revolution but something far more complicated and reactionary. . . . Jim Crow legislation and disfranchisement laws between 1881 and 1910 swept through with little opposition. . . . The caste system in the South increased the whole ideology of caste throughout the United States until laboring men felt themselves degraded to work with black men. Moreover, the attempt of Negroes to enter the employing class as merchants and landholders was made impossible by severe competition and monopoly.

"Social Planning for the Negro, Past and Present," *Journal of Negro Education* 5 (January 1936) 110–25; *Writings by W.E.B. Du Bois in Periodicals Edited by Others*, vol. 3 (1982) 30, 33.

558. THE ROSENBERGS

In the case of Julius and Ethel Rosenberg we reach the zenith of deliberate injustice. We are set to kill a mother and father and orphan their little children because we think that they believe in social remedies for evident ills which many others do not believe. . . . We promise them pardon if they will betray persons they never knew and give information they never had. . . . It is the nation itself which today should be asking pardon of the Rosenbergs rather than they and their friends should be begging for that justice which is the right of every citizen.

"Rosenberg Rally," January 8, 1953; microfilm reel no. 81, frame no. 540; W.E.B. Du Bois Papers, University of Massachusetts, Amherst.

559. RUSSIAN REVOLUTION

It is October, 1936, I am in Russia. I am here where the world's greatest experiment in organized life is making, whether it fails or not. Nothing since the discovery of America and the French Revolution is of equal importance. And yet, this experiment is being made in the midst of unexampled hostility; amid deep-seated bitterness and recrimination, such as men reserve usually for crime, degeneracy, blasphemy.

Russia and America: An Interpretation (1950, unpublished); microfilm reel no. 85, frame no. 451; W.E.B. Du Bois Papers, University of Massachusetts, Amherst.

560. SELF-DEFENSE

Brothers we are on the Great Deep. We have cast off on the vast voyage which will lead to Freedom or Death. For three centuries we have suffered and cowered. No race ever gave Passive Resistance and Submission to Evil longer, more piteous trial. Today we raise the terrible weapon of Self-Defense. When the murderer comes, he shall not longer strike us in the back. When the armed lynchers gather, we too must gather armed. When the mob moves, we propose to meet it with bricks and clubs and guns. . . . Back of the impregnable fortress of the Divine Right of Self-Defense, which is sanctioned by every law of God and man, in every land, civilized and uncivilized, we must take our unfaltering stand.

"Let Us Reason Together," *Crisis* 18 (September 1919) 231; *Selections from* The Crisis, vol. 1 (1983) 240.

561. SELF-DEPENDENCE

Philanthropy of itself . . . can never free a people. . . . The chief force behind the progress of the Negro since 1917 came from the Negro himself; his purposive and organized effort, from 1900 until today, and particularly since 1917, has formed the mainspring of Negro progress.

"The Negro Since 1900: A Progress Report," *New York Times Magazine*, November 21, 1948; *Writings by W.E.B. Du Bois in Periodicals Edited by Others*, vol. 4 (1982) 92–93.

562. SELF-DIRECTION

Against prejudice, injustice and wrong the Negro ought to protest energetically and continuously, but he must never forget that he protests because these things hinder his own efforts, and those efforts are the key to his future.

The Philadelphia Negro (1899) 390.

563. SELF-REPRESENTATION

[Between 1910 and 1930] much of the statement, assertion and habit of thought characteristic of the latter part of the nineteenth century regarding the Negro had passed away. . . . In a sense it was an epoch-making achievement. No longer was it possible or thinkable anywhere in the United States to study and discuss the Negro without letting him speak for himself and without having that speaking done by a well-equipped person, if such person was wanted.

Dusk of Dawn (1940) 283.

564. SELF-RESPECT

Every man owes a certain respect to his own soul. If he is kicked once that is not necessarily his fault. But to offer himself for repeated kicking is spiritual suicide.

To James Weldon Johnson, April 15, 1924; microfilm reel no. 13, frame no. 1057; W.E.B. Du Bois Papers, University of Massachusetts, Amherst.

565. SHACKLED HANDS

The [NAACP's magazine] *Crisis* continually has to combat the smug indifference of those people who are so afraid that mention of the evil of the world is going to induce bitterness and discontent. We are not afraid of evil and we have neither patience nor respect for those people who would let the evil of the world go swaggering on because they fear lest some poor victim may raise his shackled hands to Heaven and shake his righteous anger the foundations of hell.

Letter to Annie H. Howe, August 1, 1923, *Correspondence*, I, 275.

566. SILENCING THINKERS

Of all sins against the Holy Ghost, the stopping of thought, the silencing of
the Thinker is the worst. The Thinker may be wrong and often is; Thought may
mislead and has often done so. But with all, in the end, Thought rights itself,
and for human kind there is no other way but logical thinking to approach the
stars; than this there is no surer salvation.

"Statement for V. J. Jerome," March 9, 1953; microfilm reel no. 59, frame no. 633;
    W.E.B. Du Bois Papers, University of Massachusetts, Amherst.

567. SOCIALIST PARTY

I understand [socialism to be] an attempt to rearrange work and industry,
wages and income on a basis of reason, need and desert, rather than leaving it
to chance and the rule of the strong, as in the case today over so large a part of
the world. . . . [The Socialist Party platform] dares to mention Negro disfranchisement as a prime cause of reaction, fraud and privilege, and it is right.

To Harry W. Laidler, October 1928; microfilm reel no. 26; W.E.B. Du Bois Papers,
    University of Massachusetts, Amherst.

568. STRATEGIES AND TACTICS

Historically the strategies and techniques emphasized by the Negro minority
groups in the United States have been as follows: (1) revolt; (2) running away
to the free North and Canada; (3) colonization in Africa; (4) education for self
support; (5) emancipation; (6) enfranchisement; (7) protective laws; (8) legal
defense; (9) agitation; (10) pressure group techniques; (11) defensive and offen-
sive segregation; (12) international Negro organization; (13) international cooperation with other colored races; (14) cooperation with the white labor
movement.

To Cy W. Record, January 4, 1943; microfilm reel no. 55, frame no. 770; W.E.B. Du
    Bois Papers, University of Massachusetts, Amherst.

569. SURVEILLANCE

One of the first questions which the secret federal police [i.e., the FBI] always
ask about a suspect is "Does he associate with Negroes?"

"Colonialism and the Russian Revolution," *New World Review* (November 1956)
    18–21; *Writings by W.E.B. Du Bois in Periodicals Edited by Others*, vol. 4
    (1982) 277.

570. SYMPATHIZERS

You unfortunate folks who are not compelled to stand our campaign of lies,
but who are suffering from sheer interest in the cause will deserve undoubtedly
a very large and well-fitting crown in the next world.

To Mary W. Ovington, May 14, 1909; microfilm reel no. 2, frame no. 1114; W.E.B. Du Bois Papers, University of Massachusetts, Amherst.

571. THE TALENTED TENTH

The Negro race, like all races, is going to be saved by its exceptional men. The problem of education, then, among Negroes must first of all deal with the Talented Tenth; it is the problem of developing the Best of this race that they may guide the Mass away from the contamination and death of the Worst, in their own and other races.

"The Talented Tenth," in *The Negro Problem.* . . . (1903); *Writings by W.E.B. Du Bois in Non-Periodical Literature Edited by Others* (1982) 17.

The net result of the Fisk interlude was to broaden the scope of my program of life, not essentially to change it; to center it in a group of educated Negroes, who from their knowledge and experience would lead the mass. I never for a moment dreamed that such leadership could ever be for the sake of the educated group itself, but always for the mass.

Autobiography (1968) 123.

I believed in the higher education of a Talented Tenth who through their knowledge of modern culture could guide the American Negro into a higher civilization. I knew that without this the Negro would have to accept white leadership and that such leadership could not always be trusted to guide this group into self-realization and to its highest cultural possibilities.

Autobiography (1968) 236.

The Talented Tenth [must not] become a guild of capitalistic exploiters within the race.

Pittsburgh Courier, December 11, 1937; *Newspaper Columns by W.E.B. Du Bois* (1986) 256.

My own panacea of earlier days was flight of class from mass, through the development of a Talented Tenth; but the power of this aristocracy of talent was to lie in its knowledge and character, and not in its economic power. The problem which I did not then attack was that of leadership and authority within the group, which by implication left controls to wealth—a contingency of which I never dreamed.

"The Position of the Negro in the American Social Order: Where Do We Go from Here?" *Journal of Negro Education* 8 (July 1939) 551–70; *Writings by W.E.B. Du Bois in Periodicals Edited by Others*, vol. 3 (1982) 85.

If I were writing today about "Talented Tenth" I would still believe in the main thesis but I should make rather different emphasis. When I wrote in 1903 I assumed that educated persons especially among American Negroes would do two things: first, devote their main energy and talent to the uplift of the mass of the people; and secondly, recognize that their talent was not exceptional but should be continually enforced and increased by the talent among the masses which is so often forgotten and frustrated.

Of course those two assumptions cannot be made at any time or among any people with complete assurance. Talented Negroes like other human beings are going to produce a large number of selfish and self-seeking persons, who will not work for the best interests of the masses of the people. Secondly, there is always the temptation to assume that the few people who have gotten education and opportunity are the only ones who are capable or worthy of reaching the heights.

Letter to Cecil Peterson, January 6, 1947; *Correspondence*, III, 131–132.

Willingness to work and make personal sacrifice for solving these problems was of course, the first prerequisite and *sine qua non*. I did not stress this, I assumed it. I assumed that with knowledge, sacrifice would automatically follow. In my youth and idealism, I did not realize that selfishness is even more natural than sacrifice.

"The Talented Tenth: Memorial Address," *Boule Journal* 15 (October 1948) 3–13; *Writings by W.E.B. Du Bois in Periodicals Edited by Others*, vol. 4 (1982) 79.

My faith hitherto had been in what I once denominated the "Talented Tenth." I now realize that the ability within a people does not automatically work for its highest salvation. On the contrary, in an era like this, and in the United States, many of the educated and gifted young black folk will be as selfish and immoral as the whites who surround them and to whom Negroes have been taught to look as ideals.

In Battle for Peace (1952) 76–77.

572.   VIOLENCE

We black men say . . . we do not believe in violence. Our object is justice, not violence, and we will fight only when there is no better way.

"Social Planning for the Negro, Past and Present," *Journal of Negro Education* 5 (January 1936) 110–25; *Writings by W.E.B. Du Bois in Periodicals Edited by Others*, vol. 3 (1982) 39.

13

Christianity

573. AFRICA

Let the white world keep its missionaries at home to teach the Golden Rule to its corporate thieves. Damn the God of Slavery, Exploitation and War. Peace on Earth; no more war. The earth of Africa is for its people. Its Wealth is for the poor and not for the rich. All Hail Africa. (1955)

The World and Africa (1947, 1965) 291.

574. APOPLEXY

I have had a splendid lecture trip. . . . a lot of smug preachers at Indianapolis whom I addressed on the thesis: "Of all present forces of social uplift I have least faith in white Christian ministers." Some of them had apoplexy.

Letter to Joel E. Spingarn, February 14, 1925; *Correspondence*, I, 304.

575. BEING DEAD

Believe me, dear friend, you will die. We all of us shall die and we are going to stay dead, and our duty is to leave a decent and reasonable and good world behind us, instead of trying simply to grasp wings for ourselves.

To Mollie Keelan, September 17, 1931; microfilm reel no. 35, frame no. 6; W.E.B. Du Bois Papers, University of Massachusetts, Amherst.

576. BELIEF

What difference does it make whether the whale swallowed Jonah or Jonah swallowed the whale, so long as Justice, Mercy and Peace prevail?

"Darrow," *Crisis* 35 (June 1928) 203; *Selections from* The Crisis, vol. 2 (1983) 516.

577. BELIEF IN GOD

If by being "a believer in God," you mean a belief in a person of vast power who consciously rules the universe for the good of mankind, I answer No; I cannot disprove this assumption, but I certainly see no proof to sustain such a belief, neither in History nor in my personal experience.

If on the other hand you mean by "God" a vague Force which in some incomprehensible way, dominates all life and change, then I answer, Yes, I recognize such Force, and if you wish to call it God, I do not object.

To E. Pina Moreno, November 15, 1948; microfilm reel no. 62, frame no. 381; W.E.B.
    Du Bois Papers, University of Massachusetts, Amherst.

578. BIBLE

I do not believe that the biblical record is authentic history. I think it is very interesting myth and legend.

To A.P.B. Holly, April 7, 1925; microfilm reel no. 15, frame no. 649; W.E.B. Du Bois
    Papers, University of Massachusetts, Amherst.

579. BLACK CHURCH

The Negro churches were the birthplace of Negro schools and of all agencies which seek to promote the intelligence of the masses; and even today no agency serves to disseminate news or information so quickly and effectively among Negroes as the church.

The Philadelphia Negro (1899) 207.

The Negro church [was] . . . the first distinctly Negro American social institution.

The Gift of Black Folk (1924) 326.

There is no attempt to modernize the old religious doctrine: there is no attempt to put social organization upon a logical ethical basis. This does not mean the persistence of religion. It means the death of it, and at the same time a persistence and growth of the church. But this growth of the church is threatened by lack of educated leadership. The only revolt against religion in the Negro race is shown by the small numbers of Negroes who are willing to become ministers.

"What the New Negro Is Thinking," December 27, 1931; microfilm reel no. 80, frame
    no. 467; W.E.B. Du Bois Papers, University of Massachusetts, Amherst.

It represented the people, served and catered to them, and what was more, it escaped more than any other social institution the influence and domination of the whites. Naturally, it did not entirely escape. It had to have the cooperation of the white ruling classes. It found some support from their gifts, and the recognition that the black pastor got from the white world was almost indispensable for real success. At the same time, no Negro institution so escaped the daily dictation of the whites, and the envy and interference of the poor whites as the Negro church.

Mansart Builds a School (1959) 241.

580. BLACK MISSIONARIES

Missionary societies of the United States started out, for the most part, with the obvious policy of sending Negroes to convert Africa. Then they found out that this involved social equality between white and black missionaries; the paying of Negro missionaries on the same scale as white missionaries, and their promotion and treatment as civilized beings. With few exceptions, American white Christianity could not stand this, and they consequently changed their policy.

"Missionaries," *Crisis* 36 (May 1929) 168; *Selections from* The Crisis, vol. 2 (1983) 550.

581. BLOCKED

All that is necessary for any Christian American gentleman of high position and wide power to say in denying place and promotion to an eligible candidate is: "He is of Negro descent." The answer and excuse is final and all but universally accepted.

"On Being Ashamed of Oneself. An Essay on Race Pride." *Crisis* 40 (September 1933) 199; *Selections from* The Crisis, vol. 2 (1983) 716.

582. CASH AND CONSCIENCE

When the good New England clergyman thought it a shame that slaves should herd like animals, without a legal marriage bond, he devised a quaint ceremony for them in which Sally promised Bob to cleave to him. For life? Oh no. As long as "God in his providence" kept them on the same plantation. This was in New England where there was a good deal more conscience than in Georgia.

"The Development of a People," *International Journal of Ethics* 14 (April 1904) 292–311; *Writings by W.E.B. Du Bois in Periodicals Edited by Others*, vol. 1 (1982) 211.

583. CATHOLIC CHURCH

Because Catholicism has so much that is splendid in its past and fine in its present, it is the greater shame that "nigger" haters clothed in its episcopal robes should do to black Americans in exclusion, segregation and exclusion from opportunity all that the Ku Klux Klan ever asked.

Letter to Joseph B. Glenn, March 24, 1925; *Correspondence*, I, 311.

The Catholic Church in America stands for color separation and discrimination to a degree equalled by no other church in America, and that is saying a very

great deal. . . . The white parochial schools even in the North, exclude colored
children, the Catholic high schools will not admit them, the Catholic University
at Washington invites them elsewhere and scarcely a Catholic seminary in the
country will train a Negro priest. This is not a case of blaming the Catholic
Church for not doing all it might—it is blaming it for being absolutely and
fundamentally wrong today and in the United States on the basic demands of
human brotherhood across the color line.

Letter to Joseph B. Glenn, March 24, 1925; *Correspondence*, I, 311.

   In over 400 years the Catholic Church has ordained less than a half dozen
black Catholic priests either because they have sent us poor teachers or because
American Catholics do not want to work beside black priests and sisters or
because they think Negroes have neither brains nor morals enough to occupy
positions open freely to Poles, Irishmen and Italians.

Letter to Joseph B. Glenn, March 18, 1925; *Correspondence*, I, 309.

   Many great voices in the Catholic Church dating from the fifteenth century
have been raised against Negro slavery, but as a church it maintained a position
as neutral and submissive as could be imagined.

Annals of the American Academy of Political and Social Science, September 1944; *Book
   Reviews by W.E.B. Du Bois* (1977) 226.

   I regret that the human friendship and intellectual fellowship offered by the
Catholic Church now and in the past is not as perfect as I wish it could be.
There are separate and white congregations in the South. The Catholics refuse
to receive colored students in a large number of their schools and their training
of Negro Catholic priests in America has been ridiculously below the demand.

Letter to John R. Timpany, S.S.J., January 17, 1945; *Correspondence*, III, 27.

584.   CATHOLIC COLLEGES

   Almost all Catholic institutions refuse to accept Negro students. There is not,
I am told, a single colored candidate for the priesthood in a regular Catholic
theological seminary and of the Catholic colleges only Fordham and Detroit
admit Negroes.

"Negroes in College," *Nation* 122 (March 3, 1926) 228–30; *Writings by W.E.B. Du
   Bois in Periodicals Edited by Others*, vol. 2 (1982) 281.

585.   CHRISTIAN CHURCH

   I do not know of but one white church in the United States where Negro
members are actually welcomed, and that is John Haynes Holmes' Community
Church in New York City.

To A. J. Helm, December 23, 1929; microfilm reel no. 27, frame no. 1331; W.E.B. Du
   Bois Papers, University of Massachusetts, Amherst.

The record of the church, so far as the Negro is concerned, has been almost complete acquiescence in caste, until today there is in the United States no organization that is so completely split along the color line as the Christian church.

"Will the Church Remove the Color Line?" *Christian Century* 48 (December 9, 1931) 1554–56; *Writings by W.E.B. Du Bois in Periodicals Edited by Others*, vol. 2 (1982) 316.

The Christian Church was . . . the bulwark and backbone of human slavery in the United States.

To Dan F. Bradley, December 14, 1931; microfilm reel no. 34, frame no. 632; W.E.B. Du Bois Papers, University of Massachusetts, Amherst.

I have been recently greatly astonished and pained to find that the Federal Council of Churches of Christ in America is backing the attack on the sovereignty of Liberia, which is being made by the Firestone Rubber Company, handmaiden and forerunner of capitalistic exploitation and imperial domination of the Black race.

To Francis F. McConnell, August 4, 1933; microfilm reel no. 39, frame no. 1108; W.E.B. Du Bois Papers, University of Massachusetts, Amherst.

I am not a member of a Christian church; although I have been at times in the past; I do not subscribe to ordinary Christian doctrine.

To Virginia Shattuck, April 15, 1937; microfilm reel no. 48, frame no. 110; W.E.B. Du Bois Papers, University of Massachusetts, Amherst.

586. CHRISTIANS

I am continually astonished at the way in which men who call themselves Christians perjure themselves when it comes to great moral problems [of the day].

To Henry S. Huntington, October 8, 1925; microfilm reel no. 15, frame no. 57; W.E.B. Du Bois Papers, University of Massachusetts, Amherst.

587. THE CHURCH

From my 30th year on I have increasingly regarded the church as an institution which defended such evils as slavery, color caste, exploitation of labor and war.
Autobiography (1968) 285.

The Church as organized in modern civilized countries has become the special representative of the employing and exploiting classes. It has become mainly a center of wealth and social exclusiveness, and by this very fact, wherever you find a city of large and prosperous churches . . . you find cities where the so-called best people . . . are critical of democracy, suspicious of the labor movement, bitter against Soviet Russia, and indifferent to the Negro problem, because their economic interests have put them in opposition to forward movements and the teachers and preachers whom they hire have fed them on that kind of prejudice, or maintained significant silence.

Color and Democracy (1945) 136.

588. CHURCHES AND BLACKS

The chief effect of the attitude of white Christians toward Negroes in the United States is to establish in their minds a double standard of truth. They have come to think that one must expect in this world professions and expressions of ideals which have nothing to do with actual conduct and consequently all truth has two sides: one, an ideal expression; the other, a practical series of acts. Although the first may be of the highest and finest promise, the latter may be the most selfish and self-seeking.

Letter to William Crowe, Jr., August 9, 1939; *Correspondence*, II, 195.

589. CHURCH MEMBERSHIP

The census of 1890 showed merely twenty-four thousand Negro churches in the country, with a total enrolled membership of over two and a half million, or ten actual church members to every twenty-eight persons, and in some Southern States one in every two persons. . . . There is an organized Negro church for every sixty black families in the nation, and in some States for every forty families.

The Souls of Black Folk (1903) 194–195.

590. CREDO

I believe in Love, the Father Almighty, Maker of heaven and earth; and in Work, his only Son our Lord; who was conceived by Human Vision, born of the Virgin Need, suffered under Poverty; was crucified, died and buried. He descended into Crime; the Third Day he rose again from the dead. He ascended into heaven; and sitteth on the right hand of Love the Creator; from thence he shall come to judge the Rich and the Poor.

I believe in Human Vision, a wholly catholic faith, the Communion of Labor, the Conquest of Disease, the Resurrection of the Body and the Life Everlasting. Amen.

"Credo," February 28, 1939; microfilm reel no. 77, frame no. 726; W.E.B. Du Bois Papers, University of Massachusetts, Amherst.

591. DONE IS DONE

It is quite possible that individual life does persist [after death]. If it does, I am not enthusiastic about it. I shall live it, of course, if I must, but not by choice. For why having done one life, some folk should be so eager for another and work themselves into such a lather of excitement about it, is a little beyond me. I much prefer to do this one life reasonably well and stop.

"De Senectute," February 23, 1948; microfilm reel no. 80, frame no. 1087; W.E.B. Du Bois Papers, University of Massachusetts, Amherst.

592. EMANCIPATION PROCLAMATION

The Proclamation made four and a half million willing almost in mass to socialize their last drop of blood for their new-found country. . . . It was the Coming of the Lord.

Black Reconstruction (1935) 87.

593. EPISCOPAL CHURCH

Its record on the Negro problem has been simply shameful . . . the southern branch of the Church is a moral dead weight and the northern branch of the Church never has had the moral courage to stand against it and I doubt if it has now. . . . The Church always had been behind . . . other churches in recognizing human manhood and Christian equality.

Letter to Samuel H. Bishop, May 1, 1907; *Correspondence*, I, 131.

Considering the great wealth and prestige of the Episcopal Church their work for Negro education has been pitifully small. Even their work in proselytizing among Negroes has not been notable.

Letter to A. C. Tebeau, February 20, 1940; *Correspondence*, II, 212.

594. FAITH IN MEN

I have little faith that Christianity can settle the race problem, but I have abiding faith in men.

"Foreword" to Reverdy C. Ransom, *The Negro, the Hope or the Despair of Christianity* (Boston: Ruth Hill, 1935); *Writings in Non-Periodical Literature Edited by Others* (1982) 175.

595. GOD WHITE?

Sit not longer blind, Lord God, deaf to our prayer and dumb to our dumb suffering. Surely, Thou, too, art not white, O Lord, a pale bloodless, heartless thing!

Darkwater (1920) 27.

596. THE HEREAFTER

I have every respect for people who believe in the future life, but I cannot . . . accept their belief or their wish as knowledge. Equally, I am not impressed by those who deny the possibility of future life. I have no knowledge of the possibilities of this universe and I know of no one who has.

To Sydney Strong, February 17, 1928; microfilm reel no. 26, frame no. 569 (?); W.E.B. Du Bois Papers, University of Massachusetts, Amherst.

597. JESUS IN GEORGIA

Who can doubt that if Christ came to Georgia today one of His first deeds would be to sit down and take supper with black men and who can doubt the outcome if He did?

"Religion in the South," orig. 1907, in Booker T. Washington and Du Bois, *The Negro in the South* (New York: Citadel Press, 1970) 125–91; *Writings by W.E.B. Du Bois in Non-Periodicals Edited by Others*, vol. 2 (1982) 91–92.

598. JUBILEE SINGERS

Already Fisk had the tradition of her Jubilee Singers, who once hid in a Brooklyn organ loft, lest pious Congregationalists see their black faces before they heard their heavenly voices.

Autobiography (1968) 122.

599. MILITANT RELIGION

Organized religion in this nation, Catholic, Protestant and Jewish, is with a few exceptions determined on war with Communism especially in the Soviet Union and China. Thus the united voice of religion is against Peace; and liberal priests, ministers and rabbis are in danger of ouster.

"America and Peace" (1953); Series 3/C, Folder no. 5572, p. 8, *Unpublished Articles*; W.E.B. Du Bois Papers, University of Massachusetts, Amherst.

600. MINISTERS

Twenty years ago . . . the pulpits of Nashville, Tenn., were nearly all occupied by a class of men who were a disgrace to decent society. Today most of those pulpits are in control of honest, upright men. . . . A majority of the Negro ministers in the small towns and country districts of Georgia are not fit to be spiritual leaders of any people.

"The Minister," *Hampton Negro Conference Annual Report* 2 (September 1906) 91–92; *Writings by W.E.B. Du Bois in Periodicals Edited by Others*, vol. 1 (1982) 328.

601. MY FUNERAL

But don't stress religion or immortality or Jesus Christ or the Good God. The good life at present and progress in the future are what I want stressed.

To Shirley Graham Du Bois, June 26, 1957; microfilm reel no. 79, frame no. 606; W.E.B. Du Bois Papers, University of Massachusetts, Amherst.

602. OUTSIDE THE CIRCLE

It still remains possible in the United States for a white American to be a gentleman and a scholar, a Christian and a man of integrity, and yet flatly and openly refuse to treat as a fellow human being any person who has Negro ancestry.

Dusk of Dawn (1940) 186.

603. PAST AND FUTURE

American Negroes were not particularly impressed with Dr. Kagawa. He straddled the race question beautifully and tried to tell us what Christianity was going to do. We know what Christianity has already done.

To Y. Hikida, April 21, 1936; microfilm reel no. 45, frame no. 1046; W.E.B. Du Bois Papers, University of Massachusetts, Amherst.

604. PRACTICAL CHRISTIANITY

I wish you . . . [would talk about] more of your work among the mass of people, instead of your relations to the Lord and Jesus Christ. This devotion I understand, but I am always afraid that it is too often used as a quotation without deep meaning. We are here to work hard for a better world and not merely "to submit ourselves to Jesus Christ."

To Ernest Hutcheson, Jr., November 27, 1957; microfilm reel no. 72, frame no. 668; W.E.B. Du Bois Papers, University of Massachusetts, Amherst.

605. PRAYER

I do not believe in prayer. I do not believe that there is a personal conscious King of the world who will, upon fitting petition from me, change the course of world events to suit my needs or wishes. This, as I understand it, is the simple, honest, straightforward theory of prayer. . . . If instead of a personal God we fall back on vague impersonal Power and Law, I see nothing to which Prayer can be addressed. Shall we ask gravitation to make stones fly upward? Or did the sun stand still for Joshua?

To Sydney Strong, May 4, 1929; microfilm reel no. 29, frame no. 322; W.E.B. Du Bois Papers, University of Massachusetts, Amherst.

606. THE PREACHER

Three things characterized this religion of the slave,—the Preacher, the Music, and the Frenzy. The Preacher is the most unique personality developed by the

Negro on American soil. A leader, a politician, an orator, a "boss," an intriguer, an idealist—all these he is.

The Souls of Black Folk (1903) 190.

607. QUAKERS AND SLAVERY

The protest against the slave trade in 1688 was made by German immigrants and not by English Friends; and . . . it was eight years before the Quakers advised any limitations on the buying of slaves; sixty-six years before they made the slave trade a matter of discipline; and eighty-eight years before they made manumission compulsory.

"Puritans and Quakers," *Crisis* 37 (December 1930) 426; *Selections from* The Crisis, vol. 2 (1983) 604.

608. RELIGION

Many folk follow religious ceremonies and services; and allow their children to learn fairy tales and so-called religious truth, which in time the children come to recognize as conventional lies told by their parents and teachers for the children's good.

Autobiography (1968) 43.

I cannot believe that any chosen body of people or special organization of mankind has received a direct revelation of ultimate truth which is denied to earnest scientific effort.

Color and Democracy (1945) 137.

The majority of the best and earnest people of the world are today organized in religious groups, and . . . without the cooperation of the richness of their emotional experience, and the unselfishness of their aims, science stands helpless before crude fact and selfish endeavor.

Color and Democracy (1945) 137.

609. RELIGIOUS BELIEF

There is no religion of which I know whose dogma and creed is one in which I wholly believe. I do not believe in the existence and rulership of the one God of the Jews; I do not believe in the miraculous birth and the miracles of the Christ of the Christians; I do not believe in many of the tenets of Mohammedanism and Buddhism; and . . . I do not believe that the Guardian of the Bahai faith has any supernatural knowledge of what may happen, or is any more than a fine, conscientious and hard-working leader of men.

To Larry and Carol Hautz, September 29, 1954; microfilm reel no. 70, frame no. 674; W.E.B. Du Bois Papers, University of Massachusetts, Amherst.

610. RELIGIOUS CONVERSION

In the seventeenth century not only was there little missionary effort to convert Negro slaves, but . . . there was on the contrary positive refusal to let slaves be converted. . . . [T]his refusal was one incentive to explicit statements of the doctrine of perpetual slavery for Negroes. . . . In 1729 . . . the Crown Attorney and Solicitor General . . . [ruled] that baptism in no way changed the slave's status.

The Negro Church (1903) 9–10.

611. SPLENDID FAILURE

The attempt to make black men American citizens was in a certain sense all a failure, but a splendid failure. It did not fail where it was expected to fail. It was *Athanasius contra mundum*, with back to the wall, outnumbered ten to one, with all the wealth and all the opportunity, and all the world against him. And only in his hands and heart the consciousness of a great and just cause; fighting the battle of all the oppressed and despised humanity of every race and color, against the massed hirelings of Religion, Science, Education, Law and brute force.

Black Reconstruction (1935) 708.

612. WAKE, AWAKE

I am unable to follow the reasoning of people who use the word "spirit" and "spiritual" in a technical religious sense. It is true that after any great world calamity, when people have suffered widely, there is a tendency to relapse into superstition, obscuration, and the formal religion of creeds in a vague attempt to reassure humanity, because reason and logic seemed to have failed. This instead of being a spiritual "awakening," is to my mind, an evidence of ignorance and discouragement. On the other hand, among some people, there comes in time of stress and depression, an increase of determination to plan and work for better conditions. This is not usually called a "spiritual" awakening, but it is apt to be condemned by the ignorant as "radicalism" and an "attack" upon the established order. It is, however, a manifestation of the spirit in the highest sense and something of this I seem to see beginning today.

Letter to George Vaughn, February 23, 1934; *Correspondence*, I, 477–478.

613. WAR AND IGNORANCE

There are many, many exceptions, but, in general, it is true there is scarcely a bishop in Christendom, a priest in the church, a president, governor, mayor, or legislator in the United States, a college professor or public school teacher, who does not in the end stand by War and Ignorance as the main method for the settlement of our pressing human problem.

Black Reconstruction (1935) 678.

614. WARS

>Have all the wars of all the world,
>Down all dim time, drawn blood from Thee?
>Have all the lies and thefts and hates—
>Is this Thy Crucifixion, God,
>And not that funny, little cross,
>With vinegar and thorns?

Darkwater (1920) 251–252.

615. WHITE CHRISTIANITY

A nation's religion is its life, and as such white Christianity is a miserable failure.

Darkwater (1920) 36.

616. WHITE CHURCH

If one hundred of the best and purest colored folk of the United States should seek to apply for membership in any white church in this land tomorrow, 999 out of every 1,000 ministers would lie to keep them out. They would not only do this, but would openly and brazenly defend their action as worthy of followers of Jesus Christ.

"The Church and the Negro," *Crisis* 6 (October 1913) 290–91; *Selections from* The Crisis, vol. 1 (1983) 69.

617. WHITE PROFESSION

In religion as in democracy, the Negro has been a peculiar test of white profession. The American church, both Catholic and Protestant, has been kept from any temptation to over-righteousness and empty formalism by the fact that just as Democracy in America was tested by the Negro, so American religion has always been tested by slavery and color prejudice. . . . Until the day comes when color caste falls before reason and economic opportunity the black American will stand as the last and terrible test of the ethics of Jesus Christ.

The Gift of Black Folk (1924) 338–339.

14

Jews

618. ANALOGY

Our problem is not . . . analogous to the Jewish problem in Russia. . . .

"The Negro College and the Negro Voter," April 4, 1934; microfilm reel no. 80, frame no. 574; W.E.B. Du Bois Papers, University of Massachusetts, Amherst.

619. ANTI-SEMITISM

The source of anti-Semitism for American Negroes . . . is simply slavish imitation of whites. . . . The forces in the world back of anti-Semitism are exactly the same facts that are back of color prejudice.

Amsterdam News, October 5, 1940; *Newspaper Columns by W.E.B. Du Bois* (1986) 330.

620. BLACKS AND ISRAEL

I wish to apologize in the name of the American Negro for the apparent apostasy of Ralph Bunche, acting mediator of the United Nations in Palestine, to the clear ideals of freedom and fair play, which should have guided the descendant of an American slave.

"America's Responsibility to Israel," November 30, 1948; microfilm reel no. 80, frame no. 1159; W.E.B. Du Bois Papers, University of Massachusetts, Amherst.

621. CONSISTENCY

Why do we denounce fascism, and then in the name of democracy adopt fascist methods of political control in the South, economic dictation in the West and antisemitism throughout America?

"Democracy's Opportunity," *Christian Register* 125 (August 1946) 350–51; *Writings by W.E.B. Du Bois in Periodicals Edited by Others*, vol. 4 (1982) 13.

622. CORRECTION

I do not agree with you with regard to the [highly critical views you express on the] Jews, and hope you may live to change your opinions.

To Dr. von Leers, May 31, 1955; microfilm reel no. 71, frame no. 757; W.E.B. Du Bois Papers, University of Massachusetts, Amherst.

623. DAUGHTERS

Mr. [Thomas] Dixon says that Jews are assimilated because of their beautiful daughters. His facts are mixed. The Jews are not assimilated, because they have the power to protect those same daughters. And when Negroes have in law and in public opinion similar power to guard their families from lecherous whites, there will be far less amalgamation than today. If prominent Southerners from Thomas Jefferson down to some leaders of today had found our black daughters as unattractive as Mr. Dixon alleges, there would not be two million mulattoes in the land as unanswerable witnesses to the truth.

"The Problem of Tillman, Vardaman, and Thomas Dixon, Jr." *Central Christian Advocate* 49 (October 18, 1905) 132–25; *Writings by W.E.B. Du Bois in Periodicals Edited by Others*, vol. 1 (1982) 266.

624. DESPERATE CAUSES

The death roll of 1939 includes Joel E. Spingarn, President of the National Association for the Advancement of Colored People and noted literary critic. Mr. Spingarn was of Jewish descent and an unselfish and inspired fighter for desperate causes and universal justice.

Phylon 1 (First Quarter 1940); *Selections from* Phylon (1980) 16.

625. DISCRIMINATION IN LIBRARIES

I may have been misinformed as to the exact number of Jewish girls who have been appointed Branch Librarians, but certainly the number is surprisingly small considering the Jewish population of New York.

To Franklin F. Hopper, March 1, 1930; microfilm reel no. 31, frame no. 1090; W.E.B. Du Bois Papers, University of Massachusetts, Amherst.

626. EXPULSION OF BLACKS

There is no likelihood just now of . . . [blacks] being forcibly expelled [from the U.S.]. So far as that is concerned, there was no likelihood ten years ago of the Jews being expelled from Germany. The cases are far from parallel. There is a good deal more profit in cheap Negro labor than in Jewish fellow citizens, which brings together strange bedfellows for the protection of the Negro. On the other hand one must remember that this is a day of astonishing change, injustice and cruelty; and that many Americans of stature have favored the transportation of Negroes and they were not all of the mental caliber of the present junior senator from Mississippi [Theodore Bilbo]. As the Negro develops from an easily exploitable, profit-furnishing laborer to an intelligent self-supportive citizen, the possibility of his being pushed out of his American fatherland may easily be increased rather than diminished. We may be expelled from the United States as the Jew is being expelled from Germany.

Dusk of Dawn (1940) 306.

627. EXTERMINATION OF JEWS

Whatever we as Negroes have suffered in the world from African slave trade to Asia and America, down to the lynching and mob violence of the nineteenth and twentieth centuries, it cannot be compared to the long history of cruelty, murder and humiliation which has been visited upon the Jewish people from the days of Rome down through the Spanish expulsion, the Russian pograms, the Polish oppression and the present policy of extermination under Hitler. The present massacre and persecution of Jews is to be looked at, not simply from the point of view of what they are suffering, but, even more, from what this persecution means as an exemplification of modern civilization. There is scarcely a modern civilized land that did not have its part in laying the foundation upon which Hitler has builded.

Amsterdam News, January 16, 1943; *Newspaper Columns by W.E.B. Du Bois* (1986) 494.

628. GERMAN ANTI-SEMITISM

[In the 1890s:] There was some of it, but it was excused. It wasn't spoken about openly, and it was counteracted by the way in which they brought the Jews into their cultural life, and the Jews forced themselves into it by their ability—and also into their military life, because it was laid down as a rule for an impecunious young officer to marry a rich Jewish girl, which made a great deal of difficulty in the Hitler era, because there was so much intermarriage with Jews. . . . There was a great deal of prejudice against the Jews and against darker races and against foreigners. . . . You didn't have any people on the streets talking against Jews, because there were too many Jews in high positions and too many people married to Jews who wouldn't have any of that kind of talk. So that there was no open, verbal antisemitism, and at the same time, there was a great deal of feeling against Jews. There again, you see, it culminated on the economic level, because it was the great Jewish capitalistic organization that drove the small German shopkeeper out of business. It wasn't the fault of the Jews that they were in big business. That was the only thing they were allowed, in the Middle Ages, to go into. . . . So they went into business, and they built up big business.

"Oral History Manuscript," May 24, 1960; microfilm reel no. 88, frame nos. 1650–1651; W.E.B. Du Bois Papers, University of Massachusetts, Amherst.

629. GERMAN JEWS

No people in the world have the interest in the Jewish problem in Germany that the American Negroes have. It re-orientates the whole attitude of the modern world toward race problems. . . . Here comes an exhibition of race hatred in one of the leading countries of European civilization. This again based on the same biological and psychological foundations which scientists sought to use in blacklisting the Negro. . . . If it can happen to German Jews, there is no reason in the world why under certain circumstances it should not happen to the Irish, to the Latins, to the Slavs, and indeed, to any group of human beings over whom a temporary or imagined majority hold sway and power.

Pittsburgh Courier, February 22, 1931; *in* Aptheker (ed.), *Newspaper Columns by W.E.B. Du Bois* (1986) 32–33.

There has been no tragedy in modern times equal in its awful effects to the fight on the Jew in Germany. It is an attack on civilization, comparable only to such horrors as the Spanish Inquisition and the African slave trade. It has set civilization back a hundred years.

Pittsburgh Courier, December 19, 1936; *Newspaper Columns by W.E.B. Du Bois* (1986) 149.

630. HOLOCAUST

We rightly shrieked to civilization when American Negroes were lynched and mobbed to death at the rate of 400 to 500 a year. Today in Europe and among peaceful Jews, they are killing that number each day. . . . The present plight of the Jews is far worse than ours. Yet it springs from the same cause, and what is happening to Jews may happen to us in future. The United States and Great Britain could rescue from death and worse than death, the three or four million surviving Jews. There is room for them and room aplenty within their borders.

Amsterdam News, September 18, 1943; *Newspaper Columns by W.E.B. Du Bois* (1986) 554.

There is still possible a massacre of Negroes here worse than what 6,000,000 Jews suffered in Germany.

"On Negro America," *Sunday Compass*, July 10, 1949, 4–5; *Writings by W.E.B. Du Bois in Periodicals Edited by Others*, vol. 4 (1982) 121.

631. HUMAN RIGHTS

I have received your declaration of human rights and want to say frankly that I am greatly disappointed. You say under paragraph two of your creed: "No plea of sovereignty shall ever again be allowed to permit any nation to deprive those within its borders of these fundamental rights on the claim that these are matters of internal concern." How about depriving people outside the borders of a country of their rights?

Under paragraph five you appeal for sympathy for persons driven from the land of their birth; but how about American Negroes, Africans and Indians who have not been driven from the land of their birth but nevertheless are deprived of their rights. Under paragraph six you want redress for those who wander the earth but how about those who do not wander and are not allowed to travel and nevertheless are deprived of their fundamental human rights?

In other words, this is a very easily understood declaration of Jewish rights but it has apparently no thought of the rights of Negroes, Indians, and South Sea Islanders. Why then call it the Declaration of Human Rights?

To Joseph M. Proskauer, American Jewish Committee, November 14, 1944; microfilm reel no. 55, frame no. 877; W.E.B. Du Bois Papers, University of Massachusetts, Amherst.

632. INADVERTENCE—I

[In preparing a 50th anniversary edition of *Souls of Black Folk*, Du Bois directed that the following be added to Chapter VII, p. 134:] In the Foregoing chapter, ''Jews'' have been mentioned five times, and the late Jacob Schiff once complained that this gave an impression of anti-semitism. This at the time I stoutly denied; but as I read the passages again in the light of subsequent history, I see how I laid myself open to this possible misapprehension. What, of course, I meant to condemn was exploitation of black labor and that it was in this country and at that time in part a matter of immigrant Jews, was incidental and not essential. My inner sympathy with the Jewish people was expressed better in the last paragraph of page 227. But this illustrates how easily one slips into unconscious condemnation of a whole group.

''Changes in Souls of Black Folk,'' March 16, 1953; microfilm reel no. 69, frame no. 565; W.E.B. Du Bois Papers, University of Massachusetts, Amherst.

633. INADVERTENCE—II

At the time when I had made this study . . . in south Georgia, I came across a considerable number of immigrants from Russia who had settled in the Black Belt and who together with southern and northern whites were exploiting the Negro workers with very little mercy. I referred to these Jews and to the poor whites and Yankees several times in what became the fourth chapter of my book [*Souls of Black Folk*]. Jacob Schiff, whom I knew slightly, wrote me later pointing out that my words conveyed an impression of anti-Semitism, as I seemed to be blaming religion or race for the deeds which these men were doing. I resented this strongly, denying that any race prejudice could possibly enter my thinking. Latter Rabbi Stephen Wise repeated this charge and I promised to review my words and correct them in future editions if they seemed in error.

I never did this because as I re-read the bare facts which I had chronicled, they were true. I could not conscientiously change them. Moreover, I certainly had no conscious desire to malign Jews, knowing only too well myself what race prejudice could do. I therefore continued to let the words stand as I had written them, and did not realize until the horrible massacre of German Jews, how even unconscious repetition of current folklore such as the concept of Jews as more guilty of exploitation than others, had helped the Hitlers of the world.

In planning this reprint [of *Souls of Black Folk*], therefore, my first impulse was to eliminate all those references to Jews. But this I finally realized would be historically inaccurate. I have therefore with some regret let the passages stand as written believing that other references to Jews in this very book and my evident personal indebtedness to Jewish culture will absolve me from blame of unfairness. If it does not, the case but illustrates how easy it is, especially in race relations, inadvertently to give a totally wrong impression.

"Fifty Years After," June 1, 1953; microfilm reel no. 69, frame nos. 567–568; W.E.B. Du Bois Papers, University of Massachusetts, Amherst.

634.   INADVERTENCE—III

In chapter 7 [of *Souls of Black Folk*], Jews are mentioned several times and some have got an impression of anti-Semitism. This at the time I stoutly denied; but as I read the passages again in the light of subsequent history, I see how I laid myself open to this possible misapprehension. What, of course, I meant to condemn was the exploitation of black labor, that it was in this country and at that time in part a matter of immigrant Jews, was incidental and not essential.* But this illustrates how easily one slips into unconscious condemnation of a whole group. So too, I had at the time no clear conception of the fundamental relations of Capitalism and Socialism.

"Fifty Years After," July 17, 1953; microfilm reel no. 69, frame no. 744; W.E.B. Du Bois Papers, University of Massachusetts, Amherst. This was adopted from the version dated June 1, 1953; Inadvertence, II, above.
*Lined out by Du Bois was the sentence: "My inner sympathy with the Jewish people was expressed better in the last paragraph of page 227."

635.   INTERNAL SEGREGATION

[Protesting exclusion of five black students from the senior prom at the Brooklyn Girls' High School, including Du Bois's daughter.] Are you [the principal] voting to see if the Jewish girls shall be invited to their own class promenade or the Irish girls or the red-headed girls? This is not democracy; it is sheer tyranny. Democracy is not the right to insult a senior who was able enough to write the class song by holding an election to determine as to whether she can attend a class function.

To William L. Falter, April 14, 1920; microfilm reel no. 8, frame no. 1199; W.E.B. Du Bois Papers, University of Massachusetts, Amherst.

636. JEWISH AND BLACK MEMORY

There must be for a long time, Jewish education and Negro education in a world which in many and differing ways despises and belittles both groups. Jewish and Negro children as well as all other children must attend the public school system of the nation. But outside these schools there must be concerted and continuous effort to afford these children such training in the history and struggles of their people; the story of their emancipation and especially the way in which many minority peoples have not only proven their right to share and even to lead civilization and yet to be as true Americans as peoples of English, German or French descent.

"Schools for Minorities," June 27, 1954; microfilm reel no. 81, frame nos. 881–882; W.E.B. Du Bois Papers, University of Massachusetts, Amherst.

637. JEWISH HISTORY

[In Du Bois's course Sociology 471, Race Problems in Present-Day Europe, given at Atlanta University, students analyzed anti-Semitism in Germany and Austria and] studied the Jewish problem in each European country from Roman time down to the present. . . .

To Ira De A. Reid, November 20, 1934; microfilm reel no. 41, frame no. 988; W.E.B. Du Bois Papers, University of Massachusetts, Amherst.

638. JEWS

In Fort Wayne, Indiana, I sat after the lecture with a group of Jews and talked intimately. Every problem which I called mine had its counterpart in problems which were theirs.

"Pilgrimage," *Crisis* 31 (April 1926) 267–70; *Selections from* The Crisis, vol. 2 (1983) 437.

639. JEWS AND BLACKS

Only the Jews among us, as a class, carefully select and support talent and genius among the young; the Negroes are following this example as far as their resources and knowledge allow. It is for this very reason that jealousy of the gifted Jew and ambitious Negro is closing doors of opportunity in their faces. This led to the massacre of Jews in Germany.

"Roosevelt," January 30, 1948; microfilm reel no. 80, frame no. 1078; W.E.B. Du Bois Papers, University of Massachusetts, Amherst.

640. JEWS IN EUROPE

Let Negroes remember one thing: the greatest social evil of this evil war, is the attack on the Jewish people. It is the most unforgivable and unwarranted result of this collapse of civilization. The man or race that condones it, is lost.

Amsterdam News, January 4, 1944; *Newspaper Columns by W.E.B. Du Bois*, (1986)
    581.

641. JEWS IN GERMANY

It seems impossible that in the middle of the 20th century a country like
Germany could turn to race hate as a political expedient. Surely, the example
of America is enough to warn the world. . . . It all reminds the American Negro
that after all race prejudice has nothing to do with accomplishment or desert,
with genius or ability. It is an ugly, dirty thing. It feeds on envy and hate.

"The Jews," *Crisis* 40 (May 1933) 117; *Selections from* The Crisis, vol. 2 (1983) 701.

There is a campaign of race prejudice carried on, openly, continuously and
determinedly against all non-Nordic races, but specifically against the Jews,
which surpasses in vindictive cruelty and public insult anything I have ever seen,
and I have seen much.

Pittsburgh Courier, December 5, 1936; *Newspaper Columns by W.E.B. Du Bois* (1986)
    143.

My interview . . . in the [N.Y.] "Post" was quite considerably distorted. I did
not mean to make any direct comparison between Negroes in America and Jews
in Germany but did want to emphasize the extraordinary cruelty of the Nazi
attitude toward Jews.

To Gerhard Hauptmann, February 4, 1937; microfilm reel no. 47, frame no. 586; W.E.B.
    Du Bois Papers, University of Massachusetts, Amherst.

The plight of the Jew in Germany during the Hitler regime is the greatest
human tragedy of our day. Once the world realizes its causes and extent they
will, if civilization continues, see to it that nothing like this happens again.

To Black Book Committee, March 15, 1946; microfilm reel no. 58, frame no. 599;
    W.E.B. Du Bois Papers, University of Massachusetts, Amherst.

642. LEGAL DISCRIMINATION

Mr. David Ben Gurion, Chairman of the Jewish Agency in Jerusalem, said
on the fourth of July, "Palestine is now the only place in the civilized world
where racial discrimination still exists in law." Is it possible that Mr. Ben Gurion
has not heard of the racial and caste legislation of the United States. . . . This
restrictive legislation is used not simply against Negroes but against other minority groups including Jews.

To editor of *PM*, July 8, 1947; microfilm reel no. 60, frame no. 751; W.E.B. Du Bois
    Papers, University of Massachusetts, Amherst.

643. LOBBYING FOR ISRAEL

At the request of the American Jewish Congress, [I] conferred by wire and
phone from Iowa and Chicago with the United Nations Liberian Delegation in
reference to the Palestine Partition plan.

"Department of Special Research," March 5, 1948; microfilm reel no. 62, frame no. 760; W.E.B. Du Bois Papers, University of Massachusetts, Amherst.

644.   OPPRESSIVE NAZI GERMANY

Since my arrival in Los Angeles, it has come to my attention that some persons have interpreted my articles in the *Pittsburgh Courier* as favorable to the Nazi party. I do not see how this is possible, and recommend that such persons read the articles carefully again. Certainly I regard Naziism as the most menacing single movement in the world today.

Untitled, undated [1937]; microfilm reel no. 48, frame no. 433; W.E.B. Du Bois Papers, University of Massachusetts, Amherst.

The Nazi[s] had so changed the laws that practically anything . . . [done] to Jews was legal, and what you had was legal oppression rather than the illegal cast[e] and lynching of Negroes in the United States. . . . There was on the part of the [German] populace no natural reaction of prejudice toward Negroes while there was such reaction toward Jews. This arose naturally from the frightful antisemitic propaganda.

To Leo Stein, March 10, 1937; microfilm reel no. 46, frame no. 1161; W.E.B. Du Bois Papers, University of Massachusetts, Amherst.

645.   OVERTHROWING SOCIALISM

There is no doubt but that in the state of Israel rival forces are now in deadly conflict. The power of the organized Jewish church and the power of the American capitalism have been so great that the attempt to build a modern socialism in Israel has been made difficult: There is no reason to doubt but that persons favoring reaction in Israel and in America may have easily been induced to try to overthrow Socialism in the Soviet Union and Czechoslovakia, and given money to accomplish this.

To Lorraine Cousens, February 9, 1953; microfilm reel no. 69, frame no. 738; W.E.B. Du Bois Papers, University of Massachusetts, Amherst.

646.   THE POLISH ISSUE

We have allowed ourselves in this conference to be estranged from Russia by the plight of a dozen reactionary and Jew-baiting Polish landlords, and have made no comment and taken no action on the great words spoken by [Soviet Foreign Minister V. M.] Molotov: "We must first of all see to it that dependent countries are enabled as soon as possible to take the path of national independence."

Letter to members of the U.S. delegation to the San Francisco conference on the founding of the UN, May 16, 1945; *Correspondence*, III, 11.

647. PROTOCOLS OF ZION

I do not think that you would consciously want to disseminate a proven untruth. The so-called protocols of the Elders of Zion, have been repeatedly proven by the best investigators outside the Jewish race, to be impudent and clumsy forgery. I cannot see how anybody, after investigating the evidence can assume that they are true.

To Helen W. Courtois, March 27, 1934; microfilm reel no. 41, frame no. 1206; W.E.B. Du Bois Papers, University of Massachusetts, Amherst.

648. SCRIPTURES

Very few Christian churches allowed slavery to be discussed in their pulpits. The most prominent rabbi in this city [New York City] preached a widely circulated sermon, proving from Hebrew scripture that God made Negroes "the meanest of slaves."

"Freedom of Opinion," February 14, 1955; microfilm reel no. 81, frame nos. 966–967; W.E.B. Du Bois Papers, University of Massachusetts, Amherst.

649. SOULS OF BLACK FOLK

If your agency decides to republish the book in Czechoslovakia I should like the same changes made in your edition. I am therefore sending you the revised pages, 126, 127, 132, 169, 170 and 204. In each case the actual change in phraseology is small but is important, since it will clear up any misapprehension concerning my attitude toward Jews. Also, under these circumstances, it would not be necessary for you to publish the Preface which I sent.

To Vojtech Strnad, June 8, 1953; microfilm reel no. 69, frame no. 741; W.E.B. Du Bois Papers, University of Massachusetts, Amherst. [See, also, above "Inadvertence, I, II, and III."]

650. SOVIET JEWRY

Some of those punished [for disrupting the economy in the USSR and Czechoslovakia] were Jews, but there is no reason to assume that they were punished *because* they were Jews. They were punished because they were traitors. The Soviet Union has had a splendid record of opposition to racism for 35 years. Jews have from the first stood foremost in its leadership and still do. Even in its treatment of religion, after the political and economic power of the church had been broken, Russians were free to worship.

To Lorraine Cousens, February 9, 1953; microfilm reel no. 69, frame no. 738; W.E.B. Du Bois Papers, University of Massachusetts, Amherst.

Personally, I have found no evidence of injustice toward them and I have met large numbers of Jews who agree with me. I am sure that there would be in the Soviet Union as there has been elsewhere strong opposition to the assumptions of the Jewish Orthodox Church. Whether or not this is part of the alleged attack on Yiddish I do not know.

To A. A. Roback, December 8, 1959; microfilm reel no. 73, frame no. 880; W.E.B. Du Bois Papers, University of Massachusetts, Amherst.

651. JOSEPH STALIN

Let all Negroes, Jews and Foreign-born, who have suffered in America from prejudice and intolerance, remember Joseph Stalin. This son of a slave in Georgia, as Commissar of Nationalities fought prejudice and particularism, and helped build the first modern state which outlawed race discrimination.

"Joseph Stalin," March 7, 1953; microfilm reel no. 69, frame no. 748; W.E.B. Du Bois Papers, University of Massachusetts, Amherst.

652. SYMPATHY FOR HITLER

The most disconcerting result . . . [of the Nazi attacks upon German Jews] is the repercussions of this treatment of Jews in America. There had been no doubt that among a considerable number of Americans and even among minorities like Negroes, the attitude of Hitler toward Jews has had wide sympathy, even though public discussion of the matter has been to a considerable degree suppressed. . . . There has been effort in the United States to combat anti-Semitism but it has suffered on the one hand from the "hush-hush" methods of certain Jews and from a clear lack of enthusiasm on the part of a surprising number of Gentiles.

Phylon 2 (Fourth Quarter 1941); *Selections from* Phylon (1980) 141–42.

653. UN-AMERICAN ACTIVITIES

I understand you have been asking various persons concerning their ideas of un-American activities. May I suggest the following: . . . the widespread conspiracy especially in the South to keep persons from registering as voters . . . widespread efforts to increase and advertise antisemitism . . . the opposition to Negro education particularly in the public elementary and high schools.

To Karl E. Mundt, January 2, 1945; microfilm reel no. 58, frame no. 29; W.E.B. Du Bois Papers, University of Massachusetts, Amherst.

654. UNSAFE BLACK MAJORITY

We must not make the error of the German Jews. They assumed that if the German nation received some of them as intellectual and social equals, the whole group would be safe. It only took a psychopathic criminal like Hitler to show them their tragic mistake. American Negroes may yet face a similar tragedy. They should prepare for such an eventuality.

Autobiography (1968) 393.

15

White People

655. BITTERNESS

If white people are reading my books for the purpose of learning what black folk are thinking it would be dishonest for me to hide or gloss over the bitterness which we quite naturally feel over our treatment in the United States past and present; and if knowledge of that reaction engenders further bitterness on their part I am sorry but I can do nothing about it.

Letter to Julia Belle Tutweiler, October 17, 1939; *Correspondence*, II, 197.

656. BRICKS OF MOLASSES

Until the liberal white South has the guts to stand up for democracy regardless of race there will be no solution of the Negro problem and no solution of the problem of popular government in America. You cannot build bricks of molasses.

"The Negro Citizen," in Charles S. Johnson (ed.), *The Negro in American Civilization* (New York: Holt, 1930) 461–70; *Writings by W.E.B. Du Bois in Periodicals Edited by Others*, vol. 2 (1982) 162.

657. CLEAR SIGHT

Matthew Towns: We black folk of America are the only ones of the darker world who see white folk and their civilization with level eyes and unquickened pulse. We know them.

Dark Princess (1928) 233.

658. CRIME OR COLOR?

Murder may swagger, theft may rule and prostitution may flourish and the nation gives but spasmodic, intermittent and lukewarm attention. But let the murderer be black or the thief brown or the violator of womanhood have a drop of Negro blood, and the righteousness of the indignation sweeps the world. Nor would this fact make the indignation less justifiable did not we all know that it was blackness that was condemned and not crime.

Darkwater (1920) 34–35.

659. CUSTOM

Then she made a last gesture of surrender from a Southern white to a colored person: she held out her hand.

Worlds of Color (1961) 97.

660. DEBT

This white Southern rot of talking about what black men "owe" to Southern planters ought pretty soon to die a natural and well merited death. The larger part of the debt which we owe to the South consists of ignorance, poverty and bastards.

"A Poet's Wail," *Crisis* 36 (October 1929) 349; *Selections from* The Crisis, vol. 2 (1983) 562.

661. DEFEATISM

We have within the Negro race today extraordinary defeatism. We have been brought up to assume that everything White is Right; that the one goal they have to reach is what white people have done and not what ought to be done. . . . We have got to have, for the good of the world, supervision by colored people and suppressed classes so as to make a world-wide culture worth having.

Pittsburgh Courier, May 23, 1936; *Newspaper Columns by W.E.B. Du Bois* (1986) 76.

662. A DONE DEAL

Breckinridge: "Scroggs, I promise to see to it that white men in this state get employment according to ability at decent wages; that Negro workers are not preferred before them; that we who are the old aristocracy will strive to open every path of progress to all the white people of South Carolina; and that we look forward with confidence to the day when this state will be an entirely white and prosperous community. Meantime we will take from the Negro the vote he is not fit to use and put him in his place as laborer and servant pursuing such skills as he may have. We will protect him in his humiliation and assure him a decent life and justice, so long as he is content with the sphere for which God created him."

Scroggs [Poor white leader]: "Done!"

The Ordeal of Mansart (1957) 28.

663. EQUALITY

Equality does not mean that slaves should rule Southern white men; but it does deny that a white man should own me body and soul just because he can spout Cicero.

Scientific Monthly, May 1948; *Book Reviews by W.E.B. Du Bois* (1977) 231.

664. HELL AND HEAVEN

The difference between a hospital with Southern whites in control and a hospital with colored physicians and nurses is, to the vision of most black folk, the difference between Hell and Heaven.

"The Dilemma of the Negro," *American Mercury* 3 (October 1924) 179–85; *Writings by W.E.B. Du Bois in Periodicals Edited by Others*, vol. 2 (1982) 224.

665. INDUSTRIAL REVOLUTION

We'll plant cotton mills beside the cotton fields, use whites to keep niggers in their place, and the fear of niggers to keep the poorer whites in theirs.

The Quest of the Silver Fleece (1911) 391.

666. SOUTHERN WHITES

Get your information concerning race discrimination from the colored people in North Carolina. This would involve some difficulties. They would not be frank with you unless they trusted you and it is not easy for a Southern white man to get the confidence of a Southern Negro despite all legends to the contrary.

To R. H. Woody, November 23, 1927; microfilm reel no. 23, frame no. 569; W.E.B. Du Bois Papers, University of Massachusetts, Amherst.

667. WHITE INDIFFERENCE

The most difficult social problem in the matter of Negro health is the peculiar attitude of the nation toward the well-being of the race. There have for instance, been few others in the history of civilized peoples where human suffering has been viewed with such peculiar indifference. Nearly the whole nation seemed delighted with the discredited census of 1870 because it was thought to show that the Negroes were dying off rapidly, and the country would soon be well rid of them.

The Philadelphia Negro (1899) 163.

668. THE WHITE SOUTH

The white south is the most reactionary modern social organization which exists today in the civilized areas of the world.

"Ho! Everyone That Thirsteth!" May 26, 1958; microfilm reel no. 81, frame no. 1189; W.E.B. Du Bois Papers, University of Massachusetts, Amherst.

669. WHITE WORLD

How easy . . . by emphasis and omission to make children believe that every great soul the world ever saw was a white man's soul; that every great thought the world ever knew was a white man's thought; that every great deed the world ever did was a white man's deed; that every great dream the world ever sang was a white man's dream.

Darkwater (1920) 31.

670. WHITENESS

The discovery of personal whiteness among the world's peoples is a very modern thing,—a nineteenth and twentieth century matter, indeed. The ancient world would have laughed at such a distinction. . . . Today . . . the world . . . has discovered that it is white and by that token, wonderful!

Darkwater (1920) 29–30.

671. WHITES

I am quite frank: I do not pretend to "love" white people. I think that as a race they are the most selfish of any on earth. I think that the history of the world for the last thousand years proves this beyond doubt.

"Whites in Africa after Negro Autonomy," in A. A. Roback (ed.), *In Albert Schweitzer's Realm: A Symposium* (Cambridge, Mass.: Sci-Art Publishers, 1962) 243–55; *Writings by W.E.B. Du Bois in Non-Periodical Literature Edited by Others* (1982) 295.

16

World Economy and Politics

672. ANGLO-AMERICA

If the English speaking white people hope by a union of their efforts in the 20th century to lead the world toward better government and better civilization they must at least make it plain that the lynching of Negroes has no place in that program and if they do not make that plain then they put into the minds of every thinking Negro and into the back of minds of every brown and yellow man in the world the conviction that the union of England and America is something desperately to be feared by the darker races.

"Memo to Mr. L. T. Hobhouse, Chairman of the proposed British Committee on the Negro problem" (ca. 1922); microfilm reel no. 10, frame nos. 1160–62; W.E.B. Du Bois Papers, University of Massachusetts, Amherst.

673. BRETTON WOODS PROPOSALS

We recognize the necessity for economic reconstruction after the war and we believe that so far as technical banking is concerned the Bretton Woods proposals are good. But we deplore the fact that the well-being of groups like the seven hundred and fifty million colonial peoples is entirely ignored in these proposals and it is assumed that the social and ethical questions connected with their labor, wages and social conditions have nothing to do with economic proposals. This is simply a continuation of the insistence of nineteenth century economists that economic science has nothing to do with social uplift.

To Rex Stout, March 30, 1945; microfilm reel no. 58, frame no. 325; W.E.B. Du Bois Papers, University of Massachusetts, Amherst.

674. BUSINESS ETHICS

The establishment of world credit systems is built on splendid and realizable faith in fellow-men. But it is, after all, so low and elementary a step that sometimes it looks merely like honor among thieves, for the revelations of highway robbery and low cheating in the business world and in all its great modern centers have raised in the hearts of all true men in our day an exceeding great cry for revolution in our basic methods and conceptions of industry and commerce.

Darkwater (1920) 37.

675. CARIBBEAN AREA

United States capital and English investment in Jamaica, Cuba, Puerto Rico, Haiti and the Dominican Republic, rules like a tyrant, to establish color caste, keep down wages and deny labor the right to organize. Political power is mainly in the hands of the whites and property holding mulattoes. In Cuba and Puerto Rico where the dark proletariat has some power and is trying to exercise it, the whole power of property and foreign investment is holding them in check.

"The Future of Africa in America" (1941); Series 3/C, Folder no. 5552, p. 12, *Unpublished Articles*; W.E.B. Du Bois Papers, University of Massachusetts, Amherst.

676. CHANGED BALANCE

Whether we like it or not, most of the people of the world today live under socialism or communism. We cannot stop this by force and should not if we could. We can so improve our own system of economy that the world will see the advantage of it over all others if this proves true.

National Guardian, July 11, 1951; *Newspaper Columns by W.E.B. Du Bois* (1986) 883.

677. CODES OF MORALS

It is strange that modern civilization still sanctions a code of morals between nations which if used between men would bring the severest condemnation; to steal a book is theft, but to steal an island is missionary enterprise; to tell a neighbor an untruth is to lie, but to tell a neighboring country a whole portfolio full is to be diplomatic.

"Douglass as a Statesman," March 9, 1895; Group no. 312, Series no. 22, box no. 373, folder no. 5, pp. 9–10; W.E.B. Du Bois Papers, University of Massachusetts, Amherst.

678. COLONIAL OPPRESSION

The oppressed Negro in America and English colonies is oppressed as a group and within that group is a potential educated leadership which stands with the group and fights for it. In [colonial] black France, on the other hand, the dark masses have no leaders. Their logical leaders, like Diague, Candace and others are more French than the French, and feel quite naturally much nearer the French people than to black Africa or brown Martinique.

To J. G. Fleury, undated [December 1932?]; microfilm reel no. 37, frame no. 21; W.E.B. Du Bois Papers, University of Massachusetts, Amherst.

679. COLONIAL SYSTEM

Perhaps the worst thing about the colonial system was the contradiction which arose and had to arise in Europe with regard to the whole situation. Extreme poverty in colonies was a main cause of wealth and luxury in Europe. The results of this poverty were disease, ignorance, and crime. Yet these had to be represented as natural characteristics of backward peoples. Education for colonial people must inevitably mean unrest and revolt; education, therefore, had to be limited and used to inculcate obedience and servility lest the whole colonial system be overthrown.

The World and Africa (1947, 1965) 37.

680. COLONIALISM

No labor party will risk lower wages in order to improve the condition of colonial labor.

Autobiography (1968) 17.

Each nation felt its deep interests involved. But how? . . . In the possession of land overseas, in the right of colonies, the chance to levy endless tribute on the darker world,—on coolies in China, on starving peasants in India, on black savages in Africa, on dying South Sea Islanders, on Indians of the Amazon— all this and nothing more.

Darkwater (1920) 47.

681. COLONIES

Colonies, we call them, these places where "niggers" are cheap and the earth is rich; they are those outlands where like a swarm of hungry locusts white masters may settle to be served as kings, wield the lash of slavedrivers, rape girls and wives, grow as rich as Croesus and send homeward a golden stream.

Darkwater (1920) 45.

682. DAWNING

The ability today of an American to travel even in his own country is subject to such amazing and puzzling restrictions that freedom of speech seems about to disappear. Nevertheless, I am convinced that the overwhelming majority of thinking people in the United States as in Canada are beginning to tire of their slavery and to grow in the determination to speak for World Peace and Human Equality.

To James Endicott, February 1, 1960; microfilm reel no. 74, frame no. 114; W.E.B. Du Bois Papers, University of Massachusetts, Amherst.

683. DEPRESSION

It was [Herbert Hoover] the President of the United States who assured us some months ago that fundamentally American business was sound and that therefore any economic depression was bound to be a passing and temporary phenomenon. This is not true and the repeated industrial depressions, with the present one, by way of climax, prove the untruth. It is principally because fundamentally American business and industrial organization of the modern world are not sound that the whole machinery continually goes awry, and periodically breaks down in catastrophe.

"Fundamentals," *Crisis* 37 (Dec. 1930) 426; *Selections from* The Crisis, vol. 2 (1983) 606.

684. DIVIDE AND CONQUER

Within colonies, absolute conquest being costly if not impossible, the empire following old-age wisdom divides to conquer. . . . If there are no divisions, the colonial power deliberately creates them.

Color and Democracy (1945) 109.

685. DOES COMMUNISM MENACE U.S.?

It is not as though the United States did not know when the United Nations was established that Russia was a communistic country. It is no new situation that faces us. We went into the United Nations with the firm idea that it was possible for a communistic nation and a capitalistic nation to live together in this world in peace. This was not only our belief, but our propaganda until after the war was finished. Lately we have had a deliberate increase in propaganda to persuade us that communism and capitalism are mutually exclusive ways of life.

"Cooperation between the United States and the Soviet Republic in the United Nations," June 17, 1947; microfilm reel no. 80, frame no. 991; W.E.B. Du Bois Papers, University of Massachusetts, Amherst.

686. DOMESTIC AND FOREIGN

By threatening to send English capital to China and Mexico, by threatening to hire Negro laborers in America, as well as by old-age pensions and [industrial] accident insurance, we gain industrial peace at home at the mightier cost of war abroad.

"African Roots of War," *Atlantic Monthly* 115 (May 1915) 707–14; *Writings by W.E.B. Du Bois in Periodicals Edited by Others*, vol. 2 (1982) 101.

687. FOREIGN POLICY GOALS

America is generous, but its actions especially as dictated by big business are not always philanthropic. In fact what America wants from its international relations is income, wealth and power, particularly from those parts of the world where labor and materials are cheap. This is clear from our investments in oil, gold, diamonds and other metals; in fruit and sugar and dozens of other commodities.

"Colored Folk and the Rockefeller Plan" (ca. 1952); Series 3/C, Folder no. 5570, p. 2, *Unpublished Articles*; W.E.B. Du Bois Papers, University of Massachusetts, Amherst.

688. FREEDOM AND POWER

We have become the richest and most powerful nation on earth. Our supremacy has gone to our heads. We have delusions of grandeur and some of us plan to rule mankind. But we forget the reasons for our power, of which the greatest is freedom to think and speak and act over a wide, fertile land. Moreover we also forget how far our resources and power are today monopolized and concentrated in the hands of our citizens, who regard an attack on their power as an attack on the country itself.

"Broadcast," October 15, 1948; microfilm reel no. 80, frame no. 1128; W.E.B. Du Bois Papers, University of Massachusetts, Amherst.

689. GUNBOAT FINANCE

Today as yesterday, the Englishman knows that in nine cases out of ten the English navy stands ready to collect a foreign debt; and is not going to inquire too carefully as to the underlying justice of that debt. It is this that makes the English bondholder *particeps criminis* with the thieves.

To Angus Fletcher, March 25, 1926; microfilm reel no. 18, frame no. 820; W.E.B. Du Bois Papers, University of Massachusetts, Amherst.

690. IMPERIALISM

We [Americans] are imperialists, not only because of our ownership of Puerto Rico, and Alaska, and Hawaii, and our partial ownership of the Philippines, but even more because the invested capital of America is a decisive element in South Africa, in the Congo, in East Africa, and in the West Indies, not to mention South America. The attitude of the United States of America . . . is going to be decisive for colonialism.

"The Colonial Peoples," January 20, 1948; microfilm reel no. 80, frame no. 1064; W.E.B. Du Bois Papers, University of Massachusetts, Amherst.

691. INTERNATIONAL CONCERN

Any nation has a right by law to curtail the individual liberties of its citizens for the greater good of the nation; but no country has the right to break faith with itself and deny its citizens rights which its own laws guarantee and its own declaration proclaim and when it does this, is not the matter of international concern?

To Madame Vijaya Lakshmi Pandit, September 18, 1947; microfilm reel no. 60, frame no. 129; W.E.B. Du Bois Papers, University of Massachusetts, Amherst.

692. LABOR AND IMPERIALISM

Organized labor in the United States and Europe has seldom actively opposed imperialism or championed democracy among colonial peoples, even when this slave labor was in direct competition with their own.

Color and Democracy (1945) 96.

693. PROFIT AND PROGRESS

When the profit of investors in England, Belgian, French, or American colonies is threatened by education of the masses, self-government, or high wages, profit and not welfare remains the paramount concern and not the interests of colonial peoples. Thus it is clear that the first and fundamental step to colonial reform must be the removal of the dominant profit motive in colonial administration.

"A Program of Emancipation for Colonial Peoples," in Merze Tate (ed.), *Trust and Non-Self-Governing Territories* (Washington, D.C.: Howard University Press, 1948) 96–104; *Writings by W.E.B. Du Bois in Non-Periodical Literature Edited by Others* (1982) 261.

694. PROFITABLE INVESTMENT

In colonial regions not only is there opportunity for investment, but the investor is part of the government or has large influence with the government, and can secure labor at the lowest wage and for the longest hours; he can evade taxation and profit-limiting legislation. . . . The investor can often put upon the shoulders of taxpayers at home in the name of "Empire" colonial payments and improvements, especially in long-term investments such as roads and harbors, which will increase his profit.

Color and Democracy (1945) 47.

695. PUERTO RICO

Sugar is almost entirely absentee-controlled. Tobacco is 95 percent absentee-controlled; banks, 60 percent; railroads, 60 percent; public utilities, 50 percent; and steamship lines, approximately 100 percent. So that the dollars which on paper appear to give Puerto Rico a favorable trade balance are dollars which are never seen in Puerto Rico, but are given by the banks to the absentee holders of shares in industry.

Color and Democracy (1945) 38.

696. SECURING A WORLD

I was born [in 1868] in the culminating splendor of the nineteenth century, when white western Europeans ruled the world as they thought for the world's own good, when war seemed about to cease, at least war between leading white folk; and when western European civilization had apparently reached its greatest height; when men were free, if by ''men'' one understood discipline for colored folk to serve these whites. Then the picture changed.

''World Peace Council,'' May 1959; microfilm reel no. 81, frame no. 1243; W.E.B. Du Bois Papers, University of Massachusetts, Amherst.

697. SLAVERY AND CAPITALISM

I look upon the development of the African slave trade through chartered and incorporated companies as the beginning of modern international capitalism and imperialism. I think that the international relations built up through the slave trade and based on the great crops of tobacco, cotton, sugar and rice, rebuilt and re-oriented the modern world. On this economic foundation was built the problems of the distribution and production of wealth which faces the world today, and the future relationship of the white and colored races in Africa and Asia. . . . For this reason it is of great importance to study . . . the thought and action of these founders of international trade who worked for private profit through the buying and selling of men, with no greater thought of the evil involved than those who work today for profit through the buying and selling of men's color.

To Ruth Anna Fisher, December 3, 1934; microfilm reel no. 42, frame no. 281; W.E.B. Du Bois Papers, University of Massachusetts, Amherst.

698. SLUMS OF THE WORLD

Colonies are the slums of the world. They are today the places of greatest concentration of poverty, disease, and ignorance of what the human mind has come to know. They are centers of helplessness, of discouragement of initiative, of forced labor, and of legal suppression of all activities or thoughts which the master country fears or dislikes.

Color and Democracy (1945) 17.

699. SUPREME COURT'S REASONING

[Why did it rule as it did in the *Brown* decision?] Because it realized that this nation was face to face not simply with a colored minority within its bounds, growing in efficiency, but with a world which contained an overwhelming majority of rising colored peoples; that if our fiction of democracy was to retain any validity whatsoever, it must at least give lip-service to the principle of an unsegregated system of public schools, not to mention discrimination in travel, housing, and civil rights. Thus the principle of caste citizenship must be surrendered.

The court also knew that there had arisen in the world a new power of tremendous and ever-growing strength; it knew that the socialism of Europe and the communism of the Soviet Union had attacked caste and was fighting colonial serfdom of colored peoples. If then the United States could expect to convince China, India, and all Asia, Africa and Africa overseas of the superiority of our way of life, it could no longer uphold color caste.

In addition, the Supreme Court also knew that the white South never had obeyed federal law either in slavery or emancipation, or in the case of the Civil War amendments. It would not obey this decision, and the court proceeded to make it easy for the South to put off the integration of the public schools as long as it pleased and that is precisely what the South is doing.

"The *National Guardian* Dinner," November 21, 1957; microfilm reel no. 81, frame no. 1120; W.E.B. Du Bois Papers, University of Massachusetts, Amherst.

700. U.S. WORLD ROLE

The United States of America . . . arose 200 years ago as a free-thinking democracy, with limitless land and resources; but . . . sank into a vast center of capital monopolized by closed corporations, and now seeks to replace the British empire by stopping socialism with force, and ruling the world by private capital and newly invented technique.

Autobiography (1968) 16.

701. WANT AND PLENTY

There can be no doubt that we have passed in our day from a world that could hardly satisfy the physical wants of the mass of men, by the greatest effort, to a world whose technique supplies enough for all, if all can claim their right. Our great ethical question today is, therefore, how may we justly distribute the world's goods to satisfy the necessary wants of the mass of men.

Darkwater (1920) 99.

702. WORLD COLORS

If one takes total area [of the habitable world], calls the population of South America half colored and all Asia colored we have:
  Area colored world 39 million square miles
  Area white world 20 million square miles

To Harry W. Roberts, October 11, 1950; microfilm reel no. 65, frame no. 606; W.E.B.
Du Bois Papers, University of Massachusetts, Amherst.

703. WORLD LABOR

There can be no permanent uplift of American or European labor as long as
African laborers are slaves.

Darkwater (1920) 70.

704. WORLD MARKET

Thus the world market most widely and desperately sought today is the market
where labor is cheapest and most helpless and profit is most abundant.

Darkwater (1920) 48.

705. WORLD POLICY

Every country that has been conquered by Hitler and is now regaining its
freedom is tending toward greater democracy in industry, greater governmental
control of industry, and economic planning for the future. Against this democracy
in Belgium, Holland, Italy, Greece, and other countries, the organized political
and military might of the United States and Britain is apparently being organized
and exercised.

Color and Democracy (1945) 95.

706. WORLD STATE

One tremendous advantage which the United Nations has over the League of
Nations is that in 1918 it could be argued that socialism was a dream which
never had been realized in modern times. Today, on the contrary, one Socialist
state is in many respects the most powerful member of the United Nations and
cannot be ignored. A second Socialist state [i.e., China] is only temporarily
excluded and socialism is growing in other parts of the world at an irresistible
rate. With such Socialist states and the education which they promote, the peace
which is their goal and the morality toward which economic justice opens the
way, a world state would gradually be realized.

To Anna M. Graves, January 6, 1958; microfilm reel no. 73, frame no. 148; W.E.B.
Du Bois Papers, University of Massachusetts, Amherst.

17

War and Peace

707. ARMAMENT

The cost of a single battleship like the *Massachusetts* would endow all the distinctively college work necessary for Negroes during the next half-century.

"The Training of Negroes for Social Power," *Outlook* 75 (October 17, 1903) 409–14; *Writings by W.E.B. Du Bois in Periodicals Edited by Others*, vol. 1 (1982) 181.

708. ARMY DISCRIMINATION

There were 150,000 Negro stevedores in the Great War [i.e., World War I] because when the colored draftees and volunteers were brought together in the fall of 1917 the officials largely resolved to keep them from receiving military training. They were therefore put to handling supplies or ammunition, grading, ditching, cleaning, building and draining.

The Black Man and the Wounded World (unpublished), chapter 10, "The Battalions of Labor"; W.E.B. Du Bois Papers, Fisk University.

709. BLACKS IN MILITARY

No matter what the cause of war is, Negroes [are expected] . . . to support the war policy loyally and fully, because by fighting shoulder to shoulder with America, they will gain recognition as American citizens. . . . Results prove that it was justified only in the Civil War, where Negroes were after all fighting for their own freedom. In the other cases, they got little or no credit for their effort. They fought in many cases against their own conscience and simply helped further to muddle a muddled world.

To James T. Shotwell, February 26, 1936; microfilm reel no. 45, frame no. 473; W.E.B. Du Bois Papers, University of Massachusetts, Amherst.

Either race separation will disappear in the American armed forces or the
pattern will be torn to pieces in the next war.

Letter to Lawrence E. Spivak, May 22, 1945; *Correspondence*, III, 13.

710. DEFENSIVE MILITARY TRAINING

No group which expects to survive can neglect at least defensive military
training. I think therefore that we should increase the number of colored boy
scouts and girl guides, take a greater part in the militia, attend in larger numbers
the schools for the training of officers, and go in for sports and gun clubs and
aviation, etc. In all these things we will be but obeying the laws and the continual
desire of those back of the laws. I should sincerely hope that such training would
never be used except to help in the defense of this, our common country, but
on the other hand if we should have to fight for survival in the future, it would
be foolish for us to fight without training. Something in this line has already
been done. We have two or three good Negro regiments and some semi-military
bodies like the Knights of Pythias, etc. and also a few boy scouts.

"An Answer to the Memorandum on the Bettering of the Position of the Colored People
    in America," 1926; microfilm reel no. 77, frame no. 422; W.E.B. Du Bois Papers,
    University of Massachusetts, Amherst.

711. DEVELOPMENT

The cost of this exploitation was enormous. The colonial system caused ten
times more deaths than actual war.

The World and Africa (1947, 1965) 35.

712. FIGHT FOR FREEDOM

What is this dark world thinking? It is thinking that as wild and awful as this
shameful war [World War I] was, it is nothing to compare with that fight for
freedom which black and brown and yellow men must and will make unless
their oppression and humiliation and insult at the hands of the White World
cease. The Dark World is going to submit to its present treatment just as long
as it must and not one moment longer.

Darkwater (1920) 49.

713. FREE SPEECH

For the first time in 150 years, the Commissioner of Police of the City of
New York has refused a body of citizens representing the laboring group permission to hold a meeting in Union Square to express their opinion on public
matters. In this case, they wish to advocate peace through refusing to depend
upon war as an instrument of national progress. . . . Will you tell me, Sir, what
body of persons in this city is so opposed to peace, or talk about peace, that

your Police Department is unable to keep them from violence toward those who lawfully advocate peace?

To Mayor William O'Dwyer, July 29, 1950; microfilm reel no. 65, frame no. 370; W.E.B. Du Bois Papers, University of Massachusetts, Amherst.

714. GUTS AND PEACE

Outside the small group which have always cooperated, I know of no person in New York City who...[has] guts enough to form a national peace organization. If I run across one, I'll certainly write you.

To Holland Roberts, September 26, 1957; microfilm reel no. 72, frame no. 391; W.E.B. Du Bois Papers, University of Massachusetts, Amherst.

715. INDICTED FOR PEACE

[Du Bois and four others were indicted by a federal grand jury in 1951 for violating the Foreign Agents Registration Act.] The accusation is not that we have done anything treasonable, or anything that we did not have a right to do; it does not accuse the five defendants of being representatives of a foreign government, but as the curious statute says "representatives of a foreign principal," which means that if this conviction stands [it did not], anybody who repeats in the United States anything that anyone in Europe or Russia says can be accused of being an agent. . . . Freedom of speech and of thought is being curtailed in the United States.

Letter to George Padmore, April 11, 1951; *Correspondence*, III, 312–313.

716. LEAGUE OF NATIONS

A League of Nations is absolutely necessary to the salvation of the Negro race. Unless we have some supernational power to curb the anti-Negro policy of the United States and South Africa, we are doomed eventually to *fight* for our rights. . . . It will be open to larger influences of civilization and culture which are ineffective in the United States because of the prevailing barbarism of the ruling classes in the South and their overwhelming political power.

"The League of Nations," *Crisis* 18 (May 1919) 10–11; *Selections from* The Crisis, vol. 1 (1983) 191.

717. MARCHING ON

April 3rd, [1865] the Federal troops entered Richmond. Weitzel was leading, with a black regiment in his command—a long blue line with gun-barrels gleaming, and bands playing: "John Brown's body lies a-moldering in the grave but his soul goes marching on."

Black Reconstruction (1935) 111.

718. MURDER AND MANHOOD

In the minds of most people, even those of liberals, only a murder makes men. The slave pleaded; he was humble; he protected the women of the South, and the world ignored him. The slave killed white men; and behold, he was a man!

Black Reconstruction (1935) 110.

719. NATIONAL DEFENSE

Dr. Baldwin: Great nations, too poor to build schools, libraries and hospitals, were rich enough to build magnificent warships at ten million dollars apiece, to prowl the seas for prey or scare the weak into slavery. They could not cure Cancer, but they could spread syphilis. They tore the towers of cathedrals neck from jowl to erect offices for profit.

Mansart Builds a School (1959) 29.

720. PEACE

The moral decadence of the United States since 1945 is shown not only by increasing injustice in the courts and deliberate distortion of the truth, but especially by the collapse of all organized effort for peace.

"The World Peace Movement," *New World Review* (May 1955) 14; *Writings by W.E.B. Du Bois in Periodicals Edited by Others*, vol. 4 (1982) 238.

721. PEACE WITH COMMUNISM

The truth is that despite the widespread peace feeling in the United States few people, especially those of prominence, are willing to take a public stand for peace, especially if it is peace with Communism and of course that is precisely what peace means.

To Holland Roberts, January 25, 1960; microfilm reel no. 74, frame no. 200; W.E.B. Du Bois Papers, University of Massachusetts, Amherst.

722. PRELUDE TO FREEDOM

The [First] World War was primarily the jealous and avaricious struggle for the largest share in exploiting darker races. As such it is and must be but the prelude to the armed and indignant protest of these despised and raped peoples.

Darkwater (1920) 49.

723. PRIORITIES

The *first* duty of an American is to win the war and . . . to this all else is subsidiary. . . . Whatever personal and group grievances interfere with this mighty duty must wait. . . . Any man or race that seeks to turn his country's tragic predicament to his own personal gain is fatally cheating himself. . . . *First* your Country, *then* your Rights!

"Our Special Grievances," *Crisis* 16 (September 1918) 216–17; *Selections from* The Crisis, vol. 1 (1983) 162.

724. SELF-CONQUEST

We will have to gird ourselves for a bitter attack on progressives in America during these coming years when the United States is compelled to give up the crazy dream of conquering Communism by war. We are going to attempt to conquer ourselves by unprecedented injustice and suppression.

To Lee Lorch, December 1, 1954; microfilm reel no. 70, frame no. 779; W.E.B. Du Bois Papers, University of Massachusetts, Amherst.

725. WAR

The cause of war is preparation for war; and of all that Europe has done in a century there is nothing that has equaled in energy, thought, and time her preparation for wholesale murder.

Darkwater (1920) 46.

The land hogs and war profiteers are pushing us into war with Mexico just as fast as they can, with the help of a President who is the tool of Big Business and of a Secretary of State who is a misfortune. We are meddling in Nicaragua and sending there a man trained to drill midshipmen and steer ships and shoot guns, whom we install as dictator without the grace of God.

"War," *Crisis* 33 (February 1927) 179; *Selection from* The Crisis, vol. 2 (1983) 457.

726. WAR AMONG UNEQUALS

The very men who would view with displeasure if not horror increasing armaments for war between France, England, Germany and the United States, can easily be brought to see a number of vague but very real duties which England has in India and America in Manchuria and France in Indo-China.

"The Economics of War," October 26, 1931; microfilm reel no. 80, frame no. 444; W.E.B. Du Bois Papers, University of Massachusetts, Amherst.

727. WORLD WAR II

The war was won by Russian manpower working with Anglo-American science and wealth. . . . It was Russia and Russia alone . . . that saved the British Empire and the American Commonwealth from the domination of Germany, Italy and Japan.

"Democracy's Opportunity," *Christian Register* 125 (August 1946) 350–51; *Writings by W.E.B. Du Bois in Periodicals Edited by Others*. vol. 4 (1982) 12.

18

Some Other Countries

728. ASIA FOR ASIANS

I believe in Japan. It is not that I sympathize with China less but that I hate white European and American propaganda, theft and insult more. I believe in Asia for the Asiatics and despite the hell of war and the fascism of capital, I see in Japan the best agent for this end.

Letter to Waldo McNutt, February 25, 1939; *Correspondence*, II, 185.

The sudden American love for China is not repentance for the race hate that still excludes Chinese from our shores, but simply fear of losing to Japan the immense profit of exploiting Asia. The control of Asia by Asiatics could not possibly have such frightful results as the exploitation of Asia by Europe has already had.

To Joseph North, ca. August 1941; microfilm reel no. 53, frame no. 107; W.E.B. Du Bois Papers, University of Massachusetts, Amherst.

729. CHINA

[In Shanghai during 1936] I saw a little English boy of perhaps four years order three Chinese children out of his imperial way on the sidewalk . . . ; and they meekly obeyed and walked in the gutter. It looked quite like Mississippi.

Autobiography (1968) 45.

This ancient and magnificent civilization, which has again and again set goals for human culture, is today staggering and uncertain and can look for rapid rebirth only if she has the goodwill, the economic support, and the social co-operation of the United States and Western Europe.

Color and Democracy (1945) 6–7.

The Chinese will remain bound by debt, by commercial combines, and by monopoly industry in continued subjection to the great industrial nations of the West.

Color and Democracy (1945) 60.

[In 1959] we saw the planning of a nation and a system of work rising over the entrails of dead empire.

Autobiography (1968) 47.

730. CONQUERING RUSSIA

[During the 1920s, some circles in Germany advocated the] occupation and exploitation of the Russian Heartland. This was doubly attractive, because by such a venture the demands of German capital and labor could both be met and the menace of Communism destroyed forever. The lure of the program was all the greater because of the economic history of Germany since the First World War [1914–1918]. Wealth and power in western Europe had been shaken but not overthrown. In Germany it had been shattered.

Russia and America: An Interpretation (1950, unpublished); microfilm reel no. 85, frame no. 443; W.E.B. Du Bois Papers, University of Massachusetts, Amherst.

731. CUBA

The Board of Directors of the National Association for the Advancement of Colored People wishes to express its deep sympathy with the people of Cuba in their struggle for a free popular government, which will be uncoerced by domestic tyranny or by foreign interference.

Proposed resolution, December 19, 1930; microfilm reel no. 32, frame no. 97; W.E.B. Du Bois Papers, University of Massachusetts, Amherst.

The present Negro population of Cuba probably runs to about seventy percent despite official statistics. The Negroes form naturally the bulk of the poor, ignorant and untrained. The American economic penetration has monopolized the resources of the island and made the Negro's opportunity worse. There are now Negro and white jobs and open discrimination in pay.

Black Folk Then and Now (1939) 190.

732. EASTERN EUROPE

To call these [Baltic] peoples "captive" [of the USSR] is misleading. The great mass of them were the pawns of privilege and exploitation. . . . Their upper classes represented the rich and privileged among them who called the nation their property, and sought to dominate it for their own personal advantage, assuming that what was good for the ruling classes was best for all.

Autobiography (1968) 27.

733. FIGHTING RUSSIA

[On April 20, 1949, in Paris, Paul Robeson] said: "The black folk of America will never fight against the Soviet Union!" What . . . he really was saying was: From my nature and belief, it is to me inconceivable that 15,000,000 descendants of Negro slaves who know from bitter and continuing experience what race prejudice and the enslavement of Africa and Asia has done not only to my people, but to civilization and Christianity and human decency for 500 years— it is inconceivable that these people would in any single case willingly join in war against the one great modern country which has opposed prejudice in a land once riddled by it, and the conquest and subjection of colonies in a world where colonial imperialism has murdered millions and which is suffering today in the eyes of Britain, France and America, mainly for this stand.

"Paul Robeson: Right or Wrong? Right," *Negro Digest* 7 (March 1950); *Writings by W.E.B. Du Bois in Periodicals Edited by Others*, vol. 4 (1982) 136, 137.

734. FRANCE

The one splendid thing about France of today, is the persistence of freedom of thought and expression. It was like a bath in clear, cold water to be six weeks in a country where people of intelligence and conviction were not afraid to talk, where a man has a right to be a communist and defend Russia, and another has equal right to praise the United States and the Marshall Plan, neither is smeared, jailed nor driven to suicide. . . . It is permissible to stand up and advocate peace without losing your right to earn a living.

Address by W.E.B. Du Bois. Welcome Home Rally for Paul Robeson, New York, June 19, 1949; microfilm reel no. 63; frame no. 904; W.E.B. Du Bois Papers, University of Massachusetts, Amherst.

735. FRANCE AND ENGLAND

The difference between England and France in color prejudice is the fact that England has invested in color prejudice. She has large property interests whose profits depend upon keeping yellow, black and brown men "in their place." France has much less and only recent investment of this sort. And in addition to that, French-speaking mulattoes and blacks for more than two centuries have been educated in France and brought into close contact with the best classes of French people.

To Dudley S. Mackenzie, February 7, 1928; microfilm reel no. 25, frame no. 975; W.E.B. Du Bois Papers, University of Massachusetts, Amherst.

736. FRENCH RACISM

When I first went to France in 1894, it would have been unthinkable that any French hotel or boarding house would have refused to receive a black guest for any reason unconnected with his cultural and personal deportment. Today, that is no longer so. Americans are able to dictate to Frenchmen in all lines of life, and while they have not succeeded in closing entirely hotels and restaurants to Negroes, they have made it much more difficult.

T. J. G. Fleury, undated [December 1932?]; microfilm reel no. 37, frame no. 21; W.E.B. Du Bois Papers, University of Massachusetts, Amherst.

There has grown up a legend among us that France is especially Negrophile and can be depended upon to champion the Negro race.

Pittsburgh Courier, February 8, 1936; *Newspaper Columns by, W.E.B. Du Bois* (1986) 26.

737. GERMAN OPENNESS

[In 1892, while I studied in Germany its people who sang the national anthem] expressed a love of the fatherland which I as a Negro had never felt for America. And of course, what had impressed me particularly more perhaps than was altogether just was the absence of a color line and of the deep sort of race consciousness which existed in the United States. Shades of this, of course, were there in the Jewish question, but that was treated at that time with reason. There was no dream of violence or fear for the future.

"Germany," October 8, 1954; microfilm reel no. 81, frame no. 922; W.E.B. Du Bois Papers, University of Massachusetts, Amherst.

738. GERMANY

I think that the German people are a great and fine folk misled by the Hitler movement. That movement has not spoiled their essential humanity but it has gravely influenced their methods of thought and ideals of action.

To Anna M. Graves, July 9, 1946; microfilm reel no. 58, frame no. 969; W.E.B. Du Bois Papers, University of Massachusetts, Amherst.

I had strong affection for Germany, because in the days of my Sturm and Drang [Storm and Stress, 1892–1894], this was the land where I first met white folk who treated me as a human being. At the time it bolstered my faith in the world and gave me strength to face and fight its wrongdoing.

Russia and America: An Interpretation (1950, unpublished); microfilm reel no. 85, frame no. 443; W.E.B. Du Bois Papers, University of Massachusetts, Amherst.

I . . . dislike intensely the denazification procedures so far in Germany. I do not think that Nazi party members ought to be restored to power.

To Mrs. Abraham Tow, October 27, 1950; microfilm real no. 64; frame no. 794; W.E.B. Du Bois Papers, University of Massachusetts, Amherst.

739. GERMANY DEFEATED

Germans have followed 12 years of race superiority, the right of might and the use of lies. We have conquered Germany but not their ideas. We still believe in white supremacy, keeping Negroes in their places and lying about democracy, when we mean imperial control of 750 million of human beings in colonies.

Telegram to Metz T. P. Lochard, May 4, 1945; *Correspondence*, II, 39.

740. GOOD BREEDING

[Late in the 19th century] the concept of the European "gentleman" was evolved: a man well bred and of meticulous grooming, of knightly sportsmanship and invincible courage even in the face of death; but one who did not hesitate to use machine guns against assagais and to cheat "'niggers."

The World and Africa (1947, 1965) 23.

741. HAITI

The United States has violated the independence of a sister state. With absolutely no adequate excuse she had made a white American Admiral sole and irresponsible dictator of Hayti. . . . Here, then, is the outrage of uninvited American intervention, the shooting and disarming of peaceful Haytian citizens, the seizure of public funds, the veiled, but deliberate design to alienate Haytian territory at the Mole St. Nicholas, and the pushing of the monopoly chains of an American corporation which holds a filched, if not a fraudulent railway charter. SHAME ON AMERICA!

"Hayti," *Crisis* 10 (October 1915) 291; *Selections from* The Crisis, vol. 1 (1983) 106.

The United States is at war with Haiti. Congress has never sanctioned this war. [The Secretary of the Navy] has illegally and unjustly occupied a free foreign land and murdered its inhabitants by the thousands. He has deposed its officials and dispersed its legally elected representatives. He is carrying on a reign of terror, browbeating, and cruelty, at the hands of southern white naval officers and marines.

"Haiti," *Crisis* 19 (April 1920) 297–98; *Selections from* The Crisis, vol. 1 (1983) 256.

The people of Haiti have maintained, on the whole, a decent and stable government, much more stable than the governments of France or England during the 18th century.

To Anna B. Griscom, May 20, 1929; microfilm reel no. 27, frame no. 1144; W.E.B.
     Du Bois Papers, University of Massachusetts, Amherst.

[After the revolution was won by armed black slaves] the civilized world almost to a man was united against them. The United States of America refused to recognize them for sixty years. France waited thirty years and then recognized them only on condition that they pay her an indemnity of $30,000,000, which was probably three times Haiti's total annual exports at the time.

"Haiti," December 21, 1929; microfilm reel no. 80, frame no. 371; W.E.B. Du Bois
    Papers, University of Massachusetts, Amherst.

Having seized Haiti, what have we done there? With ourselves as chief creditor, we have distributed to ourselves and other creditors Haitian revenues for the payment of her debts, admitting any claim that had the slightest color of validity. Thus, she has been saddled with a funded debt which will keep her in economic slavery to the United States for many generations.

"Haiti," December 21, 1929; microfilm reel no. 80, frame no. 374; W.E.B. Du Bois
    Papers, University of Massachusetts, Amherst.

[After the end of U.S. occupation in 1934,] Haiti was compelled to accept a debt which was nothing less than highway robbery and included every alleged "contract" that it could, under the most disadvantageous terms. Haiti again became "free," but her existence depended upon a dictatorship which must, on the one hand, keep the peace; and, on the other hand, pay enormous and continuous tribute to the banks of New York. An American fiscal officer sits in Port au Prince with his hands on the treasury, seeing that the profit of foreign investors, made permanent by the debt agreement, is paid before anything can be done for Haitian labor in wage, education, health or social advance.

Black Folk Then and Now (1939) 185.

There was a time when the Negroes of Haiti kept as far as possible from intercourse with and knowledge of American Negroes; but they found out in the attempt which the United States made to conquer Haiti that it was the political power of American Negroes which blocked the effort and secured at least the beginning of their release.

Letter to E. Sylvia Pankhurst, July 31, 1946; *Correspondence*, III, 133.

742. IMPERIALISM

The people of Britain were determined to proceed on the whole along the same paths which they had followed in the past— . . . they were determined to maintain their comforts and civilization by using cheap labor and raw materials, seized without rightful compensation. . . . (1958)

Autobiography (1968) 15.

743. INDEPENDENT INDIA

American Negroes, particularly, have every reason to hail the new and free India. It is a freedom and autonomy of colored folk; it ends the day in a whole continent, when the white man by reason of the color of his skin, can bring his segregation and his cheap habits of superiority, as shown by exclusive clubs,

"Jim Crow" cars and salaams and the other paraphernalia of disgraceful human degradation. The sun of the colored man has arisen in Asia, as it will yet arise in Africa and America and the West Indies.

"The Freeing of India," *Crisis* 54 (October 1947) 301–04, 316–17; *Writings by W.E.B. Du Bois in Periodicals Edited by Others*, vol. 4 (1982) 41.

744. LIBERIA

Liberia can only be understood as it is envisaged as a part of the imperial expansion of industry, and its failure to achieve economic security and therefore political independence, is due to no racial traits or failures, but to the same forces that have made the small state and the small business almost impossible today throughout the world.

To Macmillan and Co., February 4, 1935; microfilm reel no. 44, frame no. 587; W.E.B. Du Bois Papers, University of Massachusetts, Amherst.

745. LOUISIANA AND HAITI

[The United States has] tried to displace . . . Haiti's natural leaders by foreigners, who disfranchise them, and whose attitude they quickly realize. A large proportion of these foreigners come from Louisiana. If Louisiana has any civilization to spare, she should use it at home. The state is one of the most illiterate in the United States; it has lynched nine hundred persons in the last twenty years; it has been repeatedly swept by mobs and lawlessness. With the best intentions in the world, no white man, born and trained in Louisiana, is fit to attempt the social uplift of Negroes.

"Haiti," December 21, 1929; microfilm reel no. 80, frame no. 374; W.E.B. Du Bois Papers, University of Massachusetts, Amherst.

746. MANCHUKUO

[Compared with the Japanese colony of Manchukuo, formerly the Chinese Manchuria] I have come to the firm conclusion that in no [other] colony that I have seen or read of is there such clear evidence of (1) absence of racial or color caste; (2) impartial law and order; (3) public control of private capital for the general welfare; (4) services for health, education, city-planning, housing, consumers' cooperation and other social ends; (5) the incorporation of the natives into the administration of government and social readjustment.

Pittsburgh Courier, February 13, 1937; *Newspaper Columns by W.E.B. Du Bois* (1986) 167.

747. NAZI GERMANY

I am going to write *The Courier* four letters about Germany. I have written already a word here and there about minor aspects of the German scene. I am sure my friends have understood my hesitations and reticence; it simply wasn't safe to attempt anything further. Even my mail, when Mrs. Du Bois sent me a minor receipt to sign, was opened to see if money was being smuggled in. But now I have ended my sojourn—or at least shall have long before this is published; and to insure its reaching *The Courier* on time I am taking it to a foreign land to mail.

Pittsburgh Courier, December 5, 1936; *Newspaper Columns by W.E.B. Du Bois* vol. 1 (1986) 142.

After four months in Germany 1936 I am distinctly against the Nazi regime.

Telegram to Charlotte Sanders, January 16, 1937; microfilm reel no. 48, frame no. 465; W.E.B. Du Bois Papers, University of Massachusetts, Amherst.

748. OVERSEAS COLOR LINE

There is in London and England today nothing like the hard and fast color-bar that we know in America. On the street, in restaurants, in theaters and public places one is treated with courtesy and served with alacrity. He is in England as elsewhere in Europe a matter of some curiosity according to the depth of his color. But it is curiosity and not insult.

Pittsburgh Courier, September 5, 1936; *Newspaper Columns by W.E.B. Du Bois* (1986) 111–112.

749. PROPER TITLES

I am glad of the matter which you sent to the Emperor of Ethiopia But remember that he must not be addressed as "Your Excellency." He is "His Imperial Majesty" and has a right to that title stretching back a couple of thousand years. We say "Excellency" to ambassadors but not to ruling monarchs.

To Alphaeus Hunton, June 8, 1954; microfilm reel no. 70, frame no. 544; W.E.B. Du Bois Papers, University of Massachusetts, Amherst.

750. REST IN CUBA

I am thinking of spending a quiet ten days in Cuba early in June. . . . I do not want to meet celebrities or have any attention shown me. I just want a quiet rest in a colored country.

To Rayford W. Logan, May 5, 1941; microfilm reel no. 52, frame no. 1219; W.E.B. Du Bois Papers, University of Massachusetts, Amherst.

751. RULERS AND RULED

The English middle class and the English laborers agree with the ruling class in the fear of allowing primitive and half-civilized peoples and peoples with non-European types of culture, to act and think for themselves and share in their own government.

Black Folk Then and Now (1939) 373.

752. SIERRA LEONE

Police, sanitation, the harbor, business and commerce in general and all matters to do with the natives and education are all under the protectorate Government. And not only are the courts under the white protectorate, but as jurors must be black, the white court can at its will in criminal cases abolish trial by jury, and in all cases, the white judges, sitting as a Court of Appeal pass on their own judgements! . . . At the head of this Government is the autocratic Governor who is practically a king by divine right.

Africa—Its Place in Modern History (1930) 55.

753. SOVIET REFORM

In the United States many persons have firmly convinced themselves that Russian Communism is going capitalist; that the already established differences of income level and rewards for quality of work rather than quantity will eventually be supplemented by increased private property and even to some extent by private ownership of capital.

Color and Democracy (1945) 114.

754. SOVIET UNION

Never had I seen such public interest in social matters on the part of men, women and children. . . . What amazed and uplifted me in 1926, was to see a nation stoutly facing a problem which most other nations did not dare even to admit was real: the abolition of poverty.

Autobiography (1968) 30.

Is it possible to conduct a great modern government without autocratic leadership of the rich? The answer is: this is exactly what the Soviet Union is doing today.

Autobiography (1968) 37.

Even should the Russian experiment fail and Communism be proved unable to cope with the problems of land, property, and income, Russia deserves all credit for having at least faced the problem and for having tried to solve it; and other nations must eventually face and solve the same problem if civilization is going to be preserved.

Color and Democracy (1945) 122.

755. JOSEPH STALIN

We Negro Americans are of many different political beliefs and affiliations. We unite, however, in hailing your leadership in uprooting racial discrimination and national oppression from your land of many peoples.

"Proposed 70th Birthday Greeting to Stalin," 1949; microfilm reel no. 64, frame no. 334; W.E.B. Du Bois Papers, University of Massachusetts, Amherst.

I still regard Stalin as one of the great men of the twentieth century. He was not perfect; he was probably too cruel; but he did three things: he established the first socialist state in the modern world; he broke the power of the kulaks; and he conquered Hitler. If in his later years he became an irresponsible tyrant, that was very bad and I am sorry for it. . . . As to the general fairness of these [Moscow] trials [during the 1930s], even reliable American observers like Raymond Robbins testified.

To Anna M. Graves, July 8, 1956; microfilm reel no. 71, frame no. 1177; W.E.B. Du Bois Papers, University of Massachusetts, Amherst.

756.   STATUS AND CULTURE

Equality of status, where there is as yet no real equality of culture and habit, has been endlessly inveighed against, from the French Revolution to the Emancipation of Negroes. This, in 1936, greatly bothered observers of Russia. They were obsessed by the glamor of culture and wealth in a few despite the degradation of the mass on which this culture was built.

Russia and America: An Interpretation (1950, unpublished); microfilm reel no. 85, frame no. 453; W.E.B. Du Bois Papers, University of Massachusetts, Amherst.

757.   SURVEILLANCE

When I was in England about 38 years ago, conducting the second Pan-African Congress, the Government suspecting I might be attempting to overthrow the Empire, set an intelligence agent on my trail. We came to be very good friends and later when he became District Commissioner in Uganda he sent me a beautiful leopard skin which lay on my living room floor for 30 years or more.

To Mr. and Mrs. Frederick Arkhurst, January 4, 1959; microfilm reel no. 73, frame no. 580; W.E.B. Du Bois Papers, University of Massachusetts, Amherst.

758.   TUNISIA

The secret of French power here is her refusal to draw a color line. A Negro of ability can get recognition and preferment. He can, if he has the money, attend schools in France. He can exploit his fellow Negroes as completely and cruelly as any white man if he has capital. Thus the black mass is drained of its natural leadership; the authority and ancient social customs of the tribe are replaced by Paris ideals and the black mass festers. (1955)

The World and Africa (1947, 1965), 274–75.

19

Politics

759. BADGES OF SUPERIORITY

Georgia bribes its white labor by giving it public badges of superiority. The Jim Crow legislation was not to brand the Negro as inferior and to separate the races, but rather to flatter white labor to accept public testimony of its superiority instead of higher wages and social legislation. . . . He had a right to the title of "Mister" and "Mrs." . . . He could often demand that a Negro . . . yield him precedence on the pavement and in the store. . . . No municipal improvements must invade the Negro quarter until every white quarter approached perfection or until typhoid threatened the whites.

"Georgia: Invisible Empire State," in Ernest Gruening (ed.), *These United States*, II (New York: Boni and Liveright, 1924) 322–45; *Writings by W.E.B. Du Bois in Periodicals Edited by Others*, vol. 2 (1982) 140.

760. BALANCE OF POWER

The South will not always be *solid*, and in every *division* the Negro will hold the balance of power.

"An Open Letter to the Southern People" (1887); *Against Racism* (1985) 3–4.

761. THE BALLOT

The power of the ballot we need in sheer self-defense,—else what shall save us from a second slavery?

The Souls of Black Folk (1903) 11.

762. BLACK CONGRESSMEN

Adam [Clayton] Powell . . . is going to be elected Congressman. We will then have a second Negro member in Congress. This is of great importance. It ought to be followed up by the election of Negro congressmen from Pennsylvania and St. Louis. Once we get a really vocal group of Negro representatives in Washington, the course of history in this land is going to be altered.

Amsterdam News, April 15, 1944; *Newspaper Columns by W.E.B. Du Bois* (1986) 585.

763. CITIZENSHIP

Yet this conversion of public opinion in the United States to Negro citizenship and suffrage was long and difficult. . . . Was it good policy . . . to raise a great new working, voting class? On this point there was less open argument; but it lay in the minds of business men, and influenced their outlook and action.

Black Reconstruction (1935) 258.

Unless the right to vote had been given the Negro by Federal law in 1867, he would never have got it in America. There never has been a time since when race propaganda in America offered the slightest chance for colored people to receive American citizenship. There would have been, therefore, perpetuated in the South and in America, a permanently disfranchised mass of laborers; and the dictatorship of capital would, under those circumstances, have been even more firmly implanted than it is today.

Black Reconstruction (1935) 606.

764. CORRUPTION AND WEALTH

This brings us to the center of the corruption charge, which was in fact that poor men were ruling and taxing rich men. And this was the chief reason that ridicule and scorn and crazy anger were poured upon the government. There was after the [Civil] war a severe economic strain upon the former wealthy ruling class, and if South Carolina had been ruled by angels during 1868–1876, the protest of wealth and property would have been shrill and angry, and it would have had all the justification that the war-ridden always have.

Black Reconstruction (1935) 419–420.

765. DELIBERATE RACISM

[In his 1906 campaign for Governor of Georgia, Hoke] Smith started out to attack the corporations, especially the railroads. . . . Smith's attacks were stinging, and I have no doubt but what he was offered great inducements . . . to change the direction of his attacks, and that he found that the easiest way to do this was direct his attacks upon the Negro. This brought the support of [Tom] Watson and his followers, warded off the wrath of the corporations, and made him Governor of Georgia.

To Dewey W. Grantham, Jr., September 13, 1952; microfilm reel no. 168, frame no. 322; W.E.B. Du Bois Papers, University of Massachusetts, Amherst.

766. DEMOCRATIC PARTY

The Democratic party is prepared to play the jackass in 1936 as it did in 1896 with a radical head and a reactionary rump, progressing backward and getting nowhere.

Pittsburgh Courier, February 15, 1936; *Newspaper Columns by W.E.B. Du Bois* (1986) 28.

767. EFFECTIVE ENFRANCHISEMENT

A free ballot in the hands of a free man is the one way for maintaining democracy and insuring social progress. But before such a ballot can be used the man must be free of the threat of poverty and the chains of ignorance. . . . It is the poverty of black America that is the real basis and cause of our disfranchisement. . . . So long as the mass of American Negroes are too poor to live decently, they cannot vote freely no matter how legal their political rights may be.

Amsterdam News, May 8, 1943; *Newspaper Columns by W.E.B. Du Bois* (1986) 521.

768. 1924 ELECTION

The Ku Klux Klan, supporting Republican candidates, won notable triumphs in Indiana, Kansas, Oklahoma and Colorado and suffered defeat only in Texas where the Republicans were defeated.

"The Election," *Crisis* 29 (December 1924) 55–56; *Selections from* The Crisis, vol. 1 (1983) 414.

769. HONEST ELECTIONS

The elections [of 1868] which reconstructed the South under the Congressional plan were fair and honest elections, and probably never before were such democratic elections held in the South and never since such fair elections.

Black Reconstruction (1935) 372.

770. IGNORANCE

Although the greater number of ignorant voters in the south are those of Negro blood, yet no small number of white voters are just as ignorant and just as unfit to rule. In other words it is ignorance and not blackness which menaced civilization in the south.

"The Afro-American" (ca. 1894–1896), Series 3/C, Folder no. 5502, *Unpublished Articles*; W.E.B. Du Bois Papers, University of Massachusetts, Amherst.

771. INTEGRATION

Extreme opponents of segregation act as though there was but one solution of the race problem, and that, complete integration of the black race with the white race in America, with no distinction of color in political, civil or social life. There is no doubt but what this is the great end toward which humanity is tending, and that so long as there are artificially emphasized differences of nationality, race and color, not to mention the fundamental discrimination of economic class, there will be no real Humanity. On the other hand, it is just as clear, that not for a century and more probably not for ten centuries, will any such consummation be reached. No person born will ever live to see national and racial distinction altogether abolished, and economic distinctions will last many a day.

"Segregation in the North," *Crisis* 41 (April 1934) 115–17; *Selections from* The Crisis, vol. 2 (1983) 750.

772. INFLUENCE

For three centuries disreputable Negroes have been pushed forward by influential whites and given power over their fellows in return for abject obedience to the dictates of whites.

To Louis F. Post, April 19, 1918; microfilm reel no. 7, frame no. 85; W.E.B. Du Bois Papers, University of Massachusetts, Amherst.

I have sympathy for the ideal of cold, impartial history; but that must not be allowed to degenerate as it has so often into insensibility to human suffering and injustice. The scientific treatment of human ills has got to give evil full weight and vividly realize what it means to be among the world's oppressed.

Letter to Augustus M. Kelley, September 28, 1938; *Correspondence* II, 174.

773. MISSISSIPPI SHERIFFS

A Mississippi sheriff is elected by such local persons as are allowed to vote. He serves as Sheriff and Tax-Collector for four years; he is the arresting official and jailor; he is paid by unrevealed and unlimited fees and is practically czar of the county, especially of such counties as have majority of voteless Negroes living in virtual peonage. By a late law, a sheriff who loses a prisoner by mob violence may be removed by the Governor, but seldom has a Governor dared use this power. The succeeding sheriff can refuse to punish the mob.

"The Senators from Mississippi," February 8, 1956; microfilm reel no. 81, frame no. 1004; W.E.B. Du Bois Papers, University of Massachusetts, Amherst.

774. NATIONAL CRIME

It is wrong to aid and abet a national crime simply because it is unpopular not to do so.

The Souls of Black Folk (1903) 55.

775. THE NEGRO VOTE

I must support the Tammany candidate because of the things which he had done for Harlem. Tammany, in fact, has been the only political friend of black Harlem that I have seen in the last fifteen years. It has given us colored policemen, appointments of colored men to hospital staffs, traffic lights, and whenever I have complaints or requests, I had at least a courtesy hearing.

"A Memorandum to the Executive Committee [of the League for Independent Political Action]," February 25, 1930; microfilm reel no. 31, frame no. 809; W.E.B. Du Bois Papers, University of Massachusetts, Amherst.

776. PACKAGE DEAL

The Dyer Anti-lynching Bill went through the House of Representatives and on to the floor of the Senate. There in 1924 it died with a filibuster and the abject surrender of its friends. It was not until years after that I knew what killed the anti-lynching bill. It was a bargain between the South and the West. By this bargain, lynching was let to go on uncurbed by Federal law, on condition that the Japanese be excluded from the United States.

Dusk of Dawn (1940) 266.

777. PARTY DIFFERENCES

There is little difference between Southern Democrats and Southern Republicans as far as the Negro is concerned.

To Anna V. Brown, March 7, 1938; microfilm reel no. 48, frame no. 779; W.E.B. Du Bois Papers, University of Massachusetts, Amherst.

778. PHILADELPHIA POLITICS

Why are Philadelphia politics dirty? Because the most influential and respected citizens of the town are using public business for private gain. White citizens find that franchises, concession, and favorable administration furnish them the most money. Negroes, being barred from business, largely find the actual salaries of office not only the greatest attraction, but an actual matter of bread and butter.

"The Black Vote of Philadelphia," *Charities* 15 (October 7, 1905) 31–35; *Writings by W.E.B. Du Bois in Periodicals Edited by Others*, vol. 1 (1982) 261.

779. POLITICAL AND ECONOMIC CONTROL

It was inconceivable . . . that the masters of Northern industry through their growing control of American government, were going to allow the [black and white] laborers of the South any more real control of wealth and industry than was necessary to curb the political power of the planters and their successors. As soon as the Southern landholders and merchants yielded to the Northern demands of a plutocracy, at that moment the military dictatorship [by federal troops] should be withdrawn and dictatorship of capital allowed unhampered sway.

Black Reconstruction (1935) 345–346.

780. POLITICAL PARTIES

The Negro faces two major political parties: the Democrats and the Republicans. They stand essentially for the same thing. They represent a dictatorship of organized industry which is running the United States for the benefit of the owners of wealth. Perhaps the most characteristic thing of our present era is the frankness with which this truth is today openly admitted. What difference does it make, then, whether the Negro votes the Republican or Democratic ticket? He is voting for the same essential dictatorship. Both parties agree in a policy which nullifies the popular vote, limits the wages of common labor, monopolizes capital and land, supports the state mainly by taxes upon the poor, and increases the income of the rich by privilege and administration.

"The Strategy of the Negro Vote," *Crisis* 40 (June 1933) 140–142; *Selections from* The
    Crisis, vol. 2 (1983) 707.

[In Great Barrington, Mass.] we were nearly all Republicans. Indeed, it was not respectable to be anything else; one of our prominent lawyers . . . was a Democrat and we suspected him of low origin and questionable designs.

Autobiography (1968) 91.

781. POLITICS OF SUFFERING

When a right and just cause loses, men suffer. But men also suffer when a wrong cause loses. Suffering thus in itself does not prove the justice or injustice of a cause.

Black Reconstruction (1935) 129.

782. POPULAR GOVERNMENT

If people insist on voting for men regardless of the things that those men stand for, simply because they think the men are conscientious, then democracy is not going to be able to reform itself, and popular opinion is not going to perform its just function. The tendency of the Negro vote today in the United States is that the average Negro, even when intelligent in casting his vote out of courtesy and benevolence, instead of sternly insisting that a representative must do the will of his constituents or expect to be defeated at the next election, and that such defeat is not vengeance, not revengeful, not boastful, it is simply the only way in which popular government can function.

To Mr. Loud, October 21, 1930; microfilm reel no. 32, frame no. 118; W.E.B. Du Bois
    Papers, University of Massachusetts, Amherst.

783. POPULIST PARTY

The South said: The trend to a Third Party must be stopped by splitting the labor movement. The obvious way to do this was by using the natural and doubtless God-given difference of race in the laboring class to keep them separated. Race difference must be the emphasized and enforced by law.

The Ordeal of Mansart (1957) 176.

784. POWER AND LAW

Our millionaires of the 19th century were too often men who got their wealth by cheating, force and violence. Today our rich men obey the letter of the law. But this is chiefly because the rich wield so great influence today in making the law and enforcing it.

National Guardian, December 26, 1955; *Newspaper Columns by W.E.B. Du Bois* (1986) 945.

785. PROPERTY AND POWER

Men were seeking again to reestablish the domination of property in Southern politics. By getting rid of the black labor vote, they would take their first and substantial step. By raising the race issue, they would secure domination over the white labor vote, and thus the oligarchy that ruled the South before the war would be in part restored to power.

Black Reconstruction (1935) 428–429.

786. SOCIALIST PARTY

Socialist [party] organizers in the south have not only held separate meetings for whites and blacks, but in many cases have not been allowed by the local Socialists to hold any meetings for Negroes at all. The "Ripsaw," edited by Kate Richards O'Hare and several other Socialists in Tennessee, Texas, and Oklahoma, has often carried virulent anti-Negro articles.

To Mrs. Edmund C. Evans, December 6, 1920; microfilm reel no. 8, frame no. 1260; W.E.B. Du Bois Papers, University of Massachusetts, Amherst.

787. VOTELESS NEGROES

The voteless Negro is a provocation, an invitation to oppression, a plaything for mobs and a bonanza for demagogues. They serve always to distract attention from real issues and to ride fools and rascals into political power.

"Politics and Industry," May 31, 1909; microfilm reel no. 80, frame no. 190; W.E.B. Du Bois Papers, University of Massachusetts, Amherst.

788. WEALTH AND POWER

Most modern countries are in the hands of those who control organized wealth and . . . the just and wise distribution of income is hindered by this monopoly. This power is entrenched behind barriers of legal sanction, guarded by the best brains of the country trained as lawyers, appointed to the bench, and elected to the legislature. The retention of this power is influenced tremendously by the propaganda of newspapers and news-gathering agencies, by radio and by social organization. The hand of organized wealth guides the education of youth.

Color and Democracy (1945) 75.

789. WHOLLY OWNED SUBSIDIARY

Today Congress is owned and directed by the great aggregations of Business— the Steel Trust, the Copper Syndicate, the Aluminum Monopoly, the Textile Industry, the Farming Capitalists and a dozen others, while the Consumers and mass of workers are only partially articulate and can enforce their demands only by votes which are largely ineffective; the great interests can compel action by offering legislators financial security, profitable employment and direct bribes.

Memorandum to Walter White, October 10, 1946; *Correspondence*, III, 124.

20

General

790. A CENTURY HENCE

It is impossible to know how long such a social and economic problem as the South now faces will require for its solution. A century seems long to the living, but it is quite short and reasonable in the history of the world. I should be very glad if the South straightened itself out in much less time than a century, but I doubt it. As you say, "There is but one way out of a hole, and that is up." But when you add, "We must rise soon," I would advise putting the period after "rise."

To Emmett Carter, March 1, 1956; microfilm reel no. 71, frame no. 1084; W.E.B. Du Bois Papers, University of Massachusetts, Amherst.

791. ABSOLVING PROBLEMS

We have a way in America of wanting to be "rid" of problems. It is not so much a desire to reach the best and largest solution as it is to clean the board and start a new game. For instance, most Americans are simply tired and impatient over our most sinister social problem, the Negro. They do not want to solve it, they do not want to understand it, they want to simply be done with it and hear the last of it. Of all possible attitudes this is the most dangerous, because it fails to realize the most significant fact of the opening century, viz: The Negro problem in America is but a local phase of a world problem.

"The Color Line Belts the World," *Collier's Weekly*, Oct. 20, 1906, p. 30; *Writings by W.E.B. Du Bois in Periodicals Edited by Others*, vol. 1 (1982) 330.

792. ADVANTAGE OF DISADVANTAGE

Segregated as a social group there are many semi-social functions in which the prevailing prejudice makes it pleasanter that he should serve himself if possible. Undertakers, for instance. . . . Newspapers. . . . These enterprises are peculiar instances of the "advantage of the disadvantage"—of the way in which a hostile environment has forced the Negro to do for himself.

The Negro in Business (1899) 14–15.

793. ADVICE

There is no royal way to success. If you have talent use it and use it right where you are.

To D. V. Coleman, January 8, 1925; microfilm reel no. 15, frame no. 80; W.E.B. Du Bois Papers, University of Massachusetts, Amherst.

794. AMERICAN MUSIC

There is no true American music but the wild sweet melodies of the Negro slave.

The Souls of Black Folk (1903) 11.

795. ANY OTHER NAME

No name ever hurt or helped a person or a people in the long run. . . . The word "Negro" . . . may be used in contempt but it can only become entirely contemptuous when the people who are Negroes are ashamed of themselves. Names grow and change like other human institutions. . . . Whether you like . . . [the word "Negro"] or not it will continue to be used, and the only thing that should interest you and me is whether the people who are called by that name are honest, intelligent and hard-working, or dishonest, idiotic, and lazy. Character not names are important in this world.

To R. H. Ball, September 1, 1931; microfilm reel no. 34, frame no. 549; W.E.B. Du Bois Papers, University of Massachusetts, Amherst.

The word "Negro" comes from the Latin word "niger" meaning black. It was first used as a descriptive term for Africans and others and finally it came to be a conventional name for the black race and for American descendants of black slaves, even those who had a considerable mixture of white blood.

Any name is always a convention, an agreement, a combination of letters which conveys the same idea to different people. There is nothing scientific about any name. If people agree to change it, they can.

To Ezell Bowie, October 5, 1945; microfilm reel no. 56, frame no. 1207; W.E.B. Du Bois Papers, University of Massachusetts, Amherst.

A name [of a large group] is not a matter of individual choice or even of historical accuracy, it is a matter of general understanding and agreement and the result of long and intricate growth of culture patterns. When, therefore, we say the "black race" or the "Negro people," everybody on earth understands exactly what we mean.

It is not a question of historical accuracy or scientific definition, but a clear and indisputable fact. It can be changed only by a long and intricate process involving complete change of culture patterns, and since in this case the change would have no real meaning, why worry about it?

If black people were called epilogimistes instead of Negroes they would still be the same people with the same problems, with the same past and future.

To Elechukwu Njakar, November 27, 1950; microfilm reel no. 65, frame no. 397; W.E.B. Du Bois Papers, University of Massachusetts, Amherst.

796. ART AND BEAUTY

[Art] doesn't even care anything about nature. It doesn't even have to be beautiful. It simply has to be.

To Anne F. Jenkins, April 17, 1926; microfilm reel no. 19, frame no. 26; W.E.B. Du Bois Papers, University of Massachusetts, Amherst.

797. AUSPICIOUS AUSPICES

Unless certain investigations into the condition of the Negro are done by liberal agencies, we are bound to get all our information from unfair sources.

Memorandum to James Weldon Johnson, January 15, 1925; microfilm reel no. 15, frame no. 1218; W.E.B. Du Bois Papers, University of Massachusetts, Amherst.

798. BACK-HOME PRODUCTION

In the case of my own little town the process of life, the process of work and the matter was pretty well known to everybody. We went to the store and looked over potatoes and if the price was too high you said, "I will not pay that for the potatoes. If you don't come down on your price, I will not buy them." You knew how clothes were made. Practically the whole of the processes were known to people.

"Individualism, Democracy and Social Control," March 14, 1944; microfilm reel no. 80, frame no. 866; W.E.B. Du Bois Papers, University of Massachusetts, Amherst.

799. BEAUTY

Let us train ourselves to see beauty in black.

"In Black," *Crisis* 20 (October 1920) 263–66; *Selections from* The Crisis, vol. 1 (1983) 278.

800. BEING FRANK

Great heavens, don't you love to be frank and open?

Yes, sometimes I do; once I was; but it's a luxury few of us Negroes can afford. Then, too, I insist that it's jolly to fool them.

The Quest of the Silver Fleece (1911) 280.

801. BLACK FOLK SONG

The Negro folk song—the rhythmic cry of the slave—stands today not simply as the sole American music, but as the most beautiful expression of human experience born this side of the seas. . . . It still remains as the singular spiritual heritage of the nation and the greatest gift of the Negro people.

The Souls of Black Folk (1903) 351.

802. BLACK HISTORY

Few today are interested in Negro history because they feel the matter already settled: the Negro has no history.

Black Folk Then and Now (1939) vii.

803. BLACK MIGRATION

The effort of the Southern Negro to rise has resulted in three kinds of migration: (1) Huddling in the Black Belt. (2) The rush to Town. (3) Migration to Northern Cities.

G. R. Glenn and others, *University Extension Lectures*. . . . (1900); *Writings by W.E.B. Du Bois in Non-Periodical Literature Edited by Others* (1982) 14.

804. BLACK PRESS

The difficulty with the colored press is that they cannot afford to pay reporters of a high enough grade. The one point for congratulations is the great improvement of colored papers over ten years ago.

To Harlan A. Carter, January 7, 1930 [1931?]; microfilm reel no. 34, frame no. 695; W.E.B. Du Bois Papers, University of Massachusetts, Amherst.

Today it is probably true that there is scarcely a Negro in the United States who can read and write who does not read the Negro press. It has become a vital part of his life.

"The American Negro Press," *Chicago Defender*, February 20, 27, 1943; *Writings by W.E.B. Du Bois in Periodicals Edited by Others*, vol. 3 (1982) 155.

805. BOARDS OF DIRECTORS

You know how Boards are. You can lead them to do anything, but compulsion and defiance of their authority makes a nasty situation.

To William Pickens, May 24, 1929; microfilm reel no. 28, frame no. 1213; W.E.B. Du Bois Papers, University of Massachusetts, Amherst.

I shall be very glad to serve on any Board, provided there are no meetings to attend and nothing to do.

To Maud Cuney Hare, March 3, 1930; microfilm reel no. 31, frame no. 443; W.E.B.
    Du Bois Papers, University of Massachusetts, Amherst.

806. BROADENING HUMANITY

The history of the world is the history of the discovery of the common humanity
of human beings among steadily-increasing circles of men.

Darkwater (1920) 149.

807. BUSINESS

There is practically nothing that cannot be done and be called good if it returns
large enough profits to the industrial doers.

"Business as Public Service," *Crisis* 36 (November 1929) 374–5, 392; *Selections from
    The Crisis*, vol. 2 (1983) 567.

808. BUYING AND SELLING

Perhaps the most extraordinary characteristic of current America is the attempt
to reduce life to buying and selling. Life is not love unless love is sex and bought
and sold. Life is not knowledge save knowledge of technique, of science for
destruction. Life is not beauty except beauty for sale. Life is not art unless its
price is high and it is sold for profit. All life is production for profit, and for
what is profit but for buying and selling again?

Autobiography (1968) 418.

809. CAJOLING FOOLS

But if the time spent cajoling fools were used in convincing the honest and
upright, think how much we would gain.

The Quest of the Silver Fleece (1911) 280.

810. CAPITAL IDEA

The word Negro is almost universally capitalized on the Continent and in
England . . . and it used to be in this country down until about 1840. . . .

Letter to J. Franklin Jameson, July 5, 1910; *Correspondence*, I, 172.

If . . . the reason [the *New York Times* spells Negro with a small "n"] is
because you spell "white man" with small letters then obviously your logic is
at fault. "Negro" is not the correlative of "white man" . . . and in . . . [this case
no one] would . . . expect you to use capitals. "Negro," on the other hand, is
not only the designation of a mere color but is a well-defined technical term
standing for person of Negro descent and has just as much right to a capital
letter as "Jew" or "Irish" or "Aryan" or "Caucasian" or a dozen other similar
words.

To Rollo Ogden, November 17, 1925; microfilm reel no. 15, frame no. 1195; W.E.B.
    Du Bois Papers, University of Massachusetts, Amherst.

The majority of the magazines of higher class, and a very large minority of
the daily newspapers, capitalize the word [Negro].

To Roscoe C. Bruce, October 9, 1929; microfilm reel no. 28, frame no. 328; W.E.B.
    Du Bois Papers, University of Massachusetts, Amherst.

811. CARTOONING

The work of a cartoonist is difficult. It is not a matter of drawing. A great
many successful cartoonists cannot draw at all. If a man can draw, like Thomas
Nast, then there comes an additional requirement of a keen sense of humor, a
knowledge of current events and politics, a knowledge of human character, and
the ability to express these. We have no colored cartoonists.

To A. J. Henderson, December 19, 1931; microfilm reel no. 34, frame no. 1142; W.E.B.
    Du Bois Papers, University of Massachusetts, Amherst.

812. CHOICE

A person has a right to choose his seat in the theatre. He has no right to insist
that no one shall sit near him whom he is not willing to marry. The theatre is
open for the sake of the play, and not for making matrimonial matches.

"Segregation," *Crisis* 37 (September 1930) 316; *Selections from* The Crisis, vol. 2
    (1983) 597.

813. COLLECTIVE SELF-DEFENSE

It was the silent verdict of all America that Negroes must not be allowed to
fight for themselves. They were, therefore, dissuaded from every attempt at self-
protection or aggression by their friends as well as their enemies.

Black Reconstruction (1935) 482.

814. COMFORT AND RIGHTS

We colored people have long . . . come to the conclusion that our comfort and
pleasure must not be connected in cases of discrimination where it is inevitably
our duty to insist upon our rights. This is an extremely embarrassing situation,
but we consider it both cowardly and selfish to refuse on our own account to
press for rights when our own refusal involves the hurt of hundreds of other
colored persons who will follow us.

To T. J. Knapp, March 7, 1922; microfilm reel no. 10, frame no. 1158; W.E.B. Du
    Bois Papers, University of Massachusetts, Amherst.

815. "CONSPIRACY" WITHOUT ACTION

It was once the law that if a man could not be proven to have committed a crime he could not be punished for it. Today no criminal act need be proven if a public prosecutor can prove that a man "conspired" to do what he never did do. And this "conspiracy" may be considered proven by what *one* man says, that another man thought. On such charge the Rosenbergs were murdered and [Morton] Sobell is in prison.

"*National Guardian* Dinner," November 30, 1954; microfilm reel no. 81, frame no.
    928; W.E.B. Du Bois Papers, University of Massachusetts, Amherst.

816. CONTRADICTION

The fact that people are well-meaning has never in human history hindered them from doing evil.

"The United States and War," September 11, 1958; microfilm reel no. 81, frame no.
    1199; W.E.B. Du Bois Papers, University of Massachusetts, Amherst.

817. COOPERATIVE ECONOMY

There exists today a chance for the Negroes to organize a cooperative State within their own group. By letting Negro farmers feed Negro artisans, and Negro technicians guide Negro home industries, and Negro thinkers plan this integration of cooperation, while Negro artists dramatize and beautify the struggle, economic independence can be achieved.

"A Negro Nation within the Nation," *Current History* 42 (June 1935) 265–70; *Writings
    by W.E.B. Du Bois in Periodicals Edited by Others*, vol. 3 (1982) 5–6.

818. CORRUPTION AND PROGRESS

If there was one thing that South Carolina feared more than bad Negro government, it was good Negro government.

Black Reconstruction (1935) 428.

819. COTTON

Cotton they knew—how the furry seed was planted, how it was hoed and attended as it grew, how it came up through the furrows and waxed green and lush, and then burst into a great sea of lovely flowers—white and yellow and purple. And then, finally, came the miracle. Out of the swelling pods below the flowers came great fistfuls of silver lint that burst into fine glimpses of a new world of clothes. And the people with bent backs hoed it and hoed it again and "chopped" to keep back the weeds.

Mansart Builds a School (1959) 261.

820. CRIME

Do not . . . excuse crime because you hate the conditions which gave rise to it. Crime is still crime.

Amsterdam News, August 28, 1943; *Newspaper Columns by W.E.B. Du Bois* (1986) 549.

821. CURLS

I do not know how much colored people spend for cosmetics and beauty paraphernalia but I do not think that they spend any more proportionately to take the curl out of their hair than white people do to put the curl in.

To R. H. Thomas, September 23, 1931; microfilm reel no. 35, frame no. 881; W.E.B. Du Bois Papers, University of Massachusetts, Amherst.

822. DARK HUMANITY

A belief in humanity is a belief in colored man. If the uplift of mankind must be done by men, then the destinies of this world will rest ultimately in the hands of darker nations.

Darkwater (1920) 49.

823. DEBT

The keynote of the Black Belt is debt; not commercial credit, but debt in the sense of continued inability on the part of the mass of the population to make income cover expense.

The Souls of Black Folk (1903) 137.

824. DEFINING A SCIENCE

It is impossible to tell what a science is merely by defining it—the definition is the last thing a science discovers—indeed it can truthfully be said that no science can be fully defined until it is perfect, until its work is done. The best explanation of a science then is a description of the sort of work it is doing and what it has already accomplished.

"A Program for a Sociological Society," 1897 or 1899; microfilm reel no. 80, frame no. 86; W.E.B. Du Bois Papers, University of Massachusetts, Amherst.

825. DEMAND, DON'T APOLOGIZE

Conciliation must be in any social worker's program, but on the other hand, fawning and stupid yielding to the vagaries of a master class not only secures nothing from them, but helps to submerge one's own self-respect. . . . Minorities must always "vaunt its powers," otherwise it will lose what little power it has, and while I should hate to be justly accused of bitterness and vindictiveness, nevertheless, if what I am writing in *The Crisis* comes under that head, you will, I regret to say, see as much of it in the future as you have in the past.

Letter to L. F. Strittmater, August 3, 1932; *Correspondence*, I, 461.

826. DEROGATORY WORDS

My policy when I was editor of *The Crisis* was to let a writer use the word "nigger" or "darky" if it served an artistic purpose in his story. Of course I tried not to have this occur too often. The point is if an author is quoting a Southern white man, and the white man is addressing a Negro, he will say "nigger." To make him say anything else would be rather a strain upon credulity.

To A. S. Pinkett, March 11, 1946; microfilm reel no. 46, frame no. 183; W.E.B. Du Bois Papers, University of Massachusetts, Amherst.

827. PROOF OF DESCENT

Proof of descent in this country is always difficult and in the case of Negro blood practically impossible, as there are no adequate vital statistics, particularly so far as Negroes are concerned.

To C. E. Walker, January, 6, 1927; microfilm reel no. 23, frame no. 419; W.E.B. Du Bois Papers, University of Massachusetts, Amherst.

828. DISCRIMINATION IN LIBRARIES

No one who has taken notice of the New York Public Library can long doubt but that its appointments tend to be confined to only a select part of the population and that Negroes, Jews and many other elements have a difficult road to recognition. . . .

To Franklin F. Hopper, March 11, 1930; microfilm reel no. 31, frame no. 1091; W.E.B. Du Bois Papers, University of Massachusetts, Amherst.

829. DOING AND GETTING

In this world men who can do nothing, get nothing to do.

"The Spirit of Modern Europe" (1900?); *Against Racism* (1985) 63.

830. DRAMA

Easily the most dramatic episode in American history was the sudden move to free four million black slaves in an effort to stop a great civil war, to end forty years of bitter controversy, and to appease the moral sense of civilization.

Black Reconstruction (1935) 3.

831. EMANCIPATION

The freeing of the black slave freed America.

Darkwater (1920) 100.

832.   EQUAL MANHOOD

For a brief period . . . [1866–1873] the majority of thinking Americans of the North believed in the equal manhood of Negroes. They acted accordingly with a thoroughness and clean-cut decision that no age which does not share that faith can in the slightest comprehend. . . . They . . . recognized black folk as men.

Black Reconstruction (1935) 320.

833.   EQUALITY AND POWER

Conscious self-realization and self-direction is the watchword of modern man, and the first article in the program of any group that will survive must be the great aim, equality and power among men.

"The Immediate Program of the American Negro," *Crisis* 9 (April 1915) 310–12; *Selections from* The Crisis, vol. 1 (1983) 94.

834.   ERROR

To err is human; but a human error easily slips into three crimes: the initial mistake becomes deliberate wrong; attempt is then made to cure this wrong by force rather than reason; finally the whole story is so explained and distorted as to preserve no lesson for posterity, and thus history seldom guides us aright.

"Foreword" to Howard Fast's *Freedom Road* (New York: Crown 1949) v–vi; *Writings by W.E.B. Du Bois in Non-Periodical Literature Edited by Others* (1982) 271.

835.   ESTABLISHING CULTURES

Great as has been the human advance in the last one thousand years, it is, so far as native human ability, so far as intellectual gift and moral courage are concerned, nothing as compared with any one of ten and more millenniums before, far back in the forests of tropical Africa and in hot India, where brown and black humanity first fought climate and disease and bugs and beasts; where man dared simply to live and propagate himself. There was the hardest and greatest struggle in all the human world.

Dusk of Dawn (1940) 151.

836.   FAILURE AND SUCCESS

Failure in a good cause is worth more applause than success in a bad one.

"John Brown," ca. 1909; microfilm reel no. 80, frame no. 212; W.E.B. Du Bois Papers, University of Massachusetts, Amherst.

837. THE FAILURE OF SUCCESS

The masters feared their former slaves' success far more than their anticipated failure.

Black Reconstruction (1935) 633.

838. FOLKLORE

The folklore found in the mountains and Western lumber camps is not the same as Negro folklore; and Negro spirituals are Negroes' contributions to art, even if in some cases white people have written down music.

To Mrs. C. H. Trowbridge, March 31, 1936; microfilm reel no. 46; frame no. 761; W.E.B. Du Bois Papers, University of Massachusetts, Amherst.

839. THE FOREIGN-BORN

You must not yield to the efforts to divide you from Americans or from each other. You must cease being ashamed of your fathers, their customs, and their mother tongue. Let no inner prejudices or jealousies keep you from uniting in defense of all foreign-born of every nation, color and race, and fighting a common battle against all attempts to divide Americans into a series of mutually hating groups, sitting defenseless against attack and innuendo.

To The Congress of the Foreign Born, 1948; microfilm reel no. 61; frame no. 343; W.E.B. Du Bois Papers, University of Massachusetts, Amherst.

840. FREE BUSINESS

The freeing of the nation from the strangling hands of oligarchy in the South freed not only black men but white men, not only human spirit, but business enterprise all over the land.

Black Reconstruction (1935) 210.

841. FREE NEGROES

As slavery grew to a system and the Cotton Kingdom began to expand into imperial white domination, a free Negro was a contradiction, a threat and a menace. As a thief and a vagabond, he threatened society; but as an educated property holder, a successful mechanic or even professional man, he more than threatened slavery. He contradicted and undermined it. He must not be. He must be suppressed, enslaved, colonized.

Black Reconstruction (1935) 7.

842. FREEDMEN'S BUREAU

The Freedmen's Bureau was the most extraordinary and far-reaching institution of social uplift that American has ever attempted. . . . It was a government guardianship for the relief and guidance of white and black labor from a feudal agrarianism to modern farming and industry.

Black Reconstruction (1935) 289.

843. FREEDOM

By "Freedom" for Negroes, I meant and still mean, full economic, political and social equality with American citizens, in thought, expression and action, with no discrimination based on race and color.

"My Evolving Program for Negro Freedom" in Rayford W. Logan (ed.), *What the Negro Wants* (Chapel Hill: University of North Carolina Press, 1944) 31–70; *Writings by W.E.B. Du Bois in Non-Periodical Literature Edited by Others* (1982) 237.

844. FREEDOM AND EQUALITY

Most men today cannot conceive of a freedom that does not involve somebody's slavery. They do not want equality because the thrill of their happiness comes from having things that others have not.

Darkwater (1920) 207.

845. FREEDOM OF THOUGHT

The only method . . . of insuring that thought will not mislead mankind is *not* to prevent thinking, but to ensure that opinion be honest, and that it be based on knowledge of truth. And it is right here, in the effort to insure honesty and truth, that singularly enough the world has continually gone astray and along the same paths. We have tried to stop thinking and stop men from acting according to their reasoned thought. If, of course, a man's opinion is based on what is untrue; if what you say is not what you really think, such opinions may seriously mislead. But the way to avoid this is not by stopping thought. No. It is by educating thinkers, and by persuading youth to believe that honesty is the best policy and that spying, lying and tattling is indecent for students, grown-ups or governments.

"Freedom of Opinion," February 14, 1955; microfilm reel no. 81, frame no. 964; W.E.B. Du Bois Papers, University of Massachusetts, Amherst.

846. FRYING PAN

There is an argument which both amuses and irritates me: "Aren't you better off in America than elsewhere?" "Yes," being in the frying pan makes one appreciate the fire but not necessarily love the frying pan. . . . We still object to the frying pan.

Amsterdam News, April 11, 1942; *Newspaper Columns by W.E.B. Du Bois* (1986) 422.

847.   A GANDHI PROGRAM?

A proposal has been made that American Negroes consider launching a broad national program based on non-violent, civil disobedience and no-cooperation, modeled along the lines of Gandhi. . . . Mass breaking of law or deeply ensconced custom is a serious thing to be entered upon only in great extremity and after careful thought and will to sacrifice. . . . We not only are not ready for systematic lawbreaking, but are far from convinced that this is good policy or likely to gain our ends.

Amsterdam News, March 13, 1943; *Newspaper Columns by W.E.B. Du Bois* (1986) 508.

848.   GARVEY MOVEMENT

It was interesting as the attempted revolt of a peasantry against oppression and an attempt to use commercial enterprise as a way out. Everything else was incidental and unimportant.

To Edmund D. Cronon, October 28, 1949; microfilm reel no. 63, frame no. 958; W.E.B.
     Du Bois Papers, University of Massachusetts, Amherst.

849.   GIFTS TO AMERICA

The Negro gifts to America may be classed primarily as physical labor, the struggle for freedom, the implementation of democracy, and the creative art. All these gifts were contributed now by individuals, but more effectively by group action.

"Gift of Black Folk," February 11, 1955; microfilm reel no. 81, frame no. 946; W.E.B.
     Du Bois Papers, University of Massachusetts, Amherst.

850.   THE GREAT PAY-DAY

It was the Christmas—not Christmas-tide of the North and West, but Christmas of the Southern South. It was not the festival of the Christ Child, but a time of noise and frolic and license, the great Pay-Day of the year when black men lifted their heads from a year's toiling in the earth, and, hat in hand, asked anxiously: "Master, what have I earned? Have I paid my old debts to you? Have I made my clothes and food? Have I got a little of the year's wages coming to me?" Or, more carelessly and cringingly: "Master, gimme a Christmas gift."

The Quest of the Silver Fleece (1911) 183.

851.   GROUP ECONOMY

In every city of the United States with a considerable Negro population, the colored group is serving itself with religious ministration, medical care, legal advice, and education of children; to a growing degree with food, houses, books, and newspapers. . . . This development . . . forms a large and growing part in the

economy in the case of fully one-half of the Negroes of the United States and
in the case of something between 50,000 and 100,000 town and city Negroes,
representing at least 300,000 persons the group economy approaches a complete
system.

Economic Cooperation among Negro Americans (1907) 179.

852.   GUTTER LABOR FORCE

If you put a man into the gutter and there is any manhood in him, it is going
to take at least one man to keep him down there. . . .

"Democracy in America," ca. 1928; microfilm reel no. 80, frame no. 364; W.E.B. Du
    Bois Papers, University of Massachusetts, Amherst.

853.   HAPPINESS AND HAVING

Is it possible that your happiness depends, not on what you have, but on what
others lack?

"Civil Rights," undated; microfilm reel no. 81, frame no. 1431; W.E.B. Du Bois Papers,
    University of Massachusetts, Amherst.

854.   HEALTH AND WORK

There is no earthly sense in any one ruining their health for the sake of work
worth doing, when they could do the work so much better if they were in good
health.

To Miss Jackson, May 15, 1908; microfilm reel no. 2, frame no. 233; W.E.B. Du Bois
    Papers, University of Massachusetts, Amherst.

855.   HELL

Hell is the place where people are idle—nothing to do and nothing worth the
doing.

"The Joy of Living," *Political Affairs* 44 (February 1965) 35–44, written in 1904;
    Writings by W.E.B. Du Bois in Periodicals Edited by Others, vol. 1 (1982) 219.

856.   HELL AND HEAVEN

Regardless of income, work worth while which one wants to do as compared
with highly paid drudgery is exactly the difference between heaven and hell.

Dusk of Dawn (1940) 325.

857.   HISTORIANS

I stand . . . literally aghast at what American historians have done to this field.

Black Reconstruction (1935) 725.

I have the greatest contempt for historians who try to disguise and distort history in order to make it suitable for afternoon teas.

To Charles O. Brown, February 27, 1939; microfilm reel no. 49, frame no. 1128; W.E.B. Du Bois Papers, University of Massachusetts, Amherst.

858. HISTORY

In the midst of strong feeling and deep hostility, history records not what really happened, but only what we wish to remember.

To Alfred Harcourt, October 21, 1931; microfilm reel no. 34, frame no. 1095; W.E.B. Du Bois Papers, University of Massachusetts, Amherst.

859. HONOR AND SUFFERING

It is in a sense a great honor for a man to have the opportunity to show his courage in defending the Right not simply by talking but by suffering.

"To William Patterson," August 24, 1954; microfilm reel no. 70; frame no. 974; W.E.B. Du Bois Papers, University of Massachusetts, Amherst.

860. HOUSING

A Negro slum may be in dangerous proximity to a white residence quarter, while it is quite common to find a white slum planted in the heart of a respectable Negro district. One thing, however, seldom occurs: the best of the whites and the best of the Negroes almost never live in anything like close proximity. It thus happens that in nearly every Southern town and city, both whites and blacks see commonly the worst of each other.

The Souls of Black Folk (1903) 166–167.

It would be impossible in Atlanta to find worse slums than exist in the fifth and seventh ward of Philadelphia.

"The Negro South and North," *Biblioteca Sacra* 62 (July 1905) 500–13; *Writings by W.E.B. Du Bois in Periodicals Edited by Others*, vol. 1 (1982) 253.

861. HUMOR

When in the calm afterday of thought and struggle to racial peace we look back to pay tribute to those who helped most, we shall single out for highest praise those who made the world laugh—Bob Cole, Ernest Hogan, George Walker and above all, Bert Williams. For this was not mere laughing: it was the smile that hovered above blood and tragedy, the light mask of happiness that hid breaking hearts and bitter souls. This is the top of bravery, the finest thing in service.

Untitled (ca. 1922), Series 3/C, Folder no. 5521, *Unpublished Articles*; W.E.B. Du Bois Papers, University of Massachusetts, Amherst.

This race has the greatest of the gifts of God, laughter. . . . It is frankly, boldly, deliciously human in an artificial and hypocritical land. . . . The white world has its gibes and cruel caricatures; it has its loud guffaws; but to the black world alone belongs the delicious chuckle.

Dusk of Dawn (1940) 148.

To the oppressed and unfortunate, to those who suffer, God mercifully grants the divine right of laughter. These folk are not all black nor all white, but with inborn humor, men of all colors and races face the tragedy of life and make it endurable.

"The Humor of Negroes," *Mark Twain Quarterly* 5 (Winter 1942–43) 12; *Writings by W.E.B. Du Bois in Periodicals Edited by Others*, vol. 3 (1982) 151.

862. IMBALANCE

The price of repression is greater than the cost of liberty. The degradation of men costs something both to the degraded and those who degrade.

John Brown (1909, 1962) 17.

863. INTEGRATION

Extreme opponents of segregation act as though there was but one solution of the race problem, and that, complete integration of the black race with the white race in America, with no distinction of color in political, civil or social life. There is no doubt but what this is the great end toward which humanity is tending, and that so long as there are artificially emphasized differences of nationality, race and color, not to mention the fundamental discrimination of economic class, there will be no real Humanity. On the other hand, it is just as clear, that not for a century and more probably not for ten centuries, will any such consummation be reached. No person born will ever live to see national and racial distinction altogether abolished, and economic distinctions will last many a day.

"Segregation in the North," *Crisis* 41 (April 1934) 115–17; *Selections from* The Crisis, vol. 2 (1983) 750.

All Negroes face the fact that even if they want to be integrated in American life, the overwhelming mass of the nation does not want them and in its present spirit will not have them. Therefore, it is wrong to say that we have that possibility of solution before us. We have not. What we have to decide is, whether we will leave this country, or fight for our rights, or join the revolution, or organize ourselves inside the country separately and peaceably as far as such organization is necessary and possible.

New York Herald Tribune Books, November 18, 1934; *Book Reviews by W.E.B. Du Bois* (1977) 174.

864. INTERNAL COLONY

Within every civilized land today are vast masses of people who in fact occupy a colonial status in relation to the national economy. The slums of London and New York, of Paris and Rome need the exact kind of industrial emancipation that the black people of Africa and the brown people of Asia need.

"A Program of Emancipation for Colonial Peoples" *In* Merze Tate (ed.), *Trust and Non-Self-Governing Territories* (Washington, D.C.: Howard University Press, 1948) 96–104; *Writings by W.E.B. Du Bois in Non-Periodical Literature Edited by Others* (1982) 264.

865. INTERVIEWS

The attempt of a stranger to sum up in a half hour the experience which another has spent 80 years in accumulating is invariably a mess which neither likes.

To Benjamin A. Brown, December 2, 1949; microfilm reel no. 63, frame no. 1122; W.E.B. Du Bois Papers, University of Massachusetts, Amherst.

866. INVISIBILITY

It has been the fashion . . . to attempt to ignore the Negro-American as a problem. Even when this population affects other social problems, the situation is often considered and treated as though the Negro element were not there and did not greatly modify the conditions of the problem. For instance many books on immigration to the United States ignore entirely the Negro immigrant. When foreign immigrants are considered often the Negro is regarded neither as an immigrant nor as a native American.

"The Future of Africa in America" (1941); Series 3/C, Folder no. 5552, pp. 1–2, *Unpublished Articles*; W.E.B. Du Bois Papers, University of Massachusetts, Amherst.

867. "IRISH" CONSUMPTION

Particularly with regard to consumption it must be remembered that Negroes are not the first people who have been claimed as its peculiar victims; the Irish were once thought to be doomed by that disease—but that was when Irishmen were unpopular.

The Philadelphia Negro (1899) 160.

868. JAPANESE AMERICANS

Most people do not realize that outbreaks of so-called "racial hate" are practically always organized and not spontaneous. The driving out of people of Japanese descent on the West Coast was not only the attempt to confiscate their savings without return, but to foment and prolong racial antagonism. The persons back of this wanted to keep serf Japanese labor in the Hawaiian Islands and prevent the Japanese from working anywhere in the United States outside the West Coast.

Amsterdam News, June 10, 1944; *Newspaper Columns by W.E.B. Du Bois* (1986) 591.

869. JUST DESERTS

I saw yesterday the mother of Judge [William H.] Hastie and was glad, not because a Negro had been made judge, but because a man of unusual training and fine character and undoubted ability had had the doors opened and not shut in his face.

Pittsburgh Courier, April 10, 1937; *Newspaper Columns by W.E.B. Du Bois* (1986) 186.

870. MARTIN LUTHER KING, JR.

Did this doctrine and practice of non-violence bring solution of the race problem in [Montgomery] Alabama? It did not. Black workers, many if not all, are still walking to work, and it is possible any day that their leader will be killed by hoodlums perfectly well known to the white police and the city administration, egged on by white councils of war, while most white people of the city say nothing and do nothing.

National Guardian, February 11, 1957; *Newspaper Columns by W.E.B. Du Bois* (1986) 983.

871. KNOWLEDGE AND LOGIC

What we need today is a frank admission of the limitations of scientific knowledge and a frank effort to lay down reasonable rules of logic in dealing with the unknown and the unknowable world. As it is we are hampered by a Science which claims universality, and a Philosophy which seeks to come to grips with science on its own chosen and conquered territory.

To Charles W. Hendel, December 13, 1943; microfilm reel no. 55, frame no. 20; W.E.B. Du Bois Papers, University of Massachusetts, Amherst.

872. LAND HUNGER

By far the most pressing of . . . [the freedman's] problems as a worker was that of land. This land hunger—this absolutely fundamental and essential thing to any real emancipation of the slaves—was continually pushed by all emancipated Negroes and their representatives in every Southern state.

Black Reconstruction (1935) 601.

873. LAWLESSNESS

There are . . . many other contributing causes to American lawlessness, but the caste system against Negroes is one of the most potent.

"Black America" *in* Fred J. Ringel (ed.), *America as Americans See It* (New York: Harcourt Brace Jovanovich, 1932) 140–55; *Writings by W.E.B. Du Bois in Non-Periodical Literature Edited by Others* (1982) 171.

874. LIMPID GARBAGE

The Housatonic river shall not be used as a sewer [in Great Barrington, Mass., Du Bois's birthplace]. . . . The Housatonic river is the natural Main Street of the Town of Great Barrington. It should be a clear and limpid stream, flowing gently through grass, trees and flowers; flanked by broad roadways and parks as the life stream of a town. In the midst of its passage, where now rises the monstrosity of a private school should be a lake and beach for public bathing. This would emphasize Great Barrington not as a centre for millionaires, but for money-mak[ing] but as [a] town of homes as it used to be; a place where men dreamed and thought and sought the meaning of living and cared little about how much they could make or steal.

To George P. Fitzpatrick, June 13, 1961; microfilm reel no. 75, frame no. 616; W.E.B. Du Bois Papers, University of Massachusetts, Amherst.

875. LOWLY IRISH

[The leaders of Great Barrington, Mass., Du Bois's home town] did not believe that the Irish were the same as other people. They did not allow them to be represented on the school board. The Irish were outside of democracy. Their children went to the high school but they were not altogether inside of democracy.

"Individualism, Democracy and Social Control," March 14, 1944; microfilm reel no. 80, frame no. 864; W.E.B. Du Bois Papers, University of Massachusetts, Amherst.

876. MARCHING TACTFULLY

[Emancipation of the slaves was implemented] only by the consummate tact of [a] leader of men who went no faster than his nation marched but just as fast; and also by the unwearying will of the Abolitionists, who forced the nation onward.

Black Reconstruction (1935) 84.

877. MECHANICAL COTTON PICKER

The serious problem posed by the Cotton-Picker is not new. The history of the nineteenth century is the history of the displacement of workers by machines, with the main profit of technical improvement going to the owners of machines and the impoverishment of the workers. The case of the Negro tenant farmer serves but to emphasize the problem and make it visible to all. Also because of the caste restrictions on Negroes in employment the results in poverty, ignorance and disease are more apparent and quicker.

To Bradford Jordan, February 20, 1947; microfilm reel no. 60, frame no. 186; W.E.B.
   Du Bois Papers, University of Massachusetts, Amherst.

878.   MIGHTY HUMAN RAINBOW

> Old Night, the elder sister of the Day,
> Mother of Dawn in the golden East,
> Meets in the misty twilight with her brood,
> Pale and black, tawny, red and brown,
> The mighty human rainbow of the world,
> Spanning its wilderness of storm.

Darkwater (1920) 275.

879.   MIGRATING TO CITIES

I do not think he ought to leave the South but practically all the advance made
by the Negro in the last generation has been made in cities, North and South,
and the northern cities have set the pace.

"An Answer to the Memorandum on the Bettering of the Position of the Colored People
   in America," 1926; microfilm reel no. 77, frame no. 422; W.E.B. Du Bois Papers,
   University of Massachusetts, Amherst.

880.   MULTILINGUAL STILLNESS

My good friend, Henry Hunt of Georgia . . . used to say in his often day of
trial: "I can keep still in seven different languages."

Amsterdam News, July 24, 1943; *Newspaper Columns by W.E.B. Du Bois* (1986) 540.

881.   MY COUNTRY

> My country, tis of thee,
> Rich land of slavery. . . .

"I Sing to China," May 1, 1959; microfilm reel no. 88, frame no. 1450; W.E.B. Du
   Bois Papers, University of Massachusetts, Amherst.

882.   NAACP

The NAACP has never officially opposed separate Negro organizations—such
as churches, schools and business and cultural organizations. It has never denied
the recurrent necessity of united separate action on the part of Negroes for self-
defense and self-development; but it has insistently and continually pointed out
that such action is in any case a necessary evil involving often a recognition
from within of the very color line which we are fighting without. That race pride
and race loyalty, Negro ideals and Negro unity, have a place and function today,
the NAACP never has denied and never can deny.

"A Free Forum," *Crisis* 41 (February 1934) 52–53; *Selection from* The Crisis, vol. 2
   (1983) 734.

883. NATIVE AMERICANS

The Indians of the Americas are for the most part disfranchised, landless, poverty-stricken, and illiterate, and are achieving a degree of freedom only as by the death of individuality they become integrated into the blood and culture of the whites. This is widely approved as the only sensible outcome.

Color and Democracy (1945) 71.

884. NEGRO AND AMERICAN

[The American Negro] would not Africanize America, for America has too much to teach the world and Africa. He would not bleach his Negro soul in a flood of white Americanism, for he knows that Negro blood has a message for the world. He simply wishes to make it possible for a man to be both a Negro and an American, without being cursed and spit upon by his fellows, without having the doors of Opportunity closed roughly in his face.

The Souls of Black Folk (1903) 4.

885. NEGRO OR AMERICAN?

No Negro who has given earnest thought to the situation of his people in America has failed, at some time in life, to find himself at these crossroads; has failed to ask himself at some time: what, after all, am I? Am I an American or am I a Negro? Can I be both? Or is it my duty to cease to be a Negro as soon as possible and be an American? If I strive as a Negro, am I not perpetuating the very cleft that threatened and separates black and white America?

The Conservation of Races, American Negro Academy Occasional Papers, no. 2 (Washington, D.C.: American Negro Academy, 1897); *Pamphlets and Leaflets by W.E.B. Du Bois* (1986) 5.

886. THE NEGRO PROBLEM

[In 1896] my vision was becoming clearer. The Negro problem was in my mind a matter of systematic investigation and intelligent understanding. The world was thinking wrong about race, because it did not know. The ultimate evil was stupidity. The cure for it was knowledge based on scientific investigation.

Autobiography (1968) 197.

887. NEW BLOOD

We have got to inject into the veins of this organization [NAACP] some young radical blood and it is a difficult process. But unless it is done, we are done for.

To Abram L. Harris, January 27, 1931; microfilm reel no. 36, frame no. 89; W.E.B. Du Bois Papers, University of Massachusetts, Amherst.

888. THE NINETEENTH CENTURY

The nineteenth century was the first century of human sympathy.

The Souls of Black Folk (1903) 218.

889. "NOBODY KNOWS THE TROUBLE I'VE SEEN"

When, struck with a sudden poverty, the United States refused to fulfill its promise of land to the freedmen, a brigadier-general went down to the Sea Islands to carry the news. An old woman on the outskirts of the throng began singing this song; all the mass joined with her, swaying. And the soldier wept.

The Souls of Black Folk (1903) 255.

890. OLD AGE

This tendency to look upon age as abnormal and rather useless is peculiarly American. It is true in neither France nor England, nor in most parts of the Western world, and never in Asia or Africa. But with an emphasis on Youth in America, which has long lost its meaning, it is an old American custom to write off as a liability if not total loss, the age of men in public work after they have passed fifty, and to regard them as practically dead at seventy.

In Battle for Peace (1952) 10.

891. ORGANIZATIONAL CHANGE

It is extremely difficult to make an organization grow and change in accordance with the times. Most organizations get accumulations of directors and friends, who think entirely in the past.

Letter to Owen R. Lovejoy, July 19, 1934; *Correspondence*, I, 482.

It's the same story with all organizations, as it is with some men. After they get to a certain age, they get out of touch with their surroundings, and if they can reorientate themselves, all right, and if they can't they just die, even though they are living and walking around.

To Vada and John Somerville, January 31, 1935; microfilm reel no. 44, frame no. 1067; W.E.B. Du Bois Papers, University of Massachusetts, Amherst.

892. ORGANIZE

Organization is sacrificing. Successful organized effort always means that the people who do the most work and have the most initiative often get the ... [least] credit and at critical times are asked and required to submerge their individuality and yield their judgement to the desire of others.

To R. C. Hudson, November 15, 1927; microfilm reel no. 22, frame no. 1079; W.E.B. Du Bois Papers, University of Massachusetts, Amherst.

893. ORGANIZED REACTION

For fifty years I have been in touch with social currents in the United States. Never before has organized reaction wielded the power it does today: By ownership of press and radio, by curtailment of free speech, by imprisonment of liberal thinkers and writers. It has become almost impossible today in my country even to hold a public rally for peace.

"Intervention by Dr. Du Bois," August 1950; microfilm reel no. 80, frame no. 1389; W.E.B. Du Bois Papers, University of Massachusetts, Amherst.

894. ORIGINAL INTENT

This constitutional argument was astonishing. Around and around it went in dizzy, silly dialectics. Here were grown, sensible men arguing about a written form of government adopted ninety years before, when men did not believe that slavery could outlive their generation in this country, or that civil war could possibly be its result; when no man foresaw the Industrial Revolution or the rise of the Cotton Kingdom; and yet now with incantation and abracadabra, the leaders of a nation tried to peer back into the magic crystal, and out of a bit of paper called the Constitution, find eternal and immutable law laid down for their guidance forever and ever, Amen!

Black Reconstruction (1935) 267.

895. OUT-HEROD HEROD

The black man today who dares to stand up and demand for his people those same human rights which your fathers demanded for you—age, and by God and my father's black arms at last obtained—the Negro who today demands such rights for his people is being read out of the counsels of the safe and the sane; while aid and comfort is showered on such of us who are willing to out-Herod Herod in reducing the rights and ambitions of ten million men to the privilege of being useful to white folks.

"Caste: That Is the Root of Trouble," *Des Moines Register Leader*, October 19, 1904; *Writings by W.E.B. Du Bois in Periodicals Edited by Others*, vol. 1 (1982) 233.

896. OVERFLOWING OPPRESSION

The oppression of the Negro in the United States is not simply the misfortune of the Negro. . . . Political cheating in the United States is directly traceable to cheating Negro voters in the South. . . . There is no sense in a peace program which takes no account of the worldwide economic war upon colored peoples. The insult to Japanese, Jews and southern Europeans in the pending immigration bill is a logical deduction from the American past time of Negro-baiting. It is absolutely certain that the future of liberal and radical thought in the United States is going to be made easy or impossible by the way in which American democracy treats American Negroes.

"Radicals and the Negro," *Crisis* 29 (March 1925) 200–201; *Selections from* The Crisis, vol. 1 (1983) 419–20.

897. PARKS

St. Nicholas Park is one of the most beautiful spots in New York City and almost the only place of beauty in the colored Harlem section, north of Central Park. . . . It used to be a beauty spot, but as soon as colored people began to move near it the city and police studiously neglected it, and they either openly or tacitly blamed the colored population. Of course, the colored population is not to blame. The city is to blame for its neglect.

To James V. Mulholland, October 6, 1927; microfilm reel no. 22, frame no. 948; W.E.B. Du Bois Papers, University of Massachusetts, Amherst.

898. PECULIAR COMMONALITY

[Your father Edward Parker] Kelly and I were classmates in the class of 1890 at Harvard, and we had certain peculiar interests in common, he being an Irishman, and I a Negro.

To Arthur P. Kelly, May 19, 1953; microfilm reel no. 69, frame no. 934; W.E.B. Du Bois Papers, University of Massachusetts, Amherst.

899. PERSPECTIVE ON HISTORY

I regard history as economic and psychological history and can conceive no proper study of present economics without reference to past history; I look upon cultural anthropology as a branch of history and sociology.

"What Is Graduate Instruction in Atlanta University?" January 16, 1940; microfilm reel no. 51, frame no. 127; W.E.B. Du Bois Papers, University of Massachusetts, Amherst.

900. PHILANTHROPY

[The whole philanthropic movement gave the freedman] churches before he had homes, theories of equality instead of personal security, theological bickerings instead of land and tools, and mushroom "colleges" instead of a good common school and industrial training system.

"The Afro-American" (ca. 1894–1896), Series 3/C, Folder no. 5502, *Unpublished Articles*; W.E.B. Du Bois Papers, University of Massachusetts, Amherst.

901. POLISH AMERICANS

The echo of Polish reaction is shown among the Poles in the United States: it was a Polish priest that incited the riot around the Harriet Tubman homes in Detroit. Poles have burned churches and put hindrances before Negroes in other parts of Michigan. They have been among the most unsympathetic of foreigners toward Negroes in recent times.

To Oswald Garrison Villard, April 10, 1945; microfilm reel no. 58, frame no. 149; W.E.B. Du Bois Papers, University of Massachusetts, Amherst.

902. POVERTY ˙

Poverty for an individual is understandable. There is, however, something mystic and peculiarly appalling in the poverty of an institution [like Atlanta University]; it is more than the poverty of an individual or even of a large family. It is a huge and perpetually recurring burden which can be shifted only by miracle and that miracle usually assumes the guise of a very rich and benevolent man.

The Ordeal of Mansart (1957) 181.

[In 1908:] Then, as now, the central problem of the life of my People was poverty. Today, poverty is still central, but it is a vastly broader matter, more intense, despite wealth and technique, and covering not merely American Negroes but also a large part of mankind.

"American Negroes, Socialism and Communism," May 21, 1958; microfilm reel no. 81, frame no. 1181; W.E.B. Du Bois Papers, University of Massachusetts, Amherst.

903. POWER AND DEMOCRACY

Abolitionists failed to see that after the momentary exaltation of war, the nation did not want Negroes to have civil rights and that national industry could get its way easier by alliance with Southern landholders than by sustaining Southern workers. They did not know that when they let the dictatorship of labor be overthrown in the South they surrendered the hope of democracy in America for all men.

Black Reconstruction (1935) 591–92.

904. PROBLEM NON-SOLVING

One cannot, to be sure, demand of whole nations exceptional moral foresight and heroism; but a certain hard common-sense in facing the complicated phenomena of political life must be expected in every progressive people. In some respects we as a nation seem to lack this; we have the somewhat inchoate idea that we are not destined to be harassed with great social questions, and that even if we are, and fail to answer them, the fault is with the question and not with us. Consequently, we often congratulate ourselves more on getting rid of a problem than on solving it. Such an attitude is dangerous; we have and shall have, as other peoples have had, critical, momentous, and pressing questions to answer. The riddle of the Sphinx may be postponed, it may be evasively answered now; sometime it must be fully answered.

The Suppression of the African Slave Trade (1896) 198–99.

905. PROGRESS

The American Negro has made amazing progress. White public opinion has yielded before proof of his ability. There is less crude race hatred. We have a right to note this and rejoice in it. But we are not called upon to prance down Fifth Ave., with vine leaves in our hair, nor bound in gratitude to crawl into the White House and greet Truman as "Mars Linkum."

"On Negro America," *Sunday Compass*, July 10, 1949, 4–5; *Writings by W.E.B. Du Bois in Periodicals Edited by Others*, vol. 4 (1982) 121.

906. PROTECTIVE "TARIFF"

By cooperative effort in doing their own laundry, making their own bread, preparing most of their food, making a considerable part of their clothes, doing their own repairing of all sorts, printing their own papers and books and in hundreds of other ways, the colored people of the United States, if they put their minds to it and secured the proper training, could spend a considerable part of two thousand million dollars each year hiring themselves at decent wages to perform services which the Negro group needs; and they could do this without antagonism to the white group, without any essential change of law and without a national organization involving army and police. They could even do it without the help of a protective tariff because color prejudice and race loyalty furnishes a certain amount of the same kind of protection to the Negro which the tariff furnishes manufacturers.

"The Negro and Social Reconstruction" (1936); *Against Racism* (1985) 148.

907. PUBLIC SPEAKING

You cannot become a public speaker by reading a book. Speaking to a number of persons is no different than speaking to one person. You have to have something to say and then go ahead and say it. For effective public speaking, then, you need a careful education and wide reading.

To Dudley Harris, September 10, 1932; microfilm reel no. 36, frame no. 1256; W.E.B. Du Bois Papers, University of Massachusetts, Amherst.

908. RACE AND LIFE

With the best will the factual outline of a life misses the essence of its spirit. Thus in my life the chief fact has been race—not so much scientific race, as that deep conviction of myriads of men that congenital differences among the main mass of human beings absolutely condition the individual destiny of every member of a group.

Dusk of Dawn (1940) 139.

909. RACE CONSCIOUSNESS

The group consciousness that has been aroused among Negroes is not a passing thing. There will not be a time until we are long dead that there will be less racial consciousness among Negroes than today. It is a natural phenomenon and is increasing in its intensity. It must remain as long as the great body of legislation upon which segregation and discrimination is based remains; and as long as the customs centering around that are valid.

To Jackson Davis, April 16, 1937; microfilm reel no. 47, frame no. 473; W.E.B. Du
    Bois Papers, University of Massachusetts, Amherst.

910. RACE PRIDE

I believe in Pride of race and lineage and self: in pride of self so deep as to scorn injustice to other selves; in pride of lineage so great as to despise no man's father; in pride of race so chivalrous as neither to offer bastardy to the weak nor beg wedlock of the strong knowing that men may be brothers in Christ, even though they be not brothers-in-law.

Darkwater (1920) 3.

911. RACE RIOTS

The assertion that nine-tenths of the riots of this country are caused by social relations between [female] whites and [male] Negroes is an unmitigated lie. I do not know a single riot of any size in ten years that has been so caused.

To B. L. Marchant, June 24, 1930; microfilm reel no. 31, frame no. 912; W.E.B. Du
    Bois Papers, University of Massachusetts, Amherst.

912. RACISM?

Any statement of our desire to develop American Negro culture, to keep up our ties with colored people, to remember our past, is being regarded as "racism."

"Whither Now and Why," March 31, 1960; microfilm reel no. 81, frame no. 1298;
    W.E.B. Du Bois Papers, University of Massachusetts, Amherst.

913. RADIO

My experience so far, unfortunately, has been that anything connected with the radio in the United States is a part of widespread propaganda by the rich.

To Doris Darmstadter, August 11, 1932; microfilm reel no. 36; frame no. 1011; W.E.B.
    Du Bois Papers, University of Massachusetts, Amherst.

914. RAPE

The charge of rape against colored Americans was invented by the white South after Reconstruction to excuse mob violence. No such wholesale charge was

dreamed of in slavery days and during the [Civil] war black men were often the
sole protection of white women.

"Rape," *Crisis* 18 (May 1919) 12–13; *Selections from* The Crisis, vol. 1 (1983) 193.

915.   READING ASSIGNMENT

I am glad to know you are reading but why on earth any one should want to
read moral philosophy is beyond me. You had much better take a course in Karl
Marx and [Thorstein] Veblen.

To Ruth Anna Fisher, January 5, 1938; microfilm reel no. 48, frame no. 988; W.E.B.
Du Bois Papers, University of Massachusetts, Amherst.

916.   RECONSTRUCTION

Reconstruction [was] one of the greatest attempts to spread democracy which
the modern world has seen.

The Gift of Black Folk (1924) 186.

917.   RED CROSS

During the [first world] war, the Red Cross for a long time refused to send
Negro Red Cross nurses to take care of colored soldiers in Europe. They made
every possible excuse and explanation. At the very last, a few were sent.

To Helen N. Hiller, February 7, 1931; microfilm reel no. 34, frame no. 1151; W.E.B.
Du Bois Papers, University of Massachusetts, Amherst.

918.   RELATIVES

The most necessary thing to say to relatives is that they should be at least as
polite to each other as they are to strangers.

To Henrietta Shivery, February 5, 1936; microfilm reel no. 46, frame no. 641; W.E.B.
Du Bois Papers, University of Massachusetts, Amherst.

919.   REORIENTATION

I have not yet been able satisfactorily to orientate myself in the matter of race
and culture. I had . . . to catch up from twenty years' absence from sociological
study [while I worked for NAACP]; and while I think I have made progress and
have shadows of ideas in mind, they are not yet in such shape that I should like
to state them in public.

To Charles S. Johnson, December 10, 1937; microfilm reel no. 47, frame no. 673;
W.E.B. Du Bois Papers, University of Massachusetts, Amherst.

920. RISING PEOPLE

A rising group of people are not lifted bodily from the ground like an inert solid mass, but rather stretch upward like a living past with its roots still clinging in the mould.

The Souls of Black Folk (1903) 178.

921. SCHOLARLY DISCRIMINATION

The Phelps-Stokes Fund, the Rosenwald Fund, the Funds of the General Education Board, have very seldom permitted Negroes to make investigations concerning their own race. Southern white men are almost always preferred. In the past, there might have been some excuse for this because of the scarcity of well-trained Negro scholars. There is no such excuse today.

Memorandum to Walter White, November 17, 1930; microfilm reel no. 32, frame no. 76; W.E.B. Du Bois Papers, University of Massachusetts, Amherst.

922. ARTHUR A. SCHOMBURG

Schomburg and I used to discuss books on Negroes. I helped with my knowledge of English books while his knowledge of Spanish and Latin-American books was boundless and he was ever learning more. . . . I could join with Schomburg in rejoicing when the New York Public library was convinced that the Negro race had a history and culture worth conserving.

"At the Schomburg Library," May 7, 1957; microfilm reel no. 81, frame no. 1070; W.E.B. Du Bois Papers, University of Massachusetts, Amherst.

923. SEGREGATED HOSPITAL

A segregated institution is always a step backward and eventual progress means tnat the ground lost has got to be covered again before real advance can be made. The segregated institution is practically always a poor institution, less well-organized and less well-supported.

To Clayborne George, July 9, 1929; microfilm reel no. 28, frame no. 97; W.E.B. Du Bois Papers, University of Massachusetts, Amherst.

924. SEGREGATION

Segregation of any set of human beings, be they black, white or of any color or race is a bad thing, since human contact is the thing that makes for civilization, and human contact is a thing for which all of us are striving today. Of course, some segregation must come, but we do not advocate it; we do not advertise it, and we do not think it is in itself a good thing.

Letter to Samuel May, Jr., December 10, 1907; *Correspondence*, I, 138.

. . . Race separation settles nothing. It puts off the day when reconciliation and understanding will come and substitutes a period which sometimes makes for peace and thoughtful consideration, but more often widens the gap between human beings and makes increased misunderstanding likely. . . . Before [a] plan of race segregation is adopted, its advocates should ask themselves this fundamental question: Will the project make for decreased discrimination in the long run? If the result of the action will not be decreased discrimination, or if it will directly or indirectly increase it, such action would surely be a calamity.

To the board of directors of NAACP, 1931; microfilm reel no. 35; W.E.B. Du Bois Papers, University of Massachusetts, Amherst.

We are not both speaking always of the same thing. I am using segregation in the broader sense of separate racial effort caused by outer social repulsions, whether those repulsions are a matter of law or custom or mere desire. You are using the word segregation simply as applying to compulsory separations.

Letter to Walter White, January 17, 1934; *Correspondence*, I, 476.

Having segregation forced upon us, we must not simply make the best of it. We must make our segregated institutions so fine and outstanding and put so much of belief and thought and loyalty in them, that the separation upon which they are based, and the doctrine of inferiority which led to them, will be confounded and contradicted by its inherent and evident foolishness.

"[Dr. Grimke on Segregation]," *Crisis* 41 (June 1934) 174; *Selections from* The Crisis, vol. 2 (1983) 764.

Segregation means the compulsory grouping of human beings. The evil in it comes from the compulsion and not from the grouping. The good comes from the grouping and in spite of the compulsion. . . . On the other hand, the voluntary association of people with each other is normal, necessary and beneficent. . . . The American Negro does not wish to be forced into association only with Negroes, or segregated by force from contact with the world.

Pittsburgh Courier, May 1, 1937; *Newspaper Columns by W.E.B. Du Bois* (1986) 196–97.

925. SEPARATE ECONOMY

We have already got a partially segregated Negro economy in the United States. . . . We not only build and finance Negro churches, but we furnish a considerable part of the funds for our segregated schools. We furnish most of our own professional services in medicine, pharmacy, dentistry and law. We furnish some part of our food and clothes, our home building and repairing and many retail services. We furnish books and newspapers; we furnish endless personal services like those of barbers, beauty shop keepers, hotels, restaurants. It may be said that this inner economy of the Negro serves but a small proportion

of its total needs; but it is growing and expanding in various ways; and what I propose is to so plan and guide it as to take advantage of certain obvious facts.
Dusk of Dawn (1940) 198.

926. SEPARATE STATE

Probably if Negroes started to take possession of one state it might meet mob violence from the . . . [residents] of that state while there would be every tendency in other states to drive away Negroes and segregate them in the new state. . . . It [would be] the most thickly populated state in the United States.

To James H. Jones, September 2, 1927; microfilm reel no. 22, frame no. 536; W.E.B. Du Bois Papers, University of Massachusetts, Amherst.

927. SEPARATION

White people and black people in the South do not, as a rule live on the same streets or in the same sections, do not travel together in train or streetcar, do not attend the same churches, do not listen to the same lectures, do not employ the same physicians, do not go to the same schools; do not, for the most part, work at the same kinds of work; do not read the same books and papers, are not taught the same traditions, and are not buried in the same graveyard.

"College-Bred Negro Communities," Atlanta University Leaflet, no. 23 (1910); *Pamphlets and Leaflets by W.E.B. Du Bois* (1986) 84.

928. A SEVENTH SON

After the Egyptian and Indian, the Greek and Roman, the Teuton and Mongolian, the Negro is a sort of seventh son, born with a veil, and gifted with second-sight in this American world,—a world which yields him no true self-consciousness, but only lets him see himself through the revelation of the other world. It is a peculiar sensation, this double-consciousness, this sense of always looking at one's self through the eyes of others, of measuring one's soul by the tape of the world that looks on in amused contempt and pity. One ever feels his two-ness,—an American, a Negro; two souls, two thoughts, two unreconciled strivings; two warring ideals in one dark body, whose dogged strength alone keeps it from being torn asunder.

The Souls of Black Folk (1903) 3.

929. SILENCE

But of the world swill that is in the trough [of colonialism], of the many millions of dark workers to whom almost nothing of modern protection for labor and uplift for the laboring classes has been applied, of the future of these folk, no modern statesmen has said a single word. The church is dumb, both Catholic and Protestant; philanthropy is dumb; science, physical and social, is voiceless.

Pittsburgh Courier, March 7, 1936; *Newspaper Columns by W.E.B. Du Bois* (1986) 40.

930. SILENT ACADEME

Socialism, communism, and the Soviet Union . . . are the great subjects of present curiosity and inquiry which face the modern world and ask for decision. In every case where I have in the last two or three years faced academic audiences, they either dare not bring up these subjects, or if somebody suggests that they be brought up, they dare not discuss it. . . . You are in slavery . . . you are scared, and . . . for this reason you ought to be ashamed of yourselves.

"Academic Freedom," April 26, 1952; microfilm reel no. 81, frame no. 367; W.E.B. Du Bois Papers, University of Massachusetts, Amherst.

931. SLUMS

It is often asked why so many Negroes persist in living in the slums. The answer is they do not; the slum is continually scaling off emigrants for other sections, and receiving new accretions from without. Thus the efforts for social betterment put forth here have often their best results elsewhere, since the beneficiaries move away and others fill their places. There is, of course, a permanent nucleus of inhabitants, and these, in some cases, are really respectable and decent people.

The Philadelphia Negro (1899) 60–61.

932. SOCIAL EQUALITY

Social equals . . . do not have the *right* to be invited to, or attend private receptions, or to marry persons who do not wish to marry them. Such a right would imply not merely equality—it would mean superiority. . . . On the other hand, every self-respecting person does claim the right to mingle with his fellows *if he is invited* and to be free from insult or hindrance because of his presence. When, therefore, the public is invited, or when he is privately invited to social gatherings, the Negro has a right to accept and no other guest has a right to complain; they have only the right to absent themselves.

"The Social Equality of Whites and Blacks," *Crisis* 21 (November 1920) 16–18; *Selections from* The Crisis, vol. 1 (1983) 281.

933. SOCIAL INQUIRY

We must study, we must investigate, we must attempt to solve; and the utmost that the world can demand is, not lack of human interest and moral conviction, but rather the heart-quality of fairness, and an earnest desire for the truth despite its possible unpleasantness.

The Philadelphia Negro (1899) 3.

934. SOCIAL WORK CAREER

The difficulty with social work is that it depends upon no fixed body of knowledge, but rather upon general education, general intelligence, a sympathetic disposition and experience. Under these circumstances the competition of those who are fitted or think they are fitted for it is very large, the remuneration very small and the tenure of office very uncertain.

To George W. Cuffee, February 14, 1922; microfilm reel no. 10, frame no. 1029; W.E.B. Du Bois Papers, University of Massachusetts, Amherst.

935. SOCIOLOGY

There is some suspicion when a small institution of learning offers courses in sociology. Very often such work means simply prolonged discussions of society and social units, which degenerate into bad metaphysics and false psychology, or it may take a statistical turn and the student becomes so immersed in mere figures as to forget, or be entirely unacquainted with, the concrete facts standing back of the counting.

"The Laboratory in Sociology at Atlanta University," *Annals* 21 (May 1903) 160–63; *Writings by W.E.B. Du Bois in Periodicals Edited by Others*, vol. 1 (1983) 158.

936. STILL AND CALM

If we were not dead we would lie and listen to the flowers grow. We would hear the birds sing and see how the rain rises and blushes and burns and pales and dies in beauty. We would see spring, summer, and the red riot of autumn, and then in winter, beneath the soft white snow, sleep and dream of dreams.

Darkwater (1920) 248.

937. STOCK MARKET CRASH

I am a little alarmed at your stock market experiments. Remember, that this present stock market gambling is bound to end with a crash, and if you can get out of your experiment without loss or with a small loss, you had better do so, and don't for heaven sakes try it again.

To Ellen Caly, April 6, 1929; microfilm reel no. 28, frame no. 91; W.E.B. Du Bois Papers, University of Massachusetts, Amherst. (The stock market crashed in October 1929).

I didn't lose a cent in that crash because I didn't have any bonds but I did have some real estate that sank in value so cheerfully and rapidly that I gave it away to the mortgagee, losing my modest wages of ten years.

To Isabel Eaton, September 9, 1931; microfilm reel no. 36, frame no. 8; W.E.B. Du Bois Papers, University of Massachusetts, Amherst.

938. SUCCESS

Cyrus Taylor: Success is not what a man does, but what he gets. The larger a man's income the greater his desert is required.

Worlds of Color (1961) 114.

939. SYMPATHY AND OPPRESSION

Perhaps never in the history of the world have victims given so much of help and sympathy to their former oppressors. Yet the most pitiable victims of the war were not the rich planters, but the poor workers; not the white race, but the black.

Black Reconstruction (1935) 129.

940. TAKEOVER

The white historians and social scientists are going to take over Negro history and social studies. Northwestern University has just received over a million dollars for a Department of African Studies. The Fund of the Republic has distributed other millions. Unless Negro scholars get busy their occupation will be gone.

To William M. Brewer, April 15, 1961; microfilm reel no. 74, frame no. 1042; W.E.B. Du Bois Papers, University of Massachusetts, Amherst.

941. TAKING POSITIONS

I can talk to people who disagree with me, and to those with whom I sympathize, but to those who are on the fence or are not going to be frank, I confess I have no methods of approach.

To Lee Lorch, February 15, 1955; microfilm reel no. 71, frame no. 529; W.E.B. Du Bois Papers, University of Massachusetts, Amherst.

942. TALENT

There is at least ten times as much talent undeveloped as there is in process of development.

To Cecil Peterson, January 6, 1947; microfilm reel no. 60, frame no. 747; W.E.B. Du Bois Papers, University of Massachusetts, Amherst.

943. TECHNOLOGY

The automobile is certainly bringing just retribution upon the silly profiteering of[the] Jim Crow [car]. All over and everywhere the colored people are traveling in their automobiles. . . . Especially is the automobile a boon for the colored Bishops, the officials of fraternal societies, insurance agents, and the like.

"A Pilgrimage to Negro Schools," *Crisis* 36 (February 1929) 43–44, 65–69; *Selections from* The Crisis, vol. 2 (1983) 536.

944. TELEVISION

Television is an example of the many devices which modern civilization has been able to invent but has neither the moral courage nor mental power to use for the benefit of mankind.

"On Television," *Academy Magazine* (June 1952) 11; *Writings by W.E.B. Du Bois in Periodicals Edited by Others*, vol. 4 (1982) 177.

945. TUSKEGEE MACHINE

[Wealthy northern whites who supported Booker T. Washington's projects viewed blacks in a special way.] They were good laborers and could be made of tremendous profit to the North. They could become a strong labor force and properly guided they would restrain the unbridled demands of white labor, born of the Northern labor unions and now spreading to the South and encouraged by European socialism.

Autobiography (1968) 239.

946. UNINTENDED CONSEQUENCES

When Northern armies entered the South they became armies of emancipation. It was the last thing they planned to be.

Black Reconstruction (1935) 55.

947. UNIONS AND CAPITALISM

In the United States . . . the best organizations of labor have traditionally been a part of the capitalist system and willing to exploit anybody anywhere if they could for a share in the profits.

To Alfred Baker Lewis, July 31, 1945; microfilm reel no. 57, frame no. 551; W.E.B. Du Bois Papers, University of Massachusetts, Amherst.

948. UNIONS IN NAACP

The NAACP did not recognize a union among its staff workers during the first twenty years of its organization and it was not until about 1940 that efforts were made to organize the stenographers, clerks and legal employees and was carried through finally after bitter struggles. There was the same difficulty in the Urban League.

"The American Negro and the Labor Movement," ca. 1945; microfilm reel no. 80, frame no. 902; W.E.B. Du Bois Papers, University of Massachusetts, Amherst.

949. VIOLENCE AND PROGRESS

The day when mobs can successfully cow the Negro to willing slavery is past. [In 1906] the Atlanta Negroes shot back and shot to kill, and that stopped the riot with a certain suddenness. The South is realizing that lawlessness and economic advance cannot coexist. If the wonderful industrial revolution is to develop unhindered, the South must have law and order and it must have intelligent workmen.

"The Economic Revolution in the South," in Booker T. Washington and Du Bois, *The Negro in the South* (Philadelphia, Penn.: Geo. W. Jacobs Co., 1907) 77–122; *Writings by W.E.B. Du Bois in Non-Periodical Literature Edited by Others*, (1982) 69.

950. WAGES AND SLAVES

High wages in the United States and England might be the skillfully manipulated result of slavery in Africa and of peonage in Asia.

Darkwater (1920) 47.

951. BOOKER T. WASHINGTON

The [Washington] . . . plan has given peace with lynchings, and dividends with caste. It has allowed oligarchy and rotten boroughs to become firmly established in the South; but at the same time it has enabled Negroes to find steady employment, accumulate property rapidly and be fairly well contented as a mass. The opposition [to Washington] can be blamed for bitterness, friction and cross purposes within and without the Negro group, but it has kept the ideal of a real democracy in America which should include black men, before the country; and held it there so persistently that not even the most optimistic Bourbon believes that the American Negro is ever going permanently to accept caste.

"The Social Significance of Booker T. Washington" (ca. 1920), Series 3/C, Folder no. 5513, p. 17, *Unpublished Articles*; W.E.B. Du Bois Papers, University of Massachusetts, Amherst.

His attitude toward the white race was: They are running the country, they're running the world, there isn't any use in bucking up against them, we can't do anything. All we can do is see what concessions we can get from them.

"Oral History Manuscript," June 9, 1960; microfilm reel no. 88, frame no. 1672; W.E.B. Du Bois Papers, University of Massachusetts, Amherst.

So far as Mr. Washington preaches Thrift, Patience, and Industrial Training for the masses, we must hold up his hands and strive with him, rejoicing in his honors and glorifying in the strength of this Joshua called of God and of man to lead the headless host. But so far as Mr. Washington apologizes for injustice, North or South, does not rightly value the privilege and duty of voting, belittles the emasculating effects of caste distinctions, and opposes the higher training and ambition of our brighter minds—so far as he, the South, or the Nation, does this—we must unceasingly and firmly oppress him. By every civilized and peaceful method we must strive for the rights which the world accords to men.

Autobiography (1968) 245.

952. WEALTH AND POWER

Wealth is not simply gratification; wealth is power, the power to say what shall be produced, under what conditions producers shall work, what wages they shall get and how much of the income of the state shall be spent for education and the fighting of disease. This power . . . is monopolized to a degree that is simply unbelievable until one studies it.

"The Talented Tenth. The Re-examination of a Concept," 1948; microfilm reel no. 80, frame no. 1112; W.E.B. Du Bois Papers, University of Massachusetts, Amherst.

953. WHO BROUGHT US?

O Southern Gentlemen! If you deplore their presence here, they ask, Who brought us?

The Souls of Black Folk (1903) 106.

954. WHO'S FIRST?

It makes little difference who was first in anything. The question is what deeds followed and if the deeds were chiefly war, murder and degradation of one's fellow there is little credit in invention or discovery.

To Ruth Pine, April 6, 1960; microfilm reel no. 74, frame no. 729; W.E.B. Du Bois Papers, University of Massachusetts, Amherst.

955. WILD AND WITLESS

Wild is the world and witless, terrible in its beauty and crime. . . . Behold the starving children of Europe, Asia, and Africa. Such a world, with all its contradictions, can be saved, can yet be born again; but not out of capital, interest, property, and gold, rather out of dreams and loiterings, out of simple goodness and friendship and love, out of science and missions.

Color and Democracy (1945) 142.

956. WORK RULES

Remember that the office is not a mere work shop: It is a place where good work is done, good cheer is expected, and where all of us strive for something greater than pay.

"All Employees of *The Crisis* [Magazine] Will Please Note," undated; microfilm reel no. 76, frame no. 632; W.E.B. Du Bois Papers, University of Massachusetts, Amherst.

957. WORKING AND BUYING

It would be in accordance with the dictates of ordinary good business for you to employ at least some colored persons as clerks and managers in your Harlem stores. If retail business is going into the hands of chain stores and chain stores are going to discriminate against the groups of people who are their customers, how are those customers going to earn decent wages which they could spend at your stores?

To the Great Atlantic and Pacific Tea Company, May 10, 1930; microfilm reel no. 31, frame no. 367; W.E.B. Du Bois Papers, University of Massachusetts, Amherst.

References

UNPUBLISHED MATERIAL

The Papers of W.E.B. Du Bois. New York: Microfilming Corporation of America, 1980. 89 microfilm reels. The material filmed consisted of substantially all the Du Bois manuscripts then held by the Archives Department of the University of Massachusetts, Amherst. Also consulted for this book were materials received since the date of this microfilming, such as Du Bois's FBI file. In addition, limited material in microfilm from Fisk University holdings was examined.

PUBLISHED MATERIAL

Quoted material from The Complete Published Works of W.E.B. Du Bois has been used with the permission of Kraus International Publications. The complete works were collated and edited by Herbert Aptheker and published as a series in thirty-seven volumes from 1973 to 1986. Individual titles within the series are listed here in alphabetical order by title.

Africa: Its Geography, People and Products. Africa: Its Place in Modern History. Girard, Kansas: Haldeman-Julius Publications, 1930. Millwood, N.Y.: Kraus International Publications, 1977 reprint.

Against Racism: Unpublished Essays, Papers, Addresses, 1887–1961. Edited by Herbert Aptheker. Amherst: University of Massachusetts Press, 1985. Paperback edition also available.

Atlanta University Publications, Numbers 1–20. 2 vols. Edited by W.E.B. Du Bois. Atlanta, Ga.: Atlanta University Press, 1896–1916. New York: Arno Press, 1969 reprint. Paperback edition available from Kraus International Publications.

The Autobiography of W.E.B. Du Bois. A Soliloquy on Viewing My Life from the Last Decade of Its First Century. New York: International Publishers, 1968. Millwood, N.Y.: Kraus International Publications, 1976 reprint. Paperback edition available from International Publishers.

The Black Flame: A Trilogy. 1. *The Ordeal of Mansart.* 2. *Mansart Builds a School.* 3. *Worlds of Color.* New York: Mainstream Publishers, 1957–1961. Millwood, N.Y.: Kraus International Publications, 1976 reprint.

Black Folk, Then and How: An Essay in the History and Sociology of the Negro Race. New York: Henry Holt, 1939. Millwood, N.Y.: Kraus International Publications, 1975 reprint.

Black North in Nineteen One: A Social Study. New York: Ayer Company Publishers, 1970.

Black Reconstruction: An Essay toward a History of the Part Which Black Folk Played in the Attempt to Reconstruct Democracy in America, 1860–1880. New York: Harcourt, Brace and Co., 1935. Millwood, N.Y.: Kraus International Publications, 1976 reprint. Paperback edition available from Atheneum.

Book Reviews by W.E.B. Du Bois. Millwood, N.Y.: Kraus International Publications, 1977.

John Brown. Philadelphia, Penn.: George W. Jacobs and Co., 1909. New York: International Publishers, 1962, with new preface and additions. Millwood, N.Y.: Kraus International Publications, 1974 reprint. Paperback edition available from International Publishers.

Color and Democracy: Colonies and Peace. New York: Harcourt, Brace and Co., 1945. Millwood, N.Y.: Kraus International Publications, 1975 reprint.

Contributions by W.E.B. Du Bois in Government Publications and Proceedings. Millwood, N.Y.: Kraus International Publications, 1981.

The Correspondence of W.E.B. Du Bois, 3 vols. Edited by Herbert Aptheker. Amherst: University of Massachusetts Press, 1973–1978.

Creative Writings by W.E.B. Du Bois: A Pageant, Poems, Short Stories and Playlets. White Plains, N.Y.: Kraus International Publications, 1985.

Dark Princess: A Romance. New York: Harcourt, Brace and Co., 1928. Millwood, N.Y.: Kraus International Publications, 1975 reprint.

Darkwater: Voices from Within the Veil. New York: Harcourt, Brace and Howe, 1920. Millwood, N.Y.: Kraus International Publications, 1975 reprint.

Dusk of Dawn: An Essay toward an Autobiography of a Race Concept. New York: Harcourt, Brace, and Co., 1940. Millwood, N.Y.: Kraus International Publications, 1975 reprint. Paperback edition available from Transaction Books.

The Education of Black People: Ten Critiques 1906–1960. Edited by Herbert Aptheker. Amherst: University of Massachusetts Press, 1973. Paperback edition available from Monthly Review Press.

The Gift of Black Folk: The Negroes in the Making of America. Boston, Mass.: The Stratford Co., 1924. Millwood, N.Y.: Kraus International Publications, 1975 reprint.

In Battle for Peace: The Story of My 83rd Birthday. New York: Masses and Mainstream Publishers, 1952. Millwood, N.Y.: Kraus International Publications, 1976 reprint.

The Negro. New York: Henry Holt, 1915. Millwood, N.Y.: Kraus International Publications, 1975 reprint. Paperback edition available from Oxford University Press.

Newspaper Columns by W.E.B. Du Bois. 2 vols. White Plains, N.Y.: Kraus International Publications, 1986.

Pamphlets and Leaflets by W.E.B. Du Bois. White Plains, N.Y.: Kraus International Publications, 1985.

The Philadelphia Negro. Philadelphia, Penn.: Ginn, 1899. Millwood, N.Y.: Kraus International Publications, 1973 reprint.

Prayers for Dark People. Edited by Herbert Aptheker. Amherst: University of Massachusetts Press, 1980. Paperback edition also available.

The Quest of the Silver Fleece: A Novel. Chicago, Ill.: A. C. McClurg and Co., 1911. Millwood, N.Y.: Kraus International Publications, 1975 reprint.

Selections from Phylon. Millwood, N.Y.: Kraus International Publications, 1980.

Selections from The Brownies Book. Millwood, N.Y.: Kraus International Publications, 1980.

Selections from The Crisis. 2 vols. Millwood, N.Y.: Kraus International Publications, 1983.

Selections from The Horizon. White Plains, N.Y.: Kraus International Publications, 1985.

The Souls of Black Folk: Essays and Sketches. Chicago, Ill.: A. C. McClurg and Co., 1903. Millwood, N.Y.: Kraus International Publications, 1973 reprint. Paperback edition available from Signet Classics.

The Suppression of the African Slave-Trade to the United States of America, 1638–1870. New York: Longmans, Green, 1896. Millwood, N.Y.: Kraus International Publications, 1973 reprint. Paperback edition available from Louisiana State University Press.

The World and Africa: An Inquiry into the Past, Which Africa Has Played in World History. New York: Viking Press, 1947. New York: International Publishers, 1965, enlarged edition. Paperback edition available from International Publishers. Millwood, N.Y.: Kraus International Publications, 1976 reprint.

Writings by W.E.B. Du Bois in Non-Periodical Literature Edited by Others. Edited by Herbert Aptheker. Millwood, N.Y.: Kraus International Publications, 1982.

Writings by W.E.B. Du Bois in Periodicals Edited by Others. Edited by Herbert Aptheker. 4 vols. Millwood, N.Y.: Kraus International Publications, 1982.

BIBLIOGRAPHIES

Aptheker, Herbert (comp.). *Annotated Bibliography of the Published Writings of W.E.B. Du Bois*. Millwood, N.Y.: Kraus-Thompson Organization Limited, 1973.

Partington, Paul G. (comp.). *W.E.B. Du Bois: A Bibliography of His Published Writings*. Revised edition. Whittier, Calif.: The Author, 1979. Paperback edition available.

———. *W.E.B. Du Bois: A Bibliography. Supplement*. Whittier, Calif.: The Author, 1984. Paperback edition available.

Index

The numbers that appear after each subject refer to entry numbers, not page numbers.

Abetting national crimes, 774

Abolitionists and capital, 403

Absolving social problems, 791

Academe, silent, 793

Academy Magazine, quotation from, 944

Accepting one's color, 293

Accepts Marxian doctrine, 397. *See also* Marx, Karl, 542, 915

Acheson, Dean, letter to, 518

Adler, Elmer, letter to, 109, 258

Advance, quotation from, 131, 409

Advice, 793

Advice to authors, 509

AF of L, 338

Africa, distaste for, 154

Africa in Europe, 176

Africa, poverty in, 155

Africa, size of, 152

African deaths, 153

African heritage, 168, 175

African land, stealing, 164

African superiority, 167

African world of equals, 161

Africanizing America, 884

Afro-American, quotation from 528

Albizu Campos, Pedro, 516

Allison, M. G., letter to, 53

"All Hail Africa," 573

America as America, 374

American Association of University Professors, 114

American Bar Association, 102. *See also* National Bar Association, 102

American Mercury, quotation from, 230, 664

America's Belgium, 286

Ames, Jessie D., letter to, 128

Amsterdam News, quotations from, 21, 64, 69, 123, 125, 139, 187, 257, 276, 294, 318, 437, 449, 470, 619, 627, 630, 640, 762, 767, 820, 846, 847, 868, 880

Ancient Blacks equal, 287. *See also* History of race concept, 321

Annals of the American Academy of Political and Social Science, quotations from, 583, 935

Anticommunism, 518

Anti-Semitism, 72, 621, 622, 625, 628, 631–634, 637, 647, 652. *See also* Protocols of the Elders of Zion, 647

Anti-Semitism, Black, 619

Application questionnaire, 266

Arkhurst, Mr. and Mrs. Frederick, letter to, 757

Armament, costs of, 707
Armattoe, Marina, letter to, 6
Armed self-defense, 560, 710, 813, 949
Art and beauty, 796
Art and propaganda, 506, 512
Asia for Asians, 728
Assassination, 870
Athanasius contra mundum, 611
Atlanta, hateful, 42
Atlanta justice, 148
Atlantic Monthly, quotation from, 73,
   686
Authenticity and audience, 485
Autobiography, quotations from, 7, 8,
   15, 16, 19, 20, 25, 34, 50, 52, 55, 66,
   74, 76, 78, 82, 87, 89, 92, 95, 98, 99,
   105, 118, 147, 154, 189, 213, 238,
   275, 283, 382, 385, 406, 471, 571,
   587, 598, 608, 654, 680, 700, 729,
   732, 742, 754, 780, 808, 888, 945
Autobiography, writing, 5, 486
Azikiwe, 163

Badges of superiority, 759
Baker, Eldrige Jr., letter to, 305
Baker, Ray Stannard, letter to, 431
Ball, R. H., letter to, 795
Baltic nations, 732
Banks, Virginia, letter to, 32
Baptism and slavery, 610
Barbering, segregated, 103
Bargain of 1876, 396. *See also* Recon-
   struction, 366
Baseball, 100
Beauty in black, 799
Begging by banks, 465
Begging pardon, 46
Being black, 21
Being frank, 800
Being misquoted, 71
Belboder, J. Samuel, letter to, 460
Belgian exploitation, 166
Belief in God, 577
Ben Gurion, David, 642. *See also* Israel,
   620, 643
Beneath white unions, 342
Beyond being ruled, 540
Beyond discrimination, 562

Bible, 578
Biblioteca Sacra, quotation from, 860
Big business, 398, 520. *See also* Con-
   gress wholly owned, 789
Big business foreign policy, 687
Bilbo, Theodore, 626
Bishop, Samuel H., letter to, 593
Black and Jewish daughters, 623
Black and white hospitals, 665
Black bitterness at treatment, 655
Black capitalism, 399
Black Church, 579
Black church membership, 589
Black class structure, 400
Black codes, 104
Black colleges, 187, 188, 189
Black college students, 190
Black congressmen, 762
Black education and culture, 191
Black faces, 292
Black folk and humanity, 464
Black Folk Then and Now, quotations
   from, 158, 159, 160, 171, 299, 320,
   321, 380, 731, 741, 751, 802
Black folklore, 838
Black gifts to America, 849
Black history, 501, 802
Black individuality, 137
Black investment in white business, 423
Black is beautiful, 9
Black landowners, 106, 311, 889
Black mainspring of progress, 561
Black mammy, 450
Black market, 792
Black migration, 803
Black ministers, 600
Black missionaries to Africa, 580
Black music, 794, 801
Black neither immigrant nor native, 866
Black occupation troops, 160
Black preacher, 606
Black press, 804
Black principals, 193
Black progress, 905
Black Reconstruction, 489
Black Reconstruction, quotations from,
   122, 128, 134, 211, 229, 246, 260,
   289, 319, 326, 327, 342, 352, 355,

363, 364, 366, 368, 375, 389, 395, 396, 403, 412, 424, 430, 433, 434, 440, 449, 466, 468, 482, 534, 537, 592, 611, 613, 717, 718, 763, 764, 769, 779, 781, 785, 813, 818, 830, 832, 837, 840, 841, 842, 857, 872, 876, 894, 903, 939, 946

Black strategies, 568

Black themes, place on, 505

Black themes, writings on, 508

Black violence, 572

Black voting and schooling, 318

Black womanliness, 451

Black women workers, 452

Black workers and interracial understanding, 370

Black youth, 196

Blacks and Africa, 162

Blacks and southern whites, 666

Blacks as colony, 401

Blacks as proletarians, 361

Blacks unsafe in U.S., 654

Bloody progress, 294

Boardman, Helen, letter to, 502

Boards of directors, 805

Boateng, Kwaku, letter to, 168

Book reviewing, 490

Boston Post, quotations from, 391, 405

Boston Transcript, quotation from, 404

Bottom of hardships, 420

Boule Journal, quotation from, 571

Boutté, M. V., letter to, 88

Bowie, Ezell, letter to, 795

Boyhood, 14

Bradley, Dan F., letter to, 585

Brand, Bernice E., letter to, 540

Brawn, Dr., letter to, 341

Breakfast, 3

Brewer, William, M., letter to, 940

Briscol, Sherman, letter to, 267

British imperialism, 742

British surveillance, 757

Brooklyn Girls' High School, 635

Brown, Anna V., letter to, 776

Brown, Benjamin A., letter to, 865

Brown, Charles O., letter to, 857

Brown decision (1954), 700. *See also* Desegregation, 206, 207

Brown, Ina Corinne, letter to, 270

Bruce, Roscoe C., letter to, 810

Buckner, G. W., letter to, 496

Burning Blacks, 121

Business ethics, 674

Buying and selling not all, 808

C.I.O. creates race unity, 340

Cajoling fools, 809

Calamitous book, 295

Caldwell, Maggie A., letter to, 242

Calling for war, 723. *See also* War frenzy, 101

Campaign for equality, 523

Capitalism, 527

Capitalism, American, 517. *See also*, Big business, 398, 520

Capitalism in Africa, 163

Capitalism in USSR, 753

Capitalizing "Negro", 810

Captains of souls, 16

Careful consumer, 44

Carter, Elmer A., letter to, 490

Carter, Emmett, letter to, 790

Carter, Harlan A., letter to, 804

Cartooning, 811

Cartwright, Leonard C., letter to, 444

Caste in Africa and America, 178

Caste system, 107, 147, 346, 404, 405, 406, 407, 548, 873

Catholic Church, 583

Catholic colleges, 583. *See also* Colleges and universities

Censorship, 79, 81

Central Christian Advocate, quotation from, 623

Century of human sympathy, 887

Chance to learn, 211, 264

Changed U.S. world role, 700. *See also* U.S. imperialism, 690

Charities, quotation from, 778

Cheap human toilers, 171

Cheating black farm laborers, 394

Cheating like whites, 417

Cheating the landless, 108

Chicago Defender, quotations from, 90, 249, 267, 443, 804

Chicago Globe, quotation from, 284

Childhood, pleasant, 78

China, 728, 729

Choosing seats and wives, 812

Christian Century, quotations from, 194, 585

Christian church, 585

Christian perjury, 586

Christian Register, quotations from 51, 478, 621, 727

Christianity and inhumanity, 602

Christianity's record, 603

Church and evil, 587

Churches and Blacks, 588

Church Review, quotation from, 298

Citizenship, 526, 530, 611, 763

Civil Rights movement, 525, 544

Class privilege and higher education, 259

Class structure, 408, 409, 410

Clay, Ellen, letter to, 937

Clemens, Cyril, letter to, 68

Clement, Rufus E., letter to, 276

Cleopatra's gracious smile, 296

Coleman, D. V., letter to, 793

College segregation, 227

College students, 221

College training important, 198

Colleges and universities: Atlanta, 157, 186, 247; Butler, 261; City College of New York, 197; Columbia, 87, 261; Detroit, 584; Fisk, 19, 219, 228, 598; Fordham, 584; Hampton Institute, 223; Harvard, 7, 41, 59, 62, 87, 224, 225, 226, 227, 228, 261; North Carolina, 277; Northwestern, 940; Pennsylvania, 21, 87, 92, 278; Princeton, 41, 258; Tuskegee, 945; University of Chicago, 276; Vassar, 41; Wilberforce, 12, 283; Yale, 41, 252, 261, 285

Collier's Weekly, quotation from, 791

Colonial education, 199

Colonial exploitation, 179. *See also* Land robbery in Kenya, 177

Colonial murder, 103

Colonialism, silence about, 929

Colonies are slums of world, 698

Color and Democracy, quotations from, 107, 140, 199, 298, 432, 471, 587,

608, 684, 692, 694, 695, 698, 705, 729, 753, 754, 778, 883, 955

Color line, 269, 298, 428, 737, 746, 758

Color prejudice, 299

Colored women, 453

Colored world, 702

Combat smug indifference, 565

Commerce with the stars, 467

Common core curriculum, 100

Communism, 519, 528. *See also* Socialism, 525, 527, 532, 544, 548

Communism in Ethiopia? 170

Communist party, 347

Compete for peace, 676

Compromising moral wrongs, 468

Congress wholly owned, 789. *See also* Big business, 398, 520

Conspiracy doctrine, 815

Conspiracy of silence, 474

Constitutional original intent, 894

Consumption (illness), 867

Contrived racial conflict, 348, 665. *See also* Economics of racism, 303

Controversial person, 23

Convict leasing, 110, 373, 378, 390

Cook, George W., letter to, 528

Cooke, Marvel, letter to, 519

Cooper, William J., letter to, 202, 243

Cooperative black economy, 817, 851, 906, 925

Corporations, 411

Corruption and wealth, 764

Couch, W. T., letter to, 513

Counterrevolution, 134

Course description, 204

Courtois, Helen W., letter to, 647

Courts, racial, 143

Cousens, Lorraine, letter to, 645, 650

Creating race feeling, 323

Creative refuge, 4

Crime of the nation, 255

Crime or color, 658

Crime, excusing and hating, 820

Crisis, quotations from, 1, 10, 22, 77, 119, 121, 127, 148, 151, 180, 206, 223, 267, 275, 285, 312, 338, 351, 352, 361, 399, 409, 414, 455, 458, 459, 461, 487, 501, 506, 508, 522,

557, 560, 576, 580, 581, 607, 616, 638, 641, 661, 683, 716, 723, 725, 741, 743, 768, 771, 780, 799, 807, 812, 833, 863, 882, 896, 914, 924, 932, 943
Cronon, Edmund D., letter to, 848
Crosswaith, Frank, letter to, 481
Crowe, William, Jr., letter to, 588
Cry aloud and spare not, 470
Cuba, 731
Cuffee, George W., letter to, 934
Cullen, Countee, letter to, 97
Culture, inner, 122
Cumming case (1899), 256. *See also* Educational goals, 213, 215
Cummings, S. H., letter to, 234
Curb power of wealth, 435
Curls in and out, 821
Current History, quotation from, 817
Curtailing government action, 422
Curti, Merle E., letter to, 36, 348

Dabney, Virginius, 553
Dangerous advances, 363
Dark Princess, quotation from, 657
Dark talent, 272
Darkwater, quotations from, 42, 83, 213, 215, 228, 272, 286, 297, 307, 329, 336, 350, 388, 389, 436, 438, 451, 452, 459, 462, 471, 595, 614, 615, 658, 669, 670, 674, 681, 701, 703, 704, 712, 722, 725, 822, 831, 844, 878, 910, 936, 950
Darmstadter, Doris, letter to, 913
Davidson, Mr. and Mrs. Eugene, letter to, 454
Davis, Harry E., letter to, 53
Davis, Jackson, letter to, 909
Davis, John W., letter to, 352
Deathly colonial system, 711
Debt, perpetual, 823
Defining a race, 320, 324
Defining Negro, 312
Deliberate racism, 765
Demand, don't apologize, 825
Demeaning address, 247
Democracy, 376, 412, 424, 476, 480, 483, 538, 635, 656, 705, 903, 916.

See also Oligarchy in the United States, 429, 430
Democratic party, 787
Democrats and Republicans, 776, 780
Derogatory words, 826
Des Moines Register Leader, quotations from, 404, 407, 895
Descent, proof of, 827
Desegregation, 206, 207. *See also Brown* decision (1954), 700
Designing clothes, 18
Desperate causes, 624
Dewey, John, 521
Dial, quotation from, 389
Dirty Philadelphia politics, 778
Discovery of whiteness, 670. *See also* White western European world, 696
Discrimination, 92
Discrimination in libraries, 250
Discrimination, military, 105
Discriminatory school finance, 270
Discriminatory universities, 275. *See also* Quotas, 261
Disfranchisement and schools, 208
Divide and conquer, 684
Dixon, Charles T., letter to, 553
Doctoral degree, 210
Dodd, Edward H., Jr., letter to, 79
Doing and getting, 829
Done deal, 662
Don't fight USSR, 733
Do something, 531
Double bargain, 395
Douglas, Benjamin, letter to, 200
Down-home economics, 798
Drama of history, 830
Driving a car, 2
Du Bois, Rachel Davis, letter to, 509
Du Bois, Shirley Graham, letter to, 60, 601. *See also* Shirley Graham, 457
Du Bois, Yolande, letter to, 9, 18, 30, 44, 45, 57, 64, 93, 96, 210
Du Bois's writings from 1887 through 1889, 48, 760
Du Bois's writings from 1890 through 1899, 14, 103, 113, 128, 140, 143, 255, 278, 310, 335, 371, 373, 379, 388, 389, 409, 410, 418, 427, 456,

469, 473, 477, 562, 579, 667, 770,
792, 824, 867, 885, 900, 904, 931
Du Bois's writings from 1900 through
1909, 10, 28, 51, 104, 106, 108, 110,
111, 115, 116, 120, 131, 136, 138,
145, 149, 189, 190, 212, 232, 234,
245, 247, 256, 269, 274, 279, 282,
298, 299, 313, 324, 346, 373, 378,
386, 387, 389, 390, 391, 394, 404,
405, 407, 409, 416, 420, 431, 445,
472, 478, 531, 539, 555, 570, 571,
582, 589, 593, 597, 600, 606, 610,
707, 761, 774, 778, 787, 791, 794,
801, 803, 823, 829, 836, 851, 854,
855, 860, 862, 884, 887, 889, 895,
920, 924, 928, 935, 949, 953
Du Bois's writings from 1910 through
1919, 1, 9, 26, 30, 73, 77, 110, 121,
127, 132, 148, 151, 176, 208, 214,
218, 223, 233, 236, 280, 285, 288,
290, 300, 311, 317, 331, 349, 351,
352, 356, 365, 368, 377, 381, 383,
384, 392, 458, 459, 461, 470, 474,
526, 541, 554, 560, 616, 665, 686,
716, 723, 741, 772, 800, 809, 810,
833, 850, 914, 927
Du Bois's writings from 1920 through
1929, 10, 18, 33, 42, 43, 45, 49, 53,
57, 64, 83, 88, 96, 97, 126, 128, 137,
152, 155, 195, 197, 200, 202, 206,
210, 213, 215, 219, 227, 228, 230,
235, 242, 243, 261, 265, 267, 272,
281, 286, 293, 297, 298, 305, 307,
309, 315, 323, 329, 339, 341, 343,
344, 350, 353, 359, 361, 388, 389,
399, 409, 413, 415, 436, 438, 444,
450, 451, 452, 455, 459, 462, 471,
481, 487, 493, 496, 498, 501, 506,
510, 540, 543, 554, 564, 565, 567,
574, 576, 578, 579, 580, 583, 584,
585, 586, 595, 596, 605, 614, 615,
617, 635, 638, 657, 658, 661, 664,
666, 669, 670, 672, 674, 680, 681,
689, 701, 703, 704, 710, 712, 722,
725, 735, 741, 745, 759, 768, 786,
793, 796, 797, 799, 805, 806, 807,
810, 814, 822, 827, 831, 844, 852,
861, 878, 879, 892, 896, 897, 910,

916, 923, 926, 932, 934, 936, 937,
943, 950, 951
Du Bois's writings from 1930 through
1939, 3, 13, 17, 22, 27, 44, 47, 58,
61, 62, 67, 68, 71, 80, 84, 85, 101,
119, 122, 124, 128, 134, 159, 160,
164, 166, 171, 174, 180, 193, 194,
211, 222, 229, 237, 244, 246, 248,
250, 260, 263, 266, 267, 273, 275,
276, 277, 289, 299, 302, 306, 312,
316, 319, 320, 321, 325, 326, 327,
338, 342, 345, 348, 352, 357, 358,
360, 361, 362, 363, 364, 366, 370,
375, 380, 382, 385, 389, 396, 397,
399, 403, 408, 409, 412, 414, 422,
424, 425, 426, 430, 433, 434, 439,
440, 441, 446, 447, 449, 460, 464,
466, 468, 476, 479, 482, 488, 489,
490, 503, 504, 505, 509, 512, 515,
521, 522, 528, 529, 534, 537, 542,
552, 557, 571, 575, 579, 581, 585,
588, 590, 592, 594, 603, 607, 611,
612, 613, 618, 625, 629, 637, 641,
644, 647, 655, 656, 662, 678, 683,
697, 709, 717, 718, 726, 728, 731,
736, 741, 744, 746, 747, 748, 751,
752, 763, 764, 766, 769, 771, 775,
776, 779, 780, 781, 782, 785, 795,
802, 804, 805, 811, 812, 813, 817,
818, 821, 825, 826, 828, 830, 832,
837, 838, 840, 841, 842, 857, 858,
863, 869, 872, 873, 876, 882, 891,
894, 903, 906, 907, 909, 911, 913,
915, 917, 918, 919, 921, 924, 929,
937, 939, 946, 957
Du Bois's writings from 1940 through
1949, 12, 21, 24, 38, 41, 53, 64, 65,
69, 90, 91, 93, 100, 102, 107, 109,
114, 117, 123, 125, 128, 130, 133,
135, 139, 140, 153, 157, 162, 165,
166, 167, 170, 172, 177, 178, 179,
180, 181, 182, 183, 184, 185, 187,
192, 199, 201, 204, 209, 213, 216,
221, 225, 228, 239, 240, 249, 252,
257, 258, 259, 262, 267, 270, 271,
275, 276, 287, 291, 292, 294, 296,
298, 301, 304, 314, 318, 322, 328,
330, 332, 334, 340, 347, 354, 369,

374, 388, 400, 401, 402, 409, 428,
432, 435, 437, 443, 448, 449, 457,
465, 467, 471, 475, 483, 484, 485,
491, 492, 494, 495, 497, 502, 507,
513, 514, 516, 519, 520, 523, 533,
535, 536, 538, 547, 553, 561, 563,
568, 571, 573, 577, 583, 587, 591,
593, 602, 608, 619, 620, 621, 624,
626, 627, 630, 631, 639, 640, 641,
642, 643, 646, 652, 653, 663, 673,
675, 679, 684, 685, 688, 690, 691,
692, 693, 694, 695, 698, 705, 709,
711, 727, 728, 729, 734, 738, 739,
740, 741, 743, 753, 754, 755, 758,
762, 767, 777, 788, 789, 795, 798,
804, 820, 834, 835, 839, 843, 846,
847, 848, 856, 861, 864, 865, 866,
868, 871, 875, 877, 880, 883, 899,
905, 908, 925, 942, 947, 948, 952,
955
Du Bois's writings from 1950 through
  1959, 4, 6, 23, 32, 36, 40, 41, 53, 54,
  56, 60, 63, 64, 70, 72, 75, 79, 81,
  112, 141, 144, 146, 150, 156, 161,
  163, 169, 183, 186, 191, 203, 207,
  217, 224, 226, 231, 251, 264, 284,
  285, 298, 333, 337, 342, 352, 372,
  376, 398, 409, 417, 421, 429, 442,
  453, 454, 463, 471, 480, 486, 488,
  499, 500, 517, 518, 524, 529, 544,
  548, 549, 550, 551, 558, 559, 566,
  569, 571, 579, 599, 601, 604, 609,
  622, 632, 633, 634, 636, 645, 648,
  649, 650, 651, 660, 668, 676, 687,
  696, 699, 702, 706, 713, 714, 715,
  719, 720, 724, 730, 733, 737, 738,
  750, 755, 756, 757, 765, 773, 783,
  784, 790, 795, 815, 816, 819, 845,
  849, 859, 870, 881, 890, 893, 898,
  902, 922, 930, 941, 944
Du Bois's writings from 1960 through
  1963, 2, 29, 31, 32, 37, 39, 46, 53,
  59, 66, 86, 94, 168, 188, 196, 205,
  206, 207, 220, 228, 276, 352, 409,
  414, 445, 472, 511, 525, 527, 529,
  530, 545, 555, 628, 659, 671, 682,
  721, 874, 912, 938, 940, 951, 954
Dunham, Barrows, letter to, 463

Du Sable High, 267
Dusk of Dawn, quotations from, 41, 128,
  216, 292, 301, 314, 330, 347, 409,
  448, 467, 485, 523, 563, 602, 626,
  777, 835, 856, 861, 908, 925
Dyer Anti-lynching Bill, 777

Earning money, 58
East St. Louis race riot, 350. See also
  Labor competition, 352
Eaton, Isabel, letter to, 737
Economic emancipation, 371
Economic justice and world state, 706
Economic self-interest, 473
Economics of racism, 303. See also Con-
  trived racial conflict, 348, 665
Economic theory, 95
Educated person, 212
Educate whites first, 236
Educating servile class, 223
Education, 185–285
Educational goals, 213, 215. See also
  Cumming case (1899), 256
Education for exploitation, 214
Egypt, African, 158
Elegy for me, 601
Elkin, Kyrle, letter to, 41
Eller, Dorothy M., letter to, 488
Emancipating America, 831
Emancipation, comparative, 468
Emancipation Proclamation, 592
Embree, Edwin R., letter to, 192
Employ blacks, 91, 522, 957
Endicott, James, letter to, 682
Endicott, Mary, letter to, 53
Enemy has the money, 425
Enslavement and schooling, 218
Episcopal Church, 593
Equality and power, 833
Equality of income, 533
Equal manhood, 832
Equal schooling, 217
Establishing cultures, 835
Ethics of Jesus Christ, 617
Europe discovers color, 297
Evans, Mrs. Edmund C., letter to, 786
Excluded from science, 265

Exclusion from unions, 356. *See also* Labor solidarity, 345, 362
Exclusion for Blacks, 209
Exile, 29, 31, 32
Explaining Constitutional original intent, 894
Exploit not, 33
Exploitation, 414
Exploitation and economic development, 472
Exploitation and revolution, 172
Expulsion of blacks, 626
Extending slavery, 317
Extension of thoughts of Du Bois, 15, 32, 41, 53, 64, 110, 128, 140, 180, 183, 189, 195, 206, 213, 215, 223, 228, 258, 267, 275, 276, 285, 299, 318, 342, 352, 361, 373, 388, 389, 399, 404, 409, 414, 449, 471, 488, 528, 529, 557, 579, 583, 585, 587, 593, 608, 630, 641, 644, 728, 729, 731, 738, 741, 747, 754, 755, 763, 780, 795, 804, 805, 810, 860, 861, 863, 891, 902, 924, 937, 951
Extermination of Jews, 627. *See also* Holocaust, 630, 640

FBI, 35, 569
Failure and success, 836
Failure of success, 837
Faith in men, not Christianity, 594
Falter, William L., letter to, 635
Farm tenancy, 377
Fauset, Arthur Huff, letter to, 488
Federal judge, 869
Fellow traveler, 535, 536
Ferguson, Oscar E., letter to, 198
Few read magazines, 244. *See also* Negro book club, 495
Fisher, Ruth Anna, letter to, 697, 915
Fitzpatrick, George P., letter to, 874
Fletcher, Angus, letter to, 689
Fleury, J. G., letter to, 678, 736
Forced labor, 116, 371–394
Foreign Affairs, quotations from, 164, 306, 428
Form national peace group, 714
Forthcoming tragedy, 124

Fosdick, Raymond B., letter to, 510
Franklin, John Hope, letter to, 157
14th Amendment, 526
France, 74, 735
Freedmen's Bureau, 842
Freedom and equality, 844
Freedom and slavery, 379
Freedom to learn, 262
Freeing business enterprise, 840
Free Negroes, 841
Friends and foes, 88
Friends, white, 47, 49
Frissell, A. S., letter to, 33
From Africa to hell, 375. *See also* Slavery 232, 389
Fruitless interviews, 865
Fund raising, 36
Funeral, 60
Funny little cross, 614
Future fight for freedom, 712

Gannett, Lewis, letter to, 296
Garbage, managing, 37
Garvey movement, 848
General Education Board, 254, 921
General strike of slaves, 537
Gentlemanly machine guns, 740
George, Clayborne, letter to, 923
Germany after the Nazis, 738. *See also* Nazi Germany, 747
Gesture of surrender, 659
Get rich, 402, 432
Get richer, 418
Gift of Black Folk, The, quotations from, 329, 359, 450, 471, 493, 579, 617, 916
Glenn, Joseph B., letter to, 583
Goens, Grace, letter to, 4, 31
Good black government, 818
Good, profitable business, 839
Good teacher, 89
Graduate students, 221
Grady, Henry, 421
Graham, Shirley, letter to, 457. *See also* Shirley Graham Du Bois, 60, 601
Graham, William B., letter to, 100
Grandfathers, remembering, 38
Grantham, Dewey W., Jr., letter to, 765

Graves, Anna M., letter to, 706, 738, 755
Graves, John Temple II, 553
Grayson, Mary, letter to, 237
Great experiment in slavery, 380
Great payday, 850
Great White Way, 117
Griggs, Johanna, letter to, 332
Grillo, S. Henry, letter to, 302
Griscom, Anna B., letter to, 741
Groves, Emma, letter to, 80
Gunboat finance, 689

Haggan, Frances, letter to, 554
Hall, Gus, letter to, 529
Hanus, Paul H., letter to, 223
Hapgood, Emilie, letter to, 526
Happiness and having, 853
Harcourt, Alfred, letter to, 858
Hare, Maud Cuney, letter to, 805
Harris, Abram L., letter to, 542, 886
Harris, Dudley, letter to, 907
Hart, Albert Bushnell, 62
Harvard University, 7, 41, 59, 62, 87, 224, 225, 226, 227, 228, 261
Hastie, William H., 869
Hate in Georgia, 413. See also Jesus in Georgia, 597
Hauptmann, Gerhard, letter to, 641
Hautz, Larry and Carol, letter to, 609
Hayes, Roland, letter to, 309
Health, 26, 40
Health and work, 854
Heaven and hell of work, 856
He is of Negro descent, 581
Hell and idleness, 855
Helm, A. J., letter to, 585
Hendel, Charles W., letter to, 871
Henderson, A. J., letter to, 811
Herberg, Will, letter to, 325
Higher than white, 28
Hikida, Y., letter to, 603
Hiller, Helen N., letter to, 917
Himstead, Ralph E., letter to, 114
Historians, 857
History, 858, 899
History, indispensable, 65
History of race concept, 321

History textbooks, 229
Hobhouse, L. T., letter to, 672
Hodnefiled, Jacob, letter to, 498
Hollander, A. N. der, letter to, 277
Holly, A.P.B., letter to, 578
Holmes, John Haynes, 585
Holocaust, 630, 640. See also Extermination of Jews, 627
Honesty, 43, 845
Honor and suffering, 859
Hooper, Mary Louise, letter to, 183
Hooper, William D., letter to, 531
Hopper, Franklin F., letter to, 625, 828
Horizon, quotation from, 416
Horr, Louis Harding, letter to, 150
Hospital, segregated, 923
Hotels, segregated, 119
Housing, 860
Housing, crowded, 120
Howe, Annie H., letter to, 565
Hudson, R. C., letter to, 892
Hughley, J. Neal, letter to, 515
Human degradation, 382
Human errors, 834
Humanity and history, 806
Humanity, dark, 822. See also Pan-Africanism, 180, 181, 316
Humanity overseas, 15
Human rights, 475, 631, 691
Humor, 50, 861
Huntington, Henry S., letter to, 586
Hunton, Alphaeus, letter to, 749
Hurston, Zora Neale, letter to, 293
Hutcheson, Ernest, Jr., letter to, 604

Ideals and realities, 463–484
Ignorance, poverty and bastards, 661
Ignoring colonial peoples, 673
Immigrant racism, 307
Immigrants, 839, 896
Imperialism and anthropology, 159. See also International African Institute, 182
Imperialism and nationalism, 165
Imperialism, countering, 169
Imported workers, 369
Inadvertently anti-Jewish, 632, 633, 634, 649
In Battle for Peace, quotations from, 56,

141, 224, 265, 333, 409, 429, 471, 890
Independent India, 743
Independent, quotation from, 269
Indicted for peace, 715
Individual honors, 492
Industrial peace and war, 686
Infant mortality, 111
Inferior separate schools, 235
Inheriting enemies, 45
Inhumane standards, 333
Injustice expensive, 305
Insist on our rights, 814
Integrated schools, 237, 245, 246, 253, 268. *See also* Segregated schools, 267
Integration, 771, 863
Intercollegiate Socialist, quotation from, 384, 474
Intermarriage, 308
Internal colonies, 864
International African Institute, 182. *See also* Imperialism and anthropology, 159
International Journal of Ethics, quotation from, 582
Interpretation of suppression, 130
Interracial love, 309
Irish, 83, 875, 898
Is God white? 595
Israel, 620, 643

Jackson, H. M., letter to, 152
Jackson, Miss, letter to, 854
James, William, 62
Jameson, J. Franklin, letter to, 810
Japan, 728. *See also* Asia for Asians, 728
Japanese Americans, 123, 868, 896
Japanese exclusion, 777
Jenkins, Anne F., letter to, 796
Jennings, S. W., letter to, 505
Jester, Clarissa, letter to, 235
Jesus in Georgia, 597. *See also* Hate in Georgia, 413
Jewish and black memory, 636
Jewish Life, quotation from, 72
Jews, 619–655, 896
Jews and Blacks, 638, 639

Jews in Germany, 628, 629, 641, 644, 737
Jim Crow literature, 238
Jim Crowed, Being, 291
Job seeking, 50
John Brown, quotations from, 445, 472, 555, 862
John Brown, 555
John Brown's body, 717
Johnson, Charles S., letter to, 919
Johnson, James Weldon, letter to, 315, 564, 797
Johnson, (Mrs.) J. Rosamond, letter to, 24
Johnson, Oakley, letter to, 527
Jones, James H., letter to, 926
Jones, Virginia Lacy, letter to, 499
Jones, William N., letter to, 552
Jordan, Bradford, letter to, 877
Journal of Negro Education, quotations from, 12, 268, 397, 529, 557, 571, 572
Justice and education, 125
Justifying myself, 39

Keelan, Mollie, letter to, 575
Keeping man in gutter, 852
Kelly, Arthur P., letter to, 898
Keppel, F. P., letter to, 489
Kidder, C. G., letter to, 290
King, Clemmon, letter to, 548
Kitchen, S. M., letter to, 49
KKK supported candidates, 768
Knapp, T. J., letter to, 814
Knowledge and administration, 463
Knowledge and logic, 871

Labor and colonial self-interest, 680
Labor and imperialism, 692
Labor and race, 310. *See also* Labor, white, 99
Labor competition, 352. *See also* East St. Louis race riot, 350
Labor, not race, problem, 354
Labor revolution, 355
Labor solidarity, 345, 362. *See also* Exclusion from unions, 356

Labor, white, 99. *See also* Labor and race, 310
Laidler, Harry W., letter to, 471, 567
Lamont, Corliss, letter to, 41
Land hunger, 872
Land robbery in Kenya, 177. *See also* Colonial exploitation, 179
Last great battle, 534
Last speaker, 51
Laundering shirts, 24
Lawlessness, 873
Laws helped produce racism, 335. *See also* Legal discrimination, 642
Leaderless colonials, 678
Leadership, 13
League of Nations should curb racism, 716
Learning styles, 242
Lecturing, 53, 84, 85, 201, 491, 907
Lee, Algernon, letter to, 353
Leers, Dr. von, letter to, 622
Legal defense, 141, 226
Legal discrimination, 642. *See also* Laws helped produce racism, 335
Leisure activities, 4, 14, 27, 30, 59, 68, 75, 100
Lewis, Alfred Baker, letter to, 947
Lewis, Mabel Stuart, letter to, 521
Liberate white colleges, 273
Liberia, 744
Libraries, 498, 499, 625, 828
Library of Congress, 126
Limpid garbage, 874
Lincoln, Abraham, 319, 876
Linked degradation, 357
Literacy, 192, 202, 232, 233, 239, 241, 243
Literature, 485–515
Literature, black, 488
Literature, white, 493
Little business, 113
Lochard, Metz T. P., telegram to, 739
Logan, Rayford W., letter to, 750
Lomax, Almena, letter to, 511
Long life, 55. *See also* Old age, 1, 64, 890
Lorch, Lee, letter to, 724, 941
Loud, Mr., letter to, 782

Love and marriage, 57
Lovejoy, Owen R., letter to, 891
Love of country, 56. *See also* My country, 881
Low college salaries, 187
Lynching, 128, 129

Mackenzie, Dudley S., letter to, 735
Mackonnen, T. R., letter to, 181
Make men intelligent, 263
Manchukuo, exemplary colony, 746
Mandel, William, letter to, 524
Manhood, denying, 48
Mann, Albert R., letter to, 222
Mansart Builds a School, quotations from 112, 352, 549, 579, 719, 819
Marchant, B. L., letter to, 911
Mark Twain Quarterly, quotation from, 861
Marriage, 454
Marston, M. B., letter to, 28
Martin Luther King, Jr., 870. *See also* Nonviolent civil disobedience, 544, 847
Marx, Karl, 542, 915
Mason, William, letter to, 298
Mass media, 131
Massachusetts Review, quotation from, 59
Maxey, C. L., Jr., letter to, 197
May, Samuel, Jr., letter to, 924
McCarthyism, 231, 524
McConnell, Francis, F., letter to, 585
McDermott, John Francis, letter to, 503
McGill, Ralph, 553
McNutt, Waldo, letter to, 728
Mechanical cotton picker, 877
Medical Review of Reviews, quotation from, 26
Midwest Journal, quotation from, 262
Mighty Human Rainbow, 878
Migration, 543, 879
Military discrimination, 151, 248, 708, 709
Mississippi sheriffs, 773. *See also* Police and Blacks, 138
Moe, Henry Allen, letter to, 64
More black workers, 353

Moreno, E. Pina, letter to, 577
Morgan, Al, interview with, 40
Morton, Ferdinand Q., letter to, 250
Most exploited class, 351
Mother Africa, 152–184
Mound Bayou, Miss., 545
Mulholland, James V., letter to, 897
Multicultural education, 249. *See also*
  Multicultural state, 546
Multicultural state, 546. *See also* Multi-
  cultural education, 249
Multicultural world history, 240
Multilingual silence, 880
Mundt, Karl E., letter to, 653
Murder and manhood, 718
Murphy, Carl, letter to, 291
My country, 881. *See also* Love of coun-
  try, 56
My words, 52

NAACP, 547, 882, 886
NAACP, unionizing, 948
Naming black people, 795
Narrowed opportunities, 222
Nation, quotation from, 584
National Bar Association, 102. *See also*
  American Bar Association, 102
National crimes, 313
National defense, 719
National Guardian, quotations from, 54,
  207, 409, 676, 784, 870
Native Americans, 883
Nazi Germany, 747. *See also* Germany
  after the Nazis, 738
Negro baiting, 896
Negro book club, 495. *See also* Few read
  magazines, 244
Negro business, 496
Negro Digest, quotations from, 318, 494,
  733
Negro jobs, 426
Negro law practice, 427
Negro or American, 885
Negro problem, 886
Negro, The, quotations from, 288, 367
Neither starve nor prosper, 381
Nelson, Alice Dunbar, letter to, 27, 84
New Africa, quotation from, 179

New Anglo-America, 672
New Deal, 549
New Review, quotation from, 365
New South, old goals, 359
New World Review, quotations from,
  569, 720
New York Herald Tribune Books, quota-
  tion from, 863
New York Post, quotation from, 245
New York Public Library, discrimination,
  828
New York Times Magazine, quotations
  from 275, 561
Nichols, Catherine R., letter to, 507
Nineteen centuries, 455
Njakar, Elechukwu, letter to, 795
Nkrumah, Kwame, 163
Nkrumah, Kwame, letter to, 529
No ancient racism, 322. *See also* No me-
  dieval racism, 306
No black Zion, 314
No Hereafter, 596
No medieval racism, 306. *See also* No
  ancient racism, 322
No sacrificial goat, 557
Nonviolent civil disobedience, 544, 847,
  870. *See also* Martin Luther King, Jr.,
  870
North American Review, quotation from,
  128
Northern black teachers, 195
Northern masters of South, 779. *See also*
  Northern moneymaking, 385
Northern moneymaking, 385. *See also*
  Northern masters of South, 779
North, Joseph, letter to, 728
Not counseling college, 281
Nyasaland, 156

Objecting to frying pan, 846
Objectionable words, 315
O'Dwyer, William, letter to, 713
Ogden, Rollo, letter to, 810
Old age, 1, 64, 890. *See also* Long life,
  55
Oligarchy in the United States, 429, 430.
  See also Democracy, 376, 412, 424,

476, 480, 483, 538, 635, 656, 705, 903, 916

Oligarchy regains power, 785

Olmstead, Mildred Scott, letter to, 281

On his writing, 494

Only one life, 591

On religious awakenings, 613

Oppressed and oppressor, 133

Oppressor's fear of oppressed, 431

Optimism, realistic, 17

Ordeal of Mansart, The, quotations from, 144, 352, 409, 421, 442, 453, 660, 783, 902

Ordinary human beings, 289

Organizational change, 891

Organized finance, 415

Organized reaction, 893

Organized wealth and power, 788

Ortiz, Fernando, letter to, 75

Our natural friends, 416

Outdating the Jim Crow car, 943

Out-Herod Herod, 895

Outlook, quotations from, 136, 707

Outside, inside, 550

Overthrowing socialism, 645

Ovington, Mary W., letter to, 570

Owens, Maud, letter to, 43

Padmore, George, letter to, 81, 163, 169, 715

Page, Kirby, letter to, 101

Pan-Africanism, 180, 181, 316. *See also* Humanity, dark, 822

Pandit, Vijaya Lakshmi, letter to, 691. *See also* Dark humanity, 822

Pankhurst, E. Sylvia, letter to, 23, 146, 162, 741

Pariah ideals, 478

Partington, Paul, letter to, 2

Passive resistance, 551

Paternalistic scholars, 182

Patriotic songs, 63

Patterson, William, letter to, 859

Paying for principle, 552

Peace, 73

Peace movement, absence in U.S., 720

Peace with communism, 721

Peck, Theodora, letter to, 53

Peking Review, quotation from, 70

Peonage, escaping, 392

People and packages, 136

People's Voice, quotation from, 177

Persistent racism, 479

Personal bitterness, 6

Personal brightness, 82

Personal characteristics, 35, 68

Personal exercise, 27, 30

Personal indulgence, 40

Personal integrity, 70

Personal protest, 77

Personal reserve, 76

Personal taste, 93

Peterson, Cecil, letter to, 571, 942

Phelps-Stokes Fund, 921

Phi Delta Kappa, 209

Philadelphia Negro, The, quotations from, 103, 140, 278, 409, 427, 456, 473, 562, 579, 667, 867, 931, 933

Philanthropy, misconceived, 900

Phylon, quotations from, 102, 209, 252, 304, 340, 401, 538, 624, 652

Pickens, William, letter to, 805

Pittsburgh Courier, quotations from, 13, 47, 166, 316, 345, 362, 370, 422, 439, 441, 571, 629, 641, 662, 736, 746, 747, 748, 766, 869, 924, 929

Pineapples and the poor, 360

Pine, Ruth, letter to, 954

Pinkett, A. S., letter to, 826

Plagiarism, 502

Planting cotton, 819

Poetry, 503, 504

Police and blacks, 138. *See also* Mississippi sheriffs, 773

Polish Americans, 901

Polish issue, 646

Political Affairs, quotation from, 855

Political balance of power, 760

Political handicap, 419

Politics, 759–789

Politics of suffering, 781

Polygamy, 386

Poor legislators, 440

Poor whites, 433, 434

Popular government, 782

Post, Louis F., letter to, 772

Potential plenty, 701
Poverty, 115, 139, 902
Power monopoly and labor, 387
Preece, Harold, letter to, 484
Preference for colonial wars, 726
Prejudice into discrimination, 290
Preparing for war, 725
Prescriptions, medical, 26
Press, black, 81
Private ownership and monopoly, 436
Problem non-solving, 904
Profit motive in colonial administration, 693
Profitable investment in colonies, 694
Profiting from backwardness, 679
Prohibition, not competition, 330
Pro-Negro, 510
Pronunciation of name, 61
Proper titles, 749
Prophet, Elizabeth, letter to, 67
Proskauer, Joseph M., letter to, 631
Protocols of the Elders of Zion, 647. See also Anti-Semitism, 72, 619, 621, 622, 625, 637, 652
Public education in South, 260
Public facility segregation, 135
Public, not private, duty, 279
Puerto Rico, 516, 695
Pullman Porters union, 343

Quakers and slavery, 607
Quest of the Silver Fleece, The, quotations from, 381, 665, 800, 809, 850
Quotas, 261. See also Discriminatory universities, 275

Race and class problems, 439
Race and culture, 919
Race and life, 908
Race and racism, 301
Race consciousness, 909
Race ideology, 304
Race pride, 910
Race riots, 911
Races and classes, 438
Racial forbears, 66
Racism, 72, 73, 74, 140, 323, 286–337, 765, 912

Racism and humanity, 300
Racism and labor, 364
Racism and revolution, 325
Racism, exporting, 34
Racism in England, 735
Racism in France, 734, 735
Racist conceptions, 326
Racist dogma, 327
Racist strikes, 365
Racist teachers out, 328
Radicalism, opposing, 554
Radio broadcasting, 913. See also Television, 944
Rape, charges of, 914
Reactionary white South, 668
Reconsideration of own thoughts by Du Bois: Color line problem of twentieth century, 298; Communist party, 529; Inadvertence, 632–634, 649; Talented Tenth, 571
Reconstruction, 366. See also Bargain of 1876, 396
Record, Cy W., letter to, 568
Red Cross nurses, 917
Reform, radicalism, and revolution, 516–572
Reid, Ira De A., letter to, 637
Rejecting the black past, 173
Relatives, polite to, 918
Relaxation, 75
Religion, 573–618
Religion against communism, 599
Religion and racism, 648
Religion of hate, 329
Religious belief, 609
Religious, the, 608
Repression and liberty, 862
Rest in a colored country, 750
Restricted travel, 146, 150
Rhodes, E. Washington, letter to, 195
Rich and richer, 448
Riches and the law, 784
Rising people, 920
Ritz, Leon, letter to, 53
Roback, A. A., letter to, 650
Roberts, Harry W., letter to, 702
Roberts, Holland, letter to, 714, 721
Roberts, Major, letter to, 183

Robeson, Paul, 79, 733
Robinson, Dwight P., letter to, 225
Rogers, Ben F., Jr., letter to, 62
Rose, B. Andrew, letter to, 85
Rosenberg, Julius and Ethel, 558, 815
Rosenwald Fund, 921
Rulers and ruled, 751
Ruling and other classes, 395–449
Russia and America (unpublished), quotations from, 32, 517, 550, 559, 730, 738, 756

St. Nicholas Park, 897
Sales of his books, 497
Salvation through emancipation, 441
Sanders, Charlotte, letter to, 747
Saur, Wolfgang, letter to, 500
Scholar-athletes or athlete-scholars? 185
Schomburg, Arthur A., 922
School desegregation, 257
School integration and black culture, 220
School segregation, 216
Schools, locally-controlled, 477
Schweitzer, Albert, letter to, 153, 184
Science, defining a, 824
Scientific Monthly, quotation from 663
Sea change, 25
Secular beliefs, 576
Secular credo, 590
Seek economic safety, 302
Segregated schools, 267. *See also* Integrated schools, 237, 245, 246, 253, 268
Segregation, 924, 927
Selective silence, 331
Selfish white race, 671
Self-representation, 563
Selsam, Howard, letter to, 201
Sengstacke, John H. H., letter to, 514
Separate black state, 926
Separate state, 546
Settling for too little, 541
Seventh Son, 928
Sex ratio and work, 456
Sexism, 460
Sexism on wheels, 457
Shaeffer, Mr., letter to, 37
Sharing Nazi ideas, 739

Shattuck, Virginia, letter to, 585
Shelvin, Mrs. C. B., letter to, 195
Sheperd, Jessie, letter to, 155
Shepperson, George, letter to, 156
Shivery, Henrietta, letter to, 58, 193, 918
Shooting at meetings, 132
Shotwell, James T., letter to, 709
Sierra Leone, injustice in, 752
Sigma Pi Phi, 251
Silberstein, Robert J., letter to, 491
Singing, 59
Slave and free labor, 367
Slave marriage and religion, 582
Slavery, 232, 389. *See also* From Africa to hell, 375
Slavery and capitalism, 697
Slavery and modern world economy, 383
Slavery persists, 384
Slaves' freedom efforts, 372
Slow progress in South, 790
Slums, black, 931
Small-town oppression, 144
Smith, Edwin W., letter to, 182
Smith, Lillian E., letter to, 244
Smith, Lurlani, letter to, 3, 360
Smug preachers, 574
Snowden, Frank M., Jr., letter to, 287
Social equality, 932
Social inquiry, 933
Socialism, 525, 527, 532, 544, 548. *See also* Communism, 519, 528
Socialist party, 481, 567, 786
Social work career, 934
Society creates property, 437
Sociology, 935
Some other countries, 728–758
Somerville, Vada and John, letter to, 891
Songs, black, 8
Souls of Black Folk, The, quotations from, 11, 108, 116, 138, 145, 232, 298, 299, 313, 378, 389, 420, 589, 606, 761, 774, 794, 823, 860, 887, 889, 920, 928, 953
Southern Education Board, 254
Southern recalcitrance, 205
Southern Workman, quotations from, 120, 247, 390

Speak out plainly, 332
Spingarn, Joel E., letter to, 219, 349, 574
Spiritual suicide, 564
Spivak, Lawrence E., letter to, 709
Splitting third party, 783
Spouting Cicero, 663
Spying, lying, and tattling, 845
Stalin, Joseph, 651, 755
Status and culture, 756
Status in a small town, 442
Stein, Leo, letter to, 644
Stereotype, 86
Sterling, Dorothy, letter to, 520
Still and calm, 936
Still not free, 145
Stock market and power, 443
Stock market crash, 937
Stolberg, Benjamin, letter to, 343
Stout, Rex, letter to, 673
Streator, George, letter to, 479
Strittmater, L. F., letter to, 825
Strnad, Vojtech, letter to, 649
Strong, Sydney, letter to, 596, 605
Student financial aid, 271
Student sit-ins, 142
Studied white indifference, 667
Studying slave trade, 388
Submerge individuality in organizing, 892
Success, 938
Sunday Compass, quotation from, 402, 630, 905
Supporting Tammany, 775
Suppressing progressives, 724
Suppression of peace advocacy, 713
Suppression of the African Slave Trade, The, quotations from, 388, 389, 469, 904
Supreme Court with guts, 334
Surrender and silence, 444
Survey, quotations from, 176, 383
Survival of fittest, 445
Sympathy and oppression, 939

Taking positions, 941
Talented Tenth, 571
Talent, undeveloped, 942

Taylor, Alva W., letter to, 261
Taylor, Frank E., letter to, 497
Teacher, log cabin, 20
Teaching blacks, 90
Teaching Jewish history, 637
Teaching race consciousness, 336
Teaching submission, 230
Teaching the trades, 234, 280
Tebeau, A. C., letter to, 593
Television, 944. *See also* Radio broadcasting, 913
Theft and diplomacy, 677
Thomas, R. H., letter to, 821
Thought rights itself, 566
Through a personal prism, 1–101
Thurman, A. G., letter to, 324
Timpany, John R., letter to, 583
Torrence, Ridgely, letter to, 492
Tough times for all, 484
Tow, Mrs. Abraham, letter to, 738
Travel restrictions, 682
Trivial but cosmic, 337
Trouble I've seen, The, 102–151
Trowbridge, Mrs. C. H., letter to, 838
Truth, 22, 54, 487, 845
Tunisia, 758
Tutweiler, Julia Belle, letter to, 655
Two contrasting Presidents (Lincoln and Johnson), 319
Tyrannical foreign capital, 675
Tyson, David, letter to, 328

Ultimate exploited, 368
Un-Americanism, 653
Unemployment in Depression, 112
Unequal desegregated schools, 203
Unequal schooling, 274
Unequal workplace, 349
Unfair information, 797
Unintended consequences, 946
Union exclusion and racism, 358
USSR, 10, 618, 650, 651, 730, 733, 754
USSR, historic experiment, 559
USSR, role in World War II, 727
Unions and capitalism, 947
Unions discriminate, 338, 344
Uniquely honest elections, 769
U.S. and Haiti, 741, 745

U.S. imperialism, 690. *See also* Changed U.S. world role, 700
Universal education for blacks, 194
Unpaid black toil, 391
Unpublished writings of Du Bois, quoted, 2, 3, 4, 6, 9, 17, 18, 23, 24, 27, 28, 29, 30, 31, 32, 33, 36, 37, 38, 39, 40, 41, 43, 44, 45, 46, 48, 49, 53, 57, 58, 60, 61, 62, 64, 66, 67, 68, 71, 75, 79, 80, 81, 84, 85, 86, 88, 91, 93, 96, 97, 100, 101, 109, 114, 118, 124, 126, 128, 130, 132, 133, 137, 142, 146, 150, 152, 153, 155, 156, 157, 161, 162, 163, 168, 169, 173, 175, 181, 182, 183, 184, 185, 186, 191, 192, 193, 195, 197, 198, 200, 201, 202, 203, 204, 205, 210, 213, 217, 219, 220, 221, 222, 223, 225, 226, 227, 228, 231, 234, 235, 237, 239, 240, 241, 242, 243, 244, 250, 251, 256, 258, 259, 261, 263, 266, 267, 270, 271, 273, 276, 279, 281, 282, 287, 290, 291, 293, 296, 298, 300, 302, 303, 305, 308, 309, 315, 323, 324, 325, 328, 331, 332, 337, 341, 343, 344, 348, 349, 352, 353, 357, 358, 360, 369, 372, 388, 392, 399, 400, 408, 409, 411, 415, 417, 419, 425, 431, 425, 431, 435, 444, 447, 454, 457, 460, 463, 464, 465, 471, 475, 476, 477, 479, 480, 481, 483, 484, 486, 488, 489, 490, 491, 492, 495, 496, 497, 498, 499, 500, 502, 503, 504, 505, 507, 509, 510, 511, 512, 513, 514, 515, 516, 517, 518, 519, 520, 521, 524, 525, 526, 527, 528, 529, 530, 531, 532, 533, 536, 539, 540, 541, 542, 543, 544, 546, 547, 548, 550, 552, 553, 554, 556, 558, 559, 564, 565, 566, 567, 568, 570, 571, 574, 575, 577, 578, 579, 585, 586, 590, 591, 593, 596, 599, 601, 603, 604, 605, 609, 612, 618, 620, 622, 625, 628, 631, 632, 633, 634, 635, 636, 637, 639, 641, 642, 643, 644, 645, 646, 647, 648, 649, 650, 651, 653, 655, 666, 668, 672, 673, 675, 677, 678, 682, 685, 687, 688, 689, 690, 691, 696, 697, 699, 702, 706, 708, 709, 710, 713, 714, 715, 721, 724, 726, 728, 730, 731, 734, 735, 736, 737, 738, 739, 741, 744, 745, 747, 749, 750, 755, 756, 757, 765, 770, 772, 773, 775, 776, 782, 786, 787, 789, 790, 793, 795, 796, 797, 798, 804, 805, 810, 811, 814, 815, 816, 821, 824, 825, 826, 827, 828, 836, 838, 839, 845, 848, 849, 852, 853, 854, 857, 858, 859, 861, 865, 866, 871, 874, 875, 877, 879, 886, 891, 892, 893, 897, 899, 900, 901, 902, 907, 909, 911, 912, 913, 915, 917, 918, 919, 921, 922, 923, 924, 926, 930, 934, 937, 940, 941, 942, 947, 948, 951, 952, 954, 956, 957
Unsound national economy, 683
Use and abuse, 446

Vagrancy laws, 149
Van Lennep, E. J., letter to, 533
Vaughn, George, letter to, 612
Veblen, Thorstein, 915
Veil, 11
Verse by Du Bois, 614, 878, 881
Vicious conquest, 174
Villard, Oswald Garrison, letter to, 126, 901
Violence, lurking, 127
Vocational training, 282
Voice of the Negro, quotation from, 373
Vollum, Alfred, letter to, 279
Voting rights, 458, 466, 482, 760, 761, 767, 799

Wages and slaves, 950
Wages of colonies, 681
Wagner, J. H., letter to, 543
Walden, J. A., letter to, 267
Wallace, Karl R., letter to, 447
Walton, Lester A., letter to, 323
Wanderjahre, 15
War, 614
War and ignorance, 613
War and peace, 707–727

War frenzy, 101. *See also* Calling for war, 723

War to exploit darker races, 722

Washing dirty linen, 94

Washington, Booker T., 447, 945, 951

We all shall die, 575

We know whites, 657

Wealth, 449

Wealth and power, 952

Wealthy contacts, 67

Wedding costs, 96

Wedding etiquette, 97

Well-meant evils, 816

What freedom means, 843

Wheaton, Barbara, letter to, 504

White and black colleges, 219

White and black labor, 339. *See also* Labor and race, 310

White Christianity, 615

White church, 616

White friends, 98

White illusions, 669

White is not Right, 662

White, Luther R., letter to, 495

Whiteness, discovery of, 670

White people, 655–671

White selecting black leaders, 772

White silence, 118

White slaves in seventeenth century, 393

Whites out of Africa, 184

White sympathizers, 570

White, Walter, letter to, 239, 475, 789, 921

White western European world, 696. *See also* Discovery of whiteness, 670

White workers, deliberate enemies, 341

Whittaker, John P., letter to, 185

Who brought us? 953

Who was first? 954

Why pray? 605

Wild and witless, 955

Williams, Du Bois, letter to, 38

Williams, Howard Y., 521

Womanhood, 459

Women, 450–462

Women's rights, 462

Women voters, 461

Woodson, Carter G., letter to, 425

Woody, R. H., letter to, 666

Work for a better world, 604

Working class, 338–370

Work rules, 956

World and Africa, The, quotations from 65, 165, 166, 167, 170, 172, 180, 322, 334, 393, 573, 679, 740, 758

World economic democracy, 705

World economy and politics, 672–706

World labor and African slavery, 703

World market, 704

Worlds of Color, quotations from 196, 206, 207, 276, 352, 414, 545, 659, 938

World supremacy of U.S., 688

Writer's wages, 511

Writing and money, 513

Writing as property, 514

Writing introductions, 515

Writings out of print, 500

About the Editor

MEYER WEINBERG is Pofessor Emeritus at the W.E.B. Du Bois Department of Afro-American Studies, University of Massachusetts at Amherst. He is the author or compiler of numerous works dealing with education and race/ethnicity issues.